OUT OF BOUNDS

Also by Lauren St John

SHOOTING AT CLOUDS
SEVE: THE BIOGRAPHY

LAUREN ST JOHN

INSIDE PROFESSIONAL GOLF

OUT OF BOUNDS

PARTRIDGE PRESS

LONDON · NEW YORK · TORONTO · SYDNEY · AUCKLAND

TRANSWORLD PUBLISHERS LTD
61–63 Uxbridge Road, London W5 5SA

TRANSWORLD PUBLISHERS (AUSTRALIA) PTY LTD
15–25 Helles Avenue, Moorebank, NSW 2170

TRANSWORLD PUBLISHERS (NZ) LTD
3 William Pickering Drive, Albany, Auckland

Published 1995 by Partridge Press
a division of Transworld Publishers Ltd

A catalogue record for this book is available from the British Library

ISBN 185225 2286

Typeset in 11/13pt Linotype Times by Kestrel Data, Exeter, Devon.

Printed in Great Britain by
Mackays of Chatham plc, Chatham, Kent.

Dedicated to the memory of my cousin, Deane,
who touched my life more than he ever knew

ACKNOWLEDGEMENTS

I am indebted to so many people I hardly know where to begin, but I do know that this book wouldn't have been possible without the kindness and support of four in particular: namely, Tom Ramsey, Robinson Holloway, Frank Williams and Kathie Shearer.

Having travelled the world in pursuit of the ideal tournament, I can confidently say that nowhere in golf – and probably in all sport – are the players, press and officials more warm, sociable or willing to help outsiders than on the Australian Tour. Kathie Shearer, the press officer, and Tom Ramsey, Australia's most highly regarded golf writer (who lives in a house straight out of paradise with his incredible wife Carmel), are perfect examples of that. The fact that I lasted more than a week Down Under is due almost entirely to the wit and wisdom of Kathie and the generosity of Tom, and also to my friends Doug and Annette Mackay, Conrad Jupiter's on the Gold Coast, the Hyatt Coolum, near Noosa (the best resort I've ever stayed in, and I've stayed in a few), the Australian PGA Tour and, of course, the unforgettable Laguna Quays resort on the Whitsunday Passage.

There is no way to express my gratitude to Robinson Holloway, to whom the unlucky task of ferrying me around American tournaments and shopping malls, listening to my typewriter keys after 4.00 a.m. wake-up calls, and picking up the pieces after yet another of my crises, has so often fallen. All I can say is, thanks – the next movie's on me.

I owe a great deal to Frank Williams, Greg Norman's ingenious manager, who went to untold lengths to secure an interview for me with the (recalcitrant, I believe, is the Australian word for it) Shark. Also to Nick Pitt, my sports editor at *The Sunday Times*, to the American golf writers Tim Rosaforte, Jaime Diaz and Larry Dorman, and to everyone in the Association of Golf Writers, particularly Peter Dobereiner, Liz Kahn, Renton Laidlaw, Michael McDonnell, Peter Higgs and the one and only Norman Dabell.

Lastly, but most importantly, thanks to my agent Sara Menguc and my publisher Debbie Beckerman, who make writing – which sometimes feels harder and more painful than wrestling alligators – easier.

Note to Kathie Shearer: If you need a ghost writer for *She Didn't Stand Over the Three-Foot Putts*, you know where to find me.

CONTENTS

INTRODUCTION

For the first five or six years of my golf writing career, I spent a great deal of time trying to give it up. Every season I would vow would be my last, and every new year I'd be there when the first shot was struck in earnest, standing wide-eyed and curious on the practice range, as enchanted as it is possible to be, saying quietly to myself: 'Just one more year and then I'll be able to walk away.'

It wasn't that I didn't love the game with all my heart. I'd grown up on a farm in Zimbabwe, a place of tawny grasses, dreams and droughts, and had not discovered golf until I was eighteen, and when I did the flood-tide of late addiction swept over me with the painful poignancy of youthful infatuation. In the early stages of my career, I savoured every moment of my association with the professional game. I cast myself adrift on the nomadic sea of the European Tour and I revelled in its eventful passage, its larger than life characters and the foreign lands it journeyed to. I listened in wonder to the players whose words I had poured over in magazines and imitated on the golf course. 'You can't be a fan with a typewriter,' one reporter cautioned me, but the players were my heroes, my inspiration, the wellspring of my writing, and my first book, *Shooting at Clouds*, reflected that; it is, undeniably, professional golf through rose-coloured spectacles.

But after a time, my feckless existence began to cause me pangs of guilt. To some extent, I felt the way the journeyman player must, that eventually the sweet bird of youth would fly away and I would pay a price for following the game for the sheer love of it, rarely sparing a thought for the long-term destination of my journalistic career or the day of financial reckoning. I was even more pre-occupied with the notion that real writers don't write about sport. As erroneous as that might be, it is definitely the perception of the literary community at large. If I want to be a novelist, I'd think, I'll have to wean myself off the Tour.

But I had reckoned without the pull of the road. I'd under-estimated the irresistible appeal of springtime in Augusta, the heady smell of sea-salt, crushed grass and history at the Open, the adrenalin rush of deadlines, the restless energy and individuality of each separate tour, the bonding and the camaraderie, and I hadn't banked on the yearning I'd feel whenever I was deprived of this mysterious and unpredictable game. Consequently, when I did attempt to summon the energy to leave, I was well and truly hooked.

I never did come to agree with that reporter about not having heroes among the players. If you enjoy a game wholeheartedly, it is inevitable that you're going to admire and respect many of its participants. But I did learn that in order to write well about any sport you have to peel back the layers, to consider carefully the motivations of its participants, to be unafraid to probe, to expose and to criticize. You have to love it enough to be able to follow the circuit for years and still catch your breath on a beautiful shot, still cry coming down the seventy-second hole of a major championship, still be moved by the words and deeds of men like Tom Watson, and yet understand it enough to read between the lines. And at some point I resigned myself to the fact that I'll probably always be a golf writer. That I'm hopelessly in love with the world's most noble and infuriating game, and that the dew on the range, the flash of sunlight on a steel shaft, the flowing lines of a perfect golf swing, the banter, the wanderlust, the heartache, and the colour and momentum of the entire green caravan, are now so much a part of my soul that I'll never be cured. And that's when I thought: I really don't want to be.

1

THE BATTLE OF THE BELFRY

'The Ryder Cup passed away yesterday. Not just for another two years but almost certainly forever. There is no further point to this charade.'

MICHAEL MCDONNELL on the USA's 21–11 victory at Laurel Valley, Pennsylvania, *Daily Mail*, 22 September 1975

It was a fine day for a resurrection. Through the gates of the Belfry came a capacity crowd of thirty thousand, a river of living colour, which cleaved the crisp, grey morning and brought with it an atmosphere of excitement and exhilaration, testifying not to the power of advertising but to the spirit of golf: the dream of a seed merchant had become one of the greatest sporting spectacles on earth – and one of the richest.

Money was everywhere at the 1993 Ryder Cup. It was there in the players' cashmere sweaters, in the endorsements on their squeaking leather bags, in the muffled clink of their chrome-plated clubs and in the Concorde baggage tags discarded in their rooms. It was hidden in the glossy black cover of the programme, on the price tags in the exhibition tent, in the flowers that bedecked the eighteenth, and in the Mercedes, Jaguars and Porsches that lined the drive. And it was the currency of choice in the luxurious Belfry Hotel, revealing itself in the cut of the suits, the glow of the whisky, the smell of American Express, and the deals being struck over breakfast. In the distance, a funeral pyre of smoke bubbled lifelessly from Birmingham's factory chimneys, speaking of poverty and deprivation, but here on the lush, hand-manicured fairways of the Belfry, prosperity and goodwill were not just alive; they were thriving.

Reports of the death of the Ryder Cup had not been exaggerated. At Laurel Valley in 1975 the match had become a cruel farce by noon on the final day. With cold finality, Michael McDonnell of the *Daily Mail* recorded that: 'The last rites of this contest, which has endured on American goodwill for most of its forty-eight years, were performed before lunch with a total and humiliating defeat of Britain and Ireland. We witnessed the last Ryder Cup in which only the British Isles are involved. If this contest is to survive, then we need a lot of world class help. It would be barefaced arrogance to argue otherwise. British professional golf has forfeited the right to maintain a solitary challenge.'

Certainly, the defeat had been embarrassing. 'Television cameras were poised to cover the last three dramatic afternoon hours of this contest and screen it coast-to-coast,' McDonnell reported. 'But by the time they were on the air, the Ryder Cup was already an exhibition match and millions of viewers switched channels to watch professional football. The American team was never under pressure yet managed to keep a straight face throughout it all. But the garden party atmosphere was captured by an odd request from American captain Arnold Palmer to his British counterpart Bernard Hunt. As it was really all over, Palmer asked if it would be all right if he took off in the afternoon to open a nearby air show by performing a couple of aerobatics over the field. Hunt could not refuse.'

It was not the first time the Ryder Cup had slumped to the level of *National Lampoon's European Vacation*. Tom Weiskopf had found the whole thing such a bore that he had turned down a place on the US team in favour of elk hunting, and when Britain and Ireland scored their first victory in twenty-four years at Lindrick in 1957, Tommy Bolt, the hot-tempered American, was so disgusted that he broke a club and boycotted the prize-giving. 'I guess you won, but I did not enjoy it a bit,' he snarled at Eric Brown, who had beaten him 4 and 3 in the singles.

'Nor would I after a licking like that,' Brown said cheerfully.

But European successes were as rare as hens' teeth. So rare, in fact, that the US team's 12½, 7½-point win at Royal Lytham in 1977 was their ninth in ten matches, the other having been halved.

At that point, Jack Nicklaus, who in a magnificent sporting gesture had conceded a putt to Tony Jacklin to ensure the tie in 1969, lost patience. He approached Lord Derby, then president of the Professional Golfers' Association, and in diplomatic terms stated the blindingly obvious: the Ryder Cup was a joke, the Americans would rather go to tenpin bowling or even to the dentist than play in another one, and the only chance it had of limping on for another year was if the doors were opened to Continental talent. Bring on Severiano Ballesteros, he said.

In golf, the wheels of political change move with the speed of evolving glaciers, but the day was fast approaching when the US Tour could no longer justify supporting an event where 150 of their players and officials spent a week without pay for the overrated pleasure of trampling on a hopeless British team, and desperate measures were called for. Even so, there were no overnight miracles. In 1979, the presence of Ballesteros and Antonio Garrido at the Greenbrier did not prevent a whitewash, and in 1981, Europe were demolished 18½, 9½, partly because they encountered arguably the best golf team ever assembled – eleven of the twelve Americans had won or would win majors – and partly as a consequence of one of the most controversial decisions in the history of the Ryder Cup: Ballesteros, winner of the 1979 Open Championship and 1980 US Masters, and Jacklin, winner of the 1969 Open and 1970 US Open, were left out of the team.

The repercussions of this were such that, thirteen years on, the members of that three-man Ryder Cup committee still point fingers at one other whenever the issue arises. It is true that Ballesteros had been at the centre of a row all year, having resigned his membership of the Tour after being banned from accepting appearance money, but his place in the team was awarded to Mark James who, along with Ken Brown, had caused what officials described as absolute havoc at the Greenbrier – something James vehemently denies. Peter Oosterhuis received the other wild card.

'Seve felt he had been betrayed,' recalled Joe Collet, Ballesteros's manager. 'To this day, [he] does not know what happened. And we never will. Because John Jacobs, Bernhard Langer and Neil Coles all tell a story which absolves them completely of any blame. So one of them is not remembering what happened correctly, put it that way.'

Jacklin was still smarting when, eighteen months later, Ken

Schofield, the executive director of the Tour, walked up to him and calmly asked if he would captain the next Ryder team. Jacklin was stunned. His immediate reaction was: 'How the hell can they invite me to do this when what's gone on's gone on?' But since he didn't hold Schofield responsible for what had happened, he agreed to at least think about the proposal. 'I was angry, angry as hell. But I kept saying, "If I do it, I want to do it my way." I said, "I want Concorde; I want an unlimited amount of clothing; I want our guys to feel equal to the Americans when they stand on the tee." And every demand I made, they accepted. It came to the point where they had accepted all that, so I was that far down the road, and then I sort of said to myself: "Now hang on. Are you going to keep a vendetta going with this thing forever?" And it was clear that the Ryder Cup was going to survive much longer than me or anybody else. So I decided at that point to let bygones be bygones.'

Thus, the Ryder Cup as we know it today was born. Jacklin was probably the only man in existence capable of persuading a very sore and bitter Ballesteros to lend his support to the team, and in Florida the Europeans played so well that Nicklaus, the US captain, kissed the divot made by the pitch shot Lanny Wadkins played to save the cup for America. 'In 1983, Jacklin was still learning,' one official said of the West Palm Beach matches; 'in '85, he pasted Trevino psychologically before he even got to the first tee.' At the Belfry, Trevino, who was a disaster as a captain, had to suffer the ignominy of watching his team go down 16, 11 to the ecstatic Europeans. Afterwards, he acquitted himself appallingly. 'Do I have to listen to this crap?' he is alleged to have asked at the victory dinner, having virtually disowned his players. But the hurting wasn't over yet. In 1987, Ballesteros, Jose Maria Olazabal and Bernhard Langer, there through Nicklaus's intervention, were in the team that took apart the Nicklaus-designed Muirfield Village and, under Jacklin's guidance, delivered a large dose of their own medicine to Captain Jack and his all-American boys, winning the trophy for the first time ever on US soil.

'Jacklin was the catalyst,' said Colin Snape, former head of the PGA. 'He made it happen.'

Within the Ryder Cup and outside of it, the die was cast. American domination of world golf had ceased, then and almost certainly for ever, and European golf was set to explode.

Thursday, 23 September 1993. In the interview room sat Mark James, brown eyes laughing. Once a teenage tearaway and the bane of officialdom, he was now a droll, elder statesman of Ryder Cup golf, there to give the rookies advice. 'The only thing that scares me about the Americans now is the clothes they wear,' James observed laconically.

A decade had made all the difference. In ten years, the underdogs had become the dogs of war – the competition between Europe and America so evenly matched that both sides had become caught in a tide of nationalistic hype that at times threatened to engulf them. During the three practice days at the Belfry, the subject most centred upon was the jingoism at Kiawah Island. Nick Faldo said that a repeat of the patriotic excesses of the 1991 match, which included members of the US team wearing Desert Storm hats, would cause the spirit of the Ryder Cup to evaporate altogether. 'Anything more like that and a few of us would turn around and say: "Thanks a lot, let's forget it." '

Faldo told the *Express* that he had been 'genuinely upset' about what happened at Kiawah, where Europe lost by a point. 'They were there to do or die. They had to win at all costs. They were so hyped up, they couldn't care less if we left there with a bad taste in our mouths . . . and a lot of us did . . . For example, at the dinner they showed us this film about the Ryder Cup without one European shot in it. Our new boys looked at us with eyes as big as saucers, as if to say: "What do we do now?" We were just short of spitting blood. We had to bite our lips and say: "OK guys, we'll accept that it's all part of it." But it shouldn't be. The players were all right, it was out of their hands. It was very much officially orientated. The captain and officials were very much involved.'

But the players were not entirely blameless. Paul Azinger, whose rivalry with Ballesteros had been at the heart of the struggle for the soul of the Ryder Cup, admitted he was guilty of War by the Shore-type aggression at Kiawah. 'On reflection, I over-reacted by whipping up feeling in the crowd,' he said, but confessed that it had been music to his ears. 'They were chanting "USA, USA" every time we walked on to the tee or holed a putt.'

This time, he promised, it would all be different. Tom Watson concurred. 'Partisanship can be beautiful,' said the US captain. 'There's nothing better than when a crowd is wholly absorbed and the players are all absorbed, but I don't want the outcome influenced by any outside agencies . . . If I miss a putt and lose a hole and the European crowd cheers, that's fine. They're cheering the implications of that missed putt. When we accelerate it into a war is when we lose the event's spirit.'

Which made it all the more ironic that it should be Watson, a gentleman golfer to the tips of his toes, who sparked the first diplomatic incident at the Belfry, by refusing to sign Sam Torrance's menu at the gala dinner on the grounds that one autograph would lead to 800, and it was Bernard Gallacher, the taciturn European captain, who smoothed ruffled feathers.

In the intervening years between Gallacher's first term as European captain, in 1991, and his return to the Belfry, he had, it has to be said, undergone several changes. He had not become a showy, innovative leader – never having had those qualities to begin with, he was always unlikely to acquire them. But he had learned to exploit his three best assets: wit, pragmatism and considerable savvy. Through trial and error he had become adept at handling the media and thinking on his feet. Whereas in the past, he had often seemed dull-witted and dour in comparison to the American captains, now he was as quick as a mongoose, a blur of sharp teeth and flashing eyes, with a particular gift for nailing the unwary to the ground. Thus, when Watson came in to offer stumbling apologies for his gaffe of the evening before ('I told Sam that I'd be happy for him to leave the menus at our team-room and I'd see they got back. I saw how embarrassed he was . . .'), Gallacher publicly took the heat out of the situation with a few well chosen words. 'If that's the incident we have this week, then that's fine. It was very small, very minor . . . Anyway, Sam's quite happy. I signed his menu for him. I know Tom Watson's signature.'

Watson had banned his team from giving a single autograph but Gallacher said that the Europeans 'were signing all night.' Why? 'Well, we're good at writing,' grinned Gallacher.

Tony Jacklin was always going to be a hard act to follow. As a captain, he had done no wrong. He led the Europeans to two historic victories, a draw and a narrow defeat, and his charismatic, hands-on approach to captaincy had won him the enthusiastic support of players, journalists and spectators alike. When he stepped down, Gallacher was viewed as the safe option. He wasn't a trailblazer, nor was he the world's most compelling speaker, but he was solid and reliable and he had the added advantage of having participated in eleven Ryder Cups – eight as a player and three as Jacklin's No. 2.

'I sort of fell into the job, mainly because of Tony's recommendation and the tournament committee voting for me to take over,' Gallacher says now. 'But the most daunting task that I had to face wasn't the captaincy of the Ryder Cup; it was actually *saving* the Ryder Cup because at the time we were in dispute with the PGA.'

For as long as they have been in existence, tournament professionals and club professionals have been uneasy bedfellows, their psychological chess games being played out over the years in the boardrooms of their respective organizations. In Britain, the European Tour Players' Division split from the PGA in 1975, becoming the PGA European Tour, whereupon the long-running feud between John Jacobs and Colin Snape was temporarily laid to rest by the resignation of Jacobs as tournament director general of the ETPD. However, in 1988 the PGA recruited John Lindsay as their new executive director and all the old jealousies reared their heads again.

'I think in retrospect, the thing probably started – and the impetus for it to go the way it did – when the match between the United States and Great Britain and Ireland was extended to take in Europe, using the Tour office, and no new contract was drafted between the British PGA and the Tour,' Ken Schofield said. 'The Ryder Cup Committee had always, and indeed still does today, had an even balance of members from the PGA and the Tour. But what happened was that during the hiatus we had between Colin Snape leaving and John Lindsay's arrival, we actually had and conducted the '87 match . . . Then John Lindsay came in and reviewed their assets, their liabilities, things that they could maximize, and he came to the conclusion that the Ryder Cup was theirs. Totally. They had the deed of trust. The deed of trust is the giving of the trophy by the St Albans seed man [Samuel Ryder] to the British Professional Golfers' Association. It's theirs. No-one ever disputes whose it is. But, you know, trophies can't sit on the wall. We were quite clear that we had always wanted fifty-fifty. And it became evident fairly quickly into John Lindsay's term that was not the route he wanted to pursue and he saw the Ryder Cup as being theirs totally. And events became public, people took strong stances and, yes, at the 1989 Ryder Cup, the only element of happiness for myself and most of my Tour senior colleagues, was that we held on to the trophy.

There was no happiness in knowing that events were unfolding behind our back to have us removed from playing an active part in it. It took until November 1990 [for the PGA] to see reason, when we again convened around a table at a Heathrow hotel, board to board, and made an agreement and had it written out while we were there, to make sure that they wouldn't again do what they did, which was to have a tacit agreement entered into in 1987, and then change all the people and the executive director of the board and say: "All bets are off." '

Lindsay had aimed to seize the reins of Ryder Cup power in 1989. From then on, the PGA would have selected the venue and made all other critical decisions, while the Tour picked up whatever crumbs were left over. Meanwhile, tradition and sportsmanship would have fallen by the wayside as greed gained the upper hand.

'They genuinely felt it was theirs – it was and remains their biggest asset, in terms of money – so clearly financial motives would come into it, yes,' Schofield agreed. 'But let's just say they had a fresh man in, with the ability to give his views as to how they should proceed, and he, for a moment in time – from May 1988 until November 1990 – conducted a policy of being, if you like, very aggressively against the Tour, and at the same time put out a smokescreen that it was the other way round. That it was, quote, "the Tour trying to take over the PGA", which was a very, very distressing time in my life, much more so than 1981 [when Ballesteros was left out of the team], however desolate that was, because the desolation on that was retrospective.'

'It got very nasty at one point and that really undermined, in my opinion, my captaincy to start off with,' said Gallacher, recalling the politics behind the scenes before Lindsay resigned and an amicable joint agreement was reached with Sandy Jones, the present executive director. 'I was very uneasy about it and at one stage I said to Ken Schofield, "I think I should resign and see how far the PGA want to take it." I felt at that time they would try and appoint their own captain . . . But Ken said that he felt it was the wrong thing for me to resign, and on reflection, maybe it was. And so that was the build-up to Kiawah. Tony Jacklin never had these problems. Tony introduced things that other captains would have liked to introduce but the European Tour wasn't in the position to do it, like going Concorde to America, like having the best clothes, like taking coaches, like having five-star treatment. Tony felt that that was a very important part of winning . . . Tony also introduced a more open captaincy, making the players feel a bit more relaxed, putting the onus on the player to prepare himself for the week. That was the obvious thing to do, instead of dressing up and sitting in stuffy dining rooms every evening. And, of course, Tony had the emergence of Seve and Nick Faldo and Sandy Lyle. I mean, a lot of people forget that in 1983, Faldo was Europe's No.1. He got maximum points at West Palm Beach and he was the best player that week, together with Seve. So you had a strong emerging team and that's what carried us through the 80s.'

Gallacher says that the person who most reminds him of Jacklin is Terry Venables, the flamboyant football manager. 'He's a street-wise type of guy, who's great with the players, but off the course the continuity breaks down. Tony's organizational skills are very much on the course. Most of the problems Tony had latterly [in his own career] came when he moved off the course into business, because he doesn't really have the concentration that's required in business to see things through to the very end. He's a great ideas guy, but he really needs somebody to pick up one of the ideas and make it work. That's the way I see Tony. Tony is an inspirational figure and he's a great captain. He likes publicity and he enjoys going to press tents.'

'And you don't?' I suggested.

'Well, I don't think I do,' Gallacher replied frankly. 'I've always seen the captain's role as being an overstated role. I think the players are the important people in the Ryder Cup, not the captain, not the officials. I've always seen my job as trying to step out of the limelight, while at the same time backing up the players because they're the ones who are actually playing in the match and putting their reputations on the line. If anything goes wrong, they're the ones who, unfortunately, have to take it.'

Friday, 24 September. Fog delayed the start of the first round by two and a half hours. This was immediately followed by what the superstitious might view as a bad omen: Sam Torrance, the first European player to tee off in the very first match, ended awkwardly on one foot as he launched his opening drive, wrenching at an already painful ingrown toenail. When he reached the ninth hole, he could hardly walk, and by the time the match had ended, Lanny Wadkins and Corey Pavin having beaten Torrance and James 4 and

3, his toe was septic. The nail was removed by the team doctor the following day, and Gallacher was informed that the Scot couldn't play unless he was given two injections per round.

Still, there were plenty of positives. Ballesteros, who had been a contentious wild card choice because his form was so horrendous, showed flashes of his old brilliance, inspiring Jose Maria Olazabal to a 4 and 3 victory in the afternoon fourballs against Tom Kite and Davis Love III whom they had lost to in the foursomes. Bernhard Langer was suffering from a neck injury and had not struck a ball in three weeks, yet he and Ian Woosnam slaughtered Azinger and Payne Stewart 7 and 5. Langer and Barry Lane, playing in his first Ryder Cup, took a hiding in the fourballs, but by then Peter Baker had made his sensational début, almost single-handedly seeing off the US Open Champion, Lee Janzen, and Jim Gallagher Jnr.

But the most electrifying match was that between Faldo and Colin Montgomerie and Azinger and Raymond Floyd. The Europeans had beaten Floyd and Fred Couples 4 and 3 in the foursomes, but in the afternoon Faldo and Azinger duelled with as much emotion and intensity as any Azinger/Ballesteros confrontation, Faldo making seven birdies on the back nine and the American seven. They were all square when darkness halted play on the eighteenth tee. When they returned early the next morning, Azinger narrowly missed a birdie putt for a win, while Faldo sunk a 10-foot par putt for a half to give Europe a one-point lead going into the second round.

'The match with Paul and Fred will live a long, long time in my memory,' a jubilant Faldo said afterwards. 'It was terrific – just what the Ryder Cup is all about.'

'It was a great, great day for golf,' Watson enthused. 'The competition was so intense that you could have written a novel about it.'

And with that, the real battle was joined.

Saturday, 25 September. Gallacher describes his style of leadership as 'consensus captaincy. I don't see my role as being: "You do this, this is the way it should be." I *can* be persuaded. I can see other people's point of view and if their point of view is better than mine, then I'll change.'

That is all well and to the good, but a captain who works on subtleties like tactical understanding, communication and mutual respect, risks being seen as soft and lacking in the conviction necessary to control strong-willed players such as Ballesteros. This is the position Gallacher found himself in on the second day of play. He was enjoying himself watching Langer and Woosnam trounce Azinger and Couples when he was summoned by Ballesteros, who was playing the fourteenth. The Spaniards were two up against Kite and Love. When Gallacher arrived, Ballesteros had just missed the green right. He walked over to the European captain and, casting pride aside, begged him not to send him out in the afternoon fourballs. He felt he had let Olazabal down.

'He appealed to me to replace him with someone else in order to allow him the time to go and work on the practice ground,' recalled Gallacher. 'And despite speaking to Seve for several minutes, trying to persuade him that that might be the wrong thing to do, I felt that Seve, who always likes to lead from the front, who's never shirked a battle, especially that week, who loves the Ryder Cup, knowing how important it is to Seve, I felt I owed it to him to agree to his request. As it turned out, he couldn't find his game. He started well at the beginning of the week, his game was quite good when he came, and it deteriorated as the week went on, and by the time the singles came he was quite distressed. And I personally wouldn't put Seve on the course when he felt like that. In actual fact, I even put Seve well down the list in the pairings for the singles to try and keep him out of the spotlight, because I've got so much respect for Seve, and I've never heard Seve ever, *ever* say to anyone that he didn't want to play.

'Bernhard Langer was a slightly different case. Langer came to the Ryder Cup not having played for five weeks and declared himself fit. I was very happy for him to be there because he's a strong influence on the team and he's got plenty of experience, and he played very well in foursomes play. So that afternoon I went to him and said, "We've got a strong lead, I'd like you and Woosie to play in the fourballs." And he just felt his fitness wasn't up to playing two rounds a day. So I had to change the pairings.'

This decision proved disastrous. Europe had emerged victorious from the foursomes, having secured a three-point lead by lunchtime, largely due to the fire and genius of Faldo and the two Spaniards, who had now won eleven of their fifteen Ryder Cup matches. But Watson, who had been rolling the dice all week in an effort to find winning combinations, hit the jackpot with John Cook and Chip Beck. They putted Faldo and Montgomerie off the course. Corey

Pavin holed a 149-yard nine-iron shot at the fifth *en route* to defeating James and Costantino Rocca, the Italian rookie, and the US swept the board 3–1 in the fourballs.

'I knew the team that I wanted to put out in the afternoon, and that was the very team that people like Tony Jacklin and people in the press with hindsight would have put out,' Gallacher said in annoyance. 'At that particular stage in the Ryder Cup, I did want to put out my renowned strength because I felt we could almost get into an unassailable position if we had a very good afternoon. I then decided that I couldn't possibly put Joakim Haeggman [the Swedish rookie] in and leave Rocca out of it, not having played at all. I just thought it was in the interests of the team that everyone should play because the match now couldn't be won before the singles.'

Sunday, 26 September. By 10.00 a.m. on the final day, jubilation had seized the European press contingent. We walked around in a state of euphoria or sat in the cafeteria and talked nonsense, occupying ourselves with a juvenile discussion on how uncanny it was that golfers always seemed to be drawn to blondes. Fred Couples, recently divorced from a fair-haired woman, was one of the few going out with a brunette.

'Can you imagine being married to Fred Couples?' I asked Robinson Holloway, a twenty-eight-year-old New Yorker.

'No,' she said. 'I can't. It would be like having a pet rock.'

At that stage, both Robinson and I were uncontracted free-lances, and in an attempt to save money, we tended to travel and occasionally stay together on the US Tour, blowing our savings in the local malls. Robinson worked almost exclusively for British papers and Reuters news agency, and thus was torn between patriotic duty and loyalty to her European friends at the Ryder Cup.

Outside, the great American golf writer Dan Jenkins had bumped into Wadkins. 'We got 'em,' Wadkins said confidently. 'We got eleven guys who can win, they've got five guys who *must* win.'

In the European team-room, it was rather more subdued. 'The feeling was, we were one point ahead going into the singles and we were optimistic,' Gallacher recalled. 'But I knew that Seve wasn't in great shape with his game and Seve knew it and the Americans knew it. And I also knew that Bernhard Langer was struggling with his fitness and we couldn't play Sam. You know, to win the Ryder Cup you need twelve guys playing well.'

The condition of Torrance's toe had worsened overnight. Upon examining it, the doctor said that the Scot could only play with the aid of pain-killing injections, which left Gallacher no option but to withdraw him. 'I couldn't possibly put anybody out, knowing he would have to come off at the tenth to have an injection,' Gallacher said perfectly reasonably. 'I mean, that's silly. So we didn't have the use of Sam all week.'

That meant that for the second consecutive Ryder Cup, the so-called 'name in the envelope' rule was triggered. Torrance was sidelined and given half a point, and Wadkins was big-hearted enough to volunteer to sit on the bench alongside him.

The envelope rule was initiated by Colin Snape in 1979. 'To me, it was quite straightforward,' said Snape. 'It was quite simply that each captain had to put a name in the envelope and then in the event of one player dropping out on the day, you married it up against the name in the other. Well, Mark James was unplayable that week. So on the morning of the last day, James was unfit and Gil Morgan was thinking he was unfit. And Billy Casper, who was the [US] captain, had put his best player down: he'd put Trevino. So there we are in the breakfast meeting, I open the envelope – James/Trevino. And John Jacobs [Europe's captain], you've got to give him his due. He went: "Oh, no, Billy! You don't really mean *Trevino*? Do you want to have another go? I tell you what, I'll just have a walk out . . ." Can you imagine it the other way round? And that was how the envelopes were launched . . . And the next time they came up was all this hoohah with Gilford.'

At Kiawah Island, Gallacher had been presented with the un-enviable decision of who to put in the envelope on the eve of the final round. David Gilford, an introspective but talented English-man, had had what Gallacher described as 'a fairly traumatic blooding'. He had played twice in the foursomes – once with Montgomerie and once with Faldo, with whom he didn't hit it off at all, Faldo being a focused individualist and Gilford being a silent loner – and come out of it with two defeats. Gallacher felt that his hands were tied. He couldn't put Paul Broadhurst in the envelope since Broadhurst had only played once and won, and the rest of the team had all had a victory or two. So he put Gilford in the envelope without telling him, never dreaming it would be triggered.

The next morning, he was talking to the BBC on the practice range when the interviewer suddenly announced that Steve Pate had withdrawn. He asked the stunned Gallacher who his name in the envelope was. Gallacher had no time to prepare poor Gilford, who collapsed sobbing in the locker-room.

'There's no question in my mind that they [the Americans] took half a point,' Gallacher said. 'I mean, if Steve Pate plays, we don't know the outcome, but if he doesn't play, he gets half a point. So they took half a point. But he *was* injured . . . But I think it was going to be a political problem if they hadn't played Steve Pate by the singles. Because he was injured [in a collision] before the opening ceremony, and it would have been a very tricky situation to have him injured two days before the Ryder Cup started and not pull someone else in, knowing full well that he wasn't going to play the whole week. I don't think our Ryder Cup committee would have accepted Steve Pate's half point if he hadn't played by Friday afternoon. So that's what made it difficult. I wasn't so concerned about the outcome of the Ryder Cup. I just felt sorry that David Gilford didn't get a chance to redeem himself in the singles.'

In *Only on Sundays*, Henry Longhurst observes that: 'A strange quality of golf is the way in which a sense either of victory or defeat can convey itself to eight people playing singles in different parts of the course then minutes apart. At Lindrick one could almost see it happening. The humble British turned like lions whose tails had been twisted long enough; the Americans disintegrated.'

At the Belfry, the reverse was true.

'I knew it was going to be tight when Barry Lane was three up and Woosie was one up against Fred Couples,' Gallacher said. 'And then Raymond Floyd unexpectedly beat Olazabal, and Chip Beck managed to hold on and beat Barry Lane, and from that moment on it looked like we were going to be beaten, even though on the scoreboard it looked like we were going to win. We were getting points – for instance, Montgomerie had a point, Woosnam had half a point, Haeggman had a point and Baker had a point – but we didn't have any points on the course. It was unfortunate that the only way out was Rocca.'

Lane was crushed after his own defeat. Several key matches had gone the way of the Americans – Ballesteros had started with four bogeys to hand a point to Gallagher, Kite had beaten Langer, and Stewart had ridden roughshod over James – but Lane had been three up over Beck with five holes to play. 'I was devastated,' he recalled later. 'I felt I had let the team down. But they were great because they had all been through it themselves. It was the best and the worst week of my life but I just can't wait to play in it again.'

The same may not be true of Rocca. He was one up against Love with two holes to play at a time when victory might still have meant that the trophy was won by Europe. When he bogeyed both, crumbling in the pressure-cooker atmosphere of the closing stages, he burst into tears. Love, who had been engulfed by his excited team-mates, broke free of them and put his arms around the bowed shoulders of the Italian. Behind them, Faldo had played his heart out against Azinger, even holing in one at the fifteenth, but by the time he halved the match on the eighteenth, it was all for nothing. Floyd had already sunk the winning putt. The US team took the match 15–13.

'Nobody can blame Costantino,' said Ballesteros, who wept with Rocca in the locker-room. 'I felt very sad for him and I feel bad about myself. You can blame me. I played very badly. I tried my best, but it was not to be. I'm sorry.'

Nevertheless, such is the team spirit of the Europeans that by the time they came into the press centre, they had recovered their humour enough to tease one another about who should be captain in 1995. Gallacher plumped for Seve.

'I do have an opinion,' Ballesteros said. 'As all of you know, my English is very poor, and we shall have to send a captain to New York, someone with a good record and someone who speaks very good English. This has to be Nick Faldo. I will go for Nick Faldo and if not Nick Faldo then Sam Torrance. Or maybe Woosie. Maybe in four years' time they can all speak Spanish.'

'I'm going to be playing next time so I'm not going to be a playing captain,' Faldo said in mock indignation. 'I have enough to think about on the course.'

Then he added more seriously: 'We were a great team, with great team spirit, but the Americans did a helluva job today. Some guys had a tough time at the end, but if you give your best – and everyone gave a 100 per cent this week – it's OK. We are a very proud team. But what the hell. It's only a game.'

There is a British rock group called Pop Will Eat Itself – their name a wry comment on the excesses and declining values of the music industry. Unless we tone down the hype surrounding it, that's what will probably become of the Ryder Cup. Jingoism and commerciality will erode the sportsmanship it was formed to showcase and cause it to self-destruct. As Watson said: 'The Ryder Cup must never lose the innocence. It must never pay professionals to take part and it must always be about who's got the most pride and who's got the most heart.'

Even at the Belfry, there were times when the responses of the players seemed less the reactions of sportsmen suspended between cold terror and absolute exhilaration than lines from a film script. The most memorable moments were those when circumstances forced real emotions and real passions out of people. There was honesty in the performances of the Ryder Cup rookies, Baker and Haeggman, because they were still young enough and idealistic enough to have retained a touching faith in the heroism in the whole thing; in the very human tears of Rocca; and, most strikingly, in the extraordinary transformation of Faldo, who, used to coping entirely by himself in an ordered world of his own creation, found himself adrift in a rudderless boat on high seas, was thrown back on his own resources, rallied and stood firm and proud against the storm. Incredible as it may seem, it was Faldo, for whom even Solitaire is a team game, who was Europe's inspirational leader.

But like all box office failures, somebody had to be held accountable when the credits rolled and the Häagen-Dazs wrappers were scraped from the seats. It is a team effort, but there is little doubt that several people weren't exactly Trojans in preventing Europe's defeat. Nobody is suggesting that those players with sore toes, backs and necks weren't trying their hardest, but the fact is these men are professional athletes, representing Europe in one of the most important sporting events in the world, and as such it is their responsibility to ensure that they are physically fit when they arrive there and have the stamina to play thirty-six holes a day. Floyd managed it and he is fifty-one years old.

In the event, it was Gallacher who received the most criticism. Jacklin wrote an article for the *Scotsman* in which he said that the players were interfering too much in the role of captain. 'This time they were consulted over everything, including pairings, and when Langer and Ballesteros asked if they could be left out of the Saturday afternoon fourballs, their request was granted. Langer often asked me if he could be excused a series of matches, but I told him that he was far too valuable to be left out. The absence of Ballesteros and Langer from a series was too big a burden for the team to carry.'

In the aftermath of the US team's victory on Sunday night, Jacklin had approached George O'Grady, deputy executive director of the Tour, and offered to captain the team at Rochester, NY. 'I only offered my services because I thought that they needed help,' Jacklin says defensively. 'I cared so much about the Ryder Cup and what we had achieved – it was not achieved by luck, it was achieved by hard work and a lot of attention to detail – and I didn't feel that was being carried on. I don't want to criticize Bernard, but some of the players can get a bit big for their boots. One of the key things about the 80s was, when it came to the Ryder Cup, egos had to be hung outside the door before the players came in the team-room.'

When it became clear that Jacklin did not have the support of the players this time round, he was happy enough to walk away. 'I don't care, but it's hard to let go of things when you've worked so hard, for no remuneration, and that's not being carried on. And now they've reduced the number of wild cards to two. It's ridiculous. Having said that, it's no damn good having three choices if you haven't got the courage to choose. I mean, do we want to win the Ryder Cup or do we want to put up a show?'

'That was disappointing,' Gallacher said. 'He said he would have put out a different team, he would have forced Seve to play, he would have forced Langer to play. Well, I don't think he would have got away with forcing Langer onto the course when he was injured . . . It doesn't take much thinking to realize that there must have been very unusual circumstances for me not to put my renowned strong players out in the afternoon. I'm not going to break up winning partnerships.'

'I was only in one of Jacklin's teams and that was the Belfry in '89,' said James. 'I don't want to say too much, but I disagreed with the pairings. Our No.1 player that year, [Ronan] Rafferty, was sitting around most of the week, looking for a partner. I couldn't believe we didn't win that . . . I think Gallacher's been a wonderful captain the last two Ryder Cups. At the Belfry, I don't think our team was very much on form and I think he went with the flow very well. I thought he got our pairings dead right. Of course he's been criticized, because we lost. What no-one mentioned was the fact that nearly every American broke par on the last day and, playing the Belfry in a reasonable wind, that sort of scoring was a tremendous feat.

They beat us because they played extremely well on the last day. I don't think there's any other reason. He's been criticized for leaving out Langer and Ballesteros on Saturday, but I mean Seve was not playing well and Langer was not happy and didn't want to play. And Langer is an extremely intelligent bloke. He is able to assess whether or not he should play. And if he says to the captain, "I don't want to play," it's difficult to argue with that. He's not a rookie that's got to be cajoled and sent out.'

Prior to arriving at the Belfry, Gallacher had insisted that regardless of the outcome he would not consider a third term as captain. He said this so often, and so vehemently, that when he agreed to captain the 1995 team at Rochester, New York, those who took a jaundiced view of his efforts at Kiawah and at the Belfry, renewed their attack. Tellingly, the players whom he had captained spoke out over and over on his behalf.

'I still believe that Gallacher is the right choice to be captain again,' Ballesteros said. 'People may look at that as choosing a losing captain. We all know that, but both times that we lost it was very close. We really nearly won in America and I think a lot of things happened on Saturday at the Belfry. Gallacher was a little unlucky. Sam Torrance was injured, I was having a bad back, Bernhard Langer was not feeling very well. A very important part of the team was injured or not feeling very good, so that was one of the problems that we faced, and then Peter Baker's daughter nearly died that night. It created a very negative atmosphere.'

'I don't really feel as bad about losing as a lot of people feel,' said Gallacher, who has agreed to captain the 1995 match in the absence of any other suitable candidate. 'I mean, to me, sport is about application and doing your best and hopefully you'll get a result . . . My whole philosophy about golf is not treating it as life and death. I just feel sorry for the players.'

2

THE KING OF SWING

'The most maddening thing about golf is the perversity with which the body refuses to obey the mind.'

PAT WARD-THOMAS, *The Long Green Fairway*

On the wall of David Leadbetter's Lake Nona academy is a *Golf World* cover, its scarlet banner headline proclaiming him 'THE KING OF SWING'. Framed photographs of his most famous pupils endorse the sentiment. 'Nice place for a walk with five shots in hand,' Nick Faldo has scrawled across a picture of the eighteenth hole at St Andrews, scene of his second Open victory in 1990, while a beaming Nick Price adds, 'I think I peaked earlier than you thought!!!' as he claims the 1992 US PGA Championship. David Frost, the possessor of one of golf's finest swings, stares intently from the cover of a 1988 edition of *Golf World*. 'Thanks for all the interest and effort you have put into my game,' he has written appreciatively. 'You're a great teacher.'

To the players he has helped become champions, Leadbetter is a genius, nothing less. 'David Leadbetter is the best teacher in the world,' Faldo states unequivocally. Others are uncertain whether to describe him as a monster, a guru, a pretender, an inventor or an opportunist; or simply the latest in a long line of distinguished teachers and gurus, all of whom represented a minute advance in our understanding of the swing but none of whom solved the whole puzzle. 'He's not a god,' Denis Pugh, a former coach at Leadbetter's academy, said. 'He's not anything other than a very good golf teacher who's got the best pupil in the world.'

Make that pupils. Over the past ten years, the greatest names in golf have enrolled at Leadbetter's élite academy. Faldo, Price and Frost have been joined in their endeavours by Tom Watson, Bernhard Langer, Ernie Els, John Cook, Craig Parry, Peter Baker, Mark McNulty, Mark O'Meara, Per-Ulrik Johansson, Catrin Nilsmark and Florence Descampe, to name but a few. There have been books (*The Golf Swing* was printed in eight languages and became the second biggest selling golf book of all time), videos (*The Full Golf Swing*, *The Short Game* and *Taking it to the Course*), instruction aids, endorsements and new academies across the globe, and all have been the result of Leadbetter's controversial theories and what is broadly known as his method – a technique based on the premise that the key to consistency under pressure is using the big muscles in the body (those in the legs and torso) to control the little ones (the hands, wrists and arms). The dog wags the tail, so to speak.

'Basically, we try to keep the clubface square for as long as possible,' explained Dennis Sheehy, who worked with Leadbetter for eleven years. 'Whereas the old teachings used your legs for power and your hands for speed, we try to eliminate the variables by using the large muscles and de-emphasizing the smaller ones.'

Pugh was sceptical. 'The method is a marketing toy,' he said disparagingly. 'Really, David Leadbetter teaches golf. He doesn't throw the book at anyone except Faldo, but then Nick's Nick. He probably knows how his television works. With Nick Price, he just says: "Move the ball back half an inch in your stance." '

The problem, as Pugh sees it, is that teaching is subjective, and that by writing books and endorsing aids, one is effectively saying that there is only one way to play golf. This did not concern the 500,000 who flocked to buy *The Golf Swing*, but it did worry some of the game's top teachers, including Eddie Birchenough, Royal Lytham's respected professional – not enough, however, to prevent Birchenough from becoming a fan of the guru and his method. 'I think Leadbetter is a superb teacher. His knowledge of the game is second to none. He's made golf teaching almost a cult.'

In 1979, when the air in Florida boiled with humidity and the sky was that intense, mercurial blue that sears the back of your eyes, an angular figure took up residence on the practice ground at Disneyworld where Phil Ritson was a teacher. An Englishman by birth, he had arrived in Orlando from Southern Africa and was aiming to try his luck on the Florida mini-tours. 'He was the guy always standing on the range, with nothing to do but watch Phil all the time and try to learn from Phil,' Pugh recalled. 'He was the tall, quiet guy, who everyone thought was a good guy, just waiting for a break.'

Leadbetter was the son of a timber merchant, who had spent most of his youth in Zimbabwe. A four-handicapper by the age of sixteen, he had played junior golf with the likes of Price, McNulty, Dennis Watson and Tony Johnstone, before embarking on an accountancy degree at the bidding of his father. In the grey corridors of business college, everything in him had ached to quit. He loathed the regimented columns, the regimented class. When the sympathetic pro at a Harare golf club offered him a job as an assistant, he had made the break for freedom without a second thought, burning his books and running away to the sunshine, the lush grass on the range, and the sweet, sweet sound of a perfectly-hit shot.

In those years, Leadbetter did not harbour dreams about wealth and glory on the international circuit. Most young professionals do at one stage or another but Leadbetter was always pessimistic about his chances, even when he was performing well on South Africa's Sunshine Circuit. Until, that is, he met Phil Ritson, the country's top teacher. Ritson was charismatic; he was influential. 'He was a very inspirational person,' Pugh said. 'If he was a football coach, he'd be a Jack Charlton sort of character. He'd have players doing things you wouldn't have thought they could do.'

Ritson took the self-conscious youngster under his wing. 'He said to me: "David, you can go as far as you want to go in this game,"' Leadbetter recalled.

Leadbetter wasn't convinced. Aware of his limitations as a player, he spent hours pouring over instruction articles and books, preparing for the day when he'd be teaching amateurs at some quiet suburban club. Hogan, Snead, Nelson, Nicklaus and Palmer were all scrutinized and analysed, and by the time he arrived in America, where he had followed Ritson, he had distilled from them what he needed and drawn his own conclusions. In Florida, Leadbetter wrestled with the mini-tours but gradually surrendered to the desire to teach rather than play. Word of his ability travelled. He graduated from a bit part at Disneyworld to his own range at Grenlefe Resort in Haines City. A one-man band with a secretary to manage his steady trickle of takings, he was giving three-hour group sessions, at $120 for six people, when an impoverished professional by the name of Dennis Sheehy presented himself for lessons.

Sheehy had come, in effect, on a pilgrimage. So revered was Leadbetter by his long-term pupils – Price, McNulty, Frost and Wayne Westner, who by now were hitting the big time – that Sheehy was prepared to offer his services as an assistant in any capacity whatsoever, and to sleep on Leadbetter's floor, or in the green-keeper's hut, or some other available corner in return for watching David teach or being taught by him. Leadbetter just smiled, shrugged and took him on board. Easygoing and kindly, in a vague, unbusinesslike way, he was to do exactly the same in later years with several other youngsters without real futures as players, most notably Simon Holmes.

This was the relaxed, enjoyable, slightly precarious position the Grenlefe academy was in on the day that Nick Faldo called and announced his intention of putting his game and, by extension, his life, into Leadbetter's hands.

'He was very intense,' said Leadbetter, recalling Faldo's arrival in 1985. 'You could see he was just totally consumed with getting to the top and being the best. His work ethic was unbelievable. It wasn't an exaggeration that he'd hit a thousand balls a day. I mean, it was *hot*. It was the middle of June and it was awful. But he'd be hitting balls and just working and working. He didn't let anything interfere with what he was doing. He said: "Listen, I know it's going to take a while but I'm not worried about it. I don't care how I play for a while." I thought: "This guy has the potential to go really far."'

With hindsight, what seems amazing, given Faldo's perfectionist nature and not inconsiderable achievements at the time, is that he should choose Leadbetter – a man based in America, whose teachings and background were so far removed from his own world – over any other coach, and, more particularly, that he should choose him on the strength of one or two casual meetings when his entire career was at stake.

'I didn't think about it at the time,' confessed Leadbetter. 'It was just a case of, here's another guy with a good reputation and I want to help him. At the time, I didn't realize the consequences of either making the guy great or failing. But if he had failed, I would have been held up as some bum who'd sort of messed up Nick Faldo.'

NOTES FROM A GURU
Extracts from Leadbetter's file on Faldo

NICK FALDO

BRITISH OPEN 90
Pre open – shorter+ feel laid off / *posture* resistance in right shoulder – feel tall as he pulls shoulder forward, keep extension in right arm.

VALDERRAMA 90
Drill getting to link 6 and hit feeling a pull.

PGA 90
Keep left knee solid. Club coming from inside – resistance back. Not inside too quick.

SKINS GAME 90
Problems – posture sloppy, weight on heels+head too far behind ball and down. Left hip closing too early on trigger.

Corrections – posture taller, weight forward on balls, head squarer and up, feel left hip move open – trigger left hip open not closed.

Problem – backswing – too much move off ball – set late + no resistance, right shoulder turns too early – face too open at the top . . . no torque (length good).

Correction – resistance with right shoulder – feel more tilt (not flat as 1st day) – sense remaining on left side + no move off ball – head steady, keep angle at back of right hand.

Problem – downswing – club dropping too much from inside, bunchy, head droopy – arms down too quickly, left leg slidey – early release + arm trapped – steep plane on release + high finish.

Correction – downswing – keep arms up as left shoulder separates – feel right shoulder stay up – no left knee slide – feel hands high throughout the downswing – after transition turn right side into ball – right bicep and chest together – pull butt-end past ball – late hit – feel tall – allow head to move forward not stay back.

GENERAL

Keep arms up and not drop down quickly causing dip – need to hold angle through impact . . . plane of shaft flatter through impact.

DRILLS – to the top 1st move leaving arms up+ hold it+ hit from there, grasp right shoulder-blade to feel right-side release.
Right arm only – shaft only to feel release.
Hit SW holding angle through impact + butt-end past the ball.
Hit shots with ball outside right foot to feel release and high hands + level shoulders with head moving forward not hanging back.
Looks great – shallow angle with driver.

Sheehy, who watched their progress – saw Faldo's raw, bleeding hands and Leadbetter's commitment – felt then that it was impossible that two such driven men could fail. 'One thing about David, and people don't really talk about this, is that he's that good and he's got that much belief in himself, that it's almost like he's fearless. When Faldo came along, both of them had so much to lose and yet they were so positive about it. And I loved that. There was just no doubt.'

The first sign that their faith and industry were to be justified came when Faldo won the Spanish Open in May 1987. The second was when he shot eighteen pars in the most violently inhospitable conditions the British Isles have to offer, two months later, to win his first Open Championship.

'The most special moment in my career was when Faldo won at Muirfield,' Leadbetter sighed. 'To me, it was the culmination of so much hard work. I mean, a lot of other things have been really great, like Nick Price winning the US PGA, but that '87 British Open was a special time because it was just like, "Wow!" I was away doing some clinic and I phoned him at Grey Walls from the airport. They said: "He's taking no phone calls." I said: "Listen, I'm sure if you tell him it's me, he'll speak to me." And he came right on the phone and he was shouting and screaming. He said: "Jeez, I can't believe this has happened!" He was in tears; so was I. That was really special. He doesn't show emotion that often, but when he does, he does – like at the Open in '92. But at Muirfield he just proved to himself – not to anybody else, but to himself – that he could actually do it.'

Not everyone was pleased that Leadbetter had, in a manner of speaking, struck gold. Ritson, for reasons of his own, ceased to speak to him at all. Nobody has yet put a copyright on method – golf's X-factor, that enigmatic, unpredictable quality in the swing, will forever defy analysis – but Ritson seemed to feel that Leadbetter had taken what he had been taught and somehow exploited it.

'Phil would probably be frustrated because David has established new heights in coaching, and he might have seen the fabulous wealth David has acquired,' Pugh explained. 'I mean, he engineered the break for David, and got him into the States. But to sort of say that David sat at his feet and slavishly learnt everything from him would not be fair to either of them.'

Leadbetter was in complete agreement. 'He influenced me a lot in my early years,' he admitted. 'I'm not saying he didn't. But he was just a stepping stone on a learning curve. I don't teach like Phil Ritson at all. I was grateful to him. In fact, he even helped me get into the country. The only reason we don't get on – as I say, it's not that I don't want to get on – is that you hear all sorts of reports: "Hey, I taught David everything he knows and now he's doing well, blah, blah, blah." To me, there's a slight amount of jealousy there. I remember him coming to me four or five years ago and saying: "I hate teaching. I'm never going to give another lesson again, and if I do I'm going to charge $1,000 an hour and I'm going to be involved in a golf course complex and design clubs . . ." And I said: "Hey, that's great. Super. All the best to you." And then two years later, it's: "Phil Ritson's making a comeback. All the teachers out there don't know what they're talking about." But, you know, that's just human nature.'

At Lake Nona, all of human life was on display. A procession of unlikely characters through the igloo that was our press tent added an exotic flavour to proceedings, and made an otherwise unendurable tournament – for no other reason than the fact that rounds commonly escalate to six and a half hours, sheer misery if one is working on British deadlines – rather enjoyable. The Zimbabwean team of McNulty and Price, friends since childhood, came in and talked about the sand greens (browns), rivalry and sun-filled days of their youth; the Jamaicans came in and explained with a resigned air how they had shot a combined 174; and the defending champions, Fred Couples and Davis Love III, came in and told us that they intended to make it a clean sweep for America in the team events of 1993 – US players had already made off with the Ryder Cup, the Walker Cup and the Dunhill Cup; the World Cup would complete the picture.

Every year, uninformed local reporters and golf writers who should know better draw comparisons between the World Cup and the Ryder Cup. This is like comparing Chaucer and John Grisham. Indeed, the only similarity between the Ryder Cup and the World Cup is the word 'Cup'. That is not to say that the latter isn't a worthy event but the standard of many players, and the ludicrous format, leaves a lot to be desired.

To all intents and purposes, the World Cup at Lake Nona was David Leadbetter's party. A handful of patriotic spectators braved the humidity to witness first hand the histrionics of Ian Woosnam or the 94 shot by Jacob Avnaim of Israel, but for the most part the thin, cosmopolitan stream of gate entrants were the goal-directed Leadbetter faithful, intent on wearing a path to golf's new Mecca.

Only one man seemed immune to the charms of the academy. He appeared on the practice ground on the afternoon of the third round, when the air was hot and damp and filled with that sweet, earthy smell that precedes enormous thunderstorms – Nick Price had spotted him in the car-park and pleaded with him to give an impromptu clinic – and before long had brought the range to a standstill, each new arrival abandoning his clubs and hurrying to join the gathered throng of disciples. 'That's Moe Norman,' one pro told a newcomer in reverential tones. 'The greatest ball-striker in the world.'

The man holding the assembled players in thrall was in his mid-sixties and dressed in heavy brown trousers and a stiff-collared white shirt, his face flushed with the effort of hitting one after another of the most beautiful golf shots it is possible to see. 'Five years, twelve hundred balls a day,' Norman puffed in response to a question about how long his method had taken to perfect. He fired off ten shots as straight and true as arrows. 'Watch this for purity . . .'

'Ohhh!' groaned the crowd appreciatively.

'Purer than the water you drink,' Norman cried, adding in his Canadian cadence: 'But I keep it so *simple* and *precise*. I'm the only golfer in history who has had his hands lower through the hitting area than he has at address.'

'How do you start down?' a South African asked respectfully.

'I'm setting the *angle* of my downswing as I go back.'

'What's the fastest part of the golf swing?'

'The *follow-through*. They think it's the backswing.'

'Talked to Hogan lately?'

'Four years ago.'

'Did you used to practise with him a lot?'

'Not a lot. He liked watching me and I liked watching him.'

It was then that the penny dropped. Norman was the legend I'd heard players refer to, the brilliant ball-striker whose genius had been denied the world. Born in Kitchener, Canada, he was, for most of his chequered career, an eccentric recluse who was so suspicious of strangers he refused to give his money to a bank and so scared of crowds that he seldom attended prize-giving ceremonies.

He habitually slept in his car. Away from the fanfare, his feats were scarcely credible. It was said that he shot 59 three or more times. Golf was so easy to him that he would wager that he could break a course record without ever having seen the course, and do exactly that. He would concede 10-foot putts in match-play and then casually roll in his own 15-footer. He would play holes backwards, taking a nine-iron off the tee and a driver off the fairway. He would deliberately putt into a greenside bunker if he was playing the final hole of a tournament with a two-stroke lead, just to make life interesting. A Coca-Cola addict who drank up to thirty Cokes a day, he once teed off a Coke bottle in the Los Angeles Open. He made history by becoming the only player ever to walk out of the Masters. Having caused a sensation at the start of the week by sacking his allotted caddie before he had even picked up the bag, he then decided that the breeze was too strong for him to continue in the third round. He was lying fifth in the tournament at the time. 'Too windy for golf. Back to Canada, back to Canada,' he said and was gone.

Golf balls flew like sparks from Norman's clubhead; the shadows of the crowd slid across his shoes. As a young man, it was his fear of people that kept him from becoming great. 'Forty-one inches back and twenty-two inches in front,' Norman explained. 'Keeps the club on line as long as possible. Wide, tight, wide. You don't see that today. Nobody believes in action-reaction any more.'

At last he took reluctant leave, offering theories and explanations for a dozen golfing dilemmas as he went.

'What's the hardest shot in golf?'

'The next one.'

'Excuse me, Mr Norman,' I said, 'but can you tell me what the secret of the golf swing is?"

Norman stopped abruptly; the crowd milled round. 'Hard work, sticking with the same thing every day you play and believing in yourself,' he replied instantly. 'People are afraid of themselves. People are afraid to *win*. They're too busy looking for obstacles. What were you thinking of when you were walking over here? Can you tell me how many steps you took? How high you lifted your feet? Were you aware of any obstruction – a car? a telephone post? No? Well, treat trees and bunkers the same way.

'Look at this little fella!' cried Norman suddenly, opening his palm and revealing a golf ball with the air of a conjuror unveiling a golden egg. 'How many people is he laughing at? Forty million people. Forty million people and they're all trying to get him. They don't know how. I'm the only guy who does. I'm the only guy who does.'

On Sunday, I walked down to Leadbetter's academy, a cool wooden bungalow more reminiscent of the home of a great Southern writer than a state-of-the-art school of golf. Fans whirred lazily, visitors lolled about in armchairs, swing videos wound and rewound and Mike Hendersen, a national junior champion who has been a regular at the academy since the age of twelve, slapped balls into the net. That Leadbetter himself was nowhere to be seen came as no surprise. A notoriously bad time-keeper, he says that his tardiness is a standing joke with Faldo and Fanny. If he tells them he'll see them at the eighth hole, Faldo replies: 'I'll expect you at the twelfth.' 'They have bets about which hole I'll appear,' Leadbetter laughs.

To journalists with distant deadlines or players without pressing problems, a lax approach to appointments might indeed seem mildly amusing – particularly since it can be justified by a punishing schedule – but there is no doubt that it is the single biggest cause of disenchantment among Leadbetter's lesser-known pupils (hence Chris Moody's caustic advertisement). Players have described the unique torture that is standing on the practice ground, hitting balls poorly, while Leadbetter and Faldo analyse and strategize interminably in the distance. Half an hour ticks by, then an hour, as Leadbetter inches his way down the range, then just when he is almost with you, someone else grabs him. There have been golfers who have actually made scheduled trips to Grenlefe or Lake Nona and have hardly seen hide nor hair of him. 'Six minutes in a year wasn't enough,' Howard Clark, a former pupil and Ryder Cup player, complained. Pugh sided with Leadbetter. 'Any player who knows David's travel schedule and who thinks that David's going to spend five hours a week with him, five months of the year, is deluding himself,' he said.

That may be so, but it doesn't alter the fact that for a golf pro with a fragile ego, lack of supervision can have dire consequences. Take the case of Ove Sellberg, for example. A talented Swede with two European Tour victories behind him, he was, none the less, someone who needed a great deal of attention to see him through the swing changes that Leadbetter wanted him to make. When that

The David Leadbetter Golf Academy

introduces the

Leadbetter Budget Plan

There is now a plan to suit any pocket.
To make himself available to a wider audience David Leadbetter is proud to announce

THE DRIVE-BY GOLF LESSON

Yes, you pay by the minute. Pay only for the time you use.
Choose from either the

ONE MINUTE LESSON
TWO MINUTE SCHOOL
THE THREE MINUTE RETREAT

All rates are fully inclusive except the one minute lesson.
There will be a supplement if David has to touch the brake.
Obviously this is not usually necessary except in extreme cases.

More fun than a drive-by shooting.
Less expensive than a drive-through McDonalds.

Phone now for a reservation.

1 800 BIG HOOK

Designed by Chris Moody, this spoof advertisement says as much about the unrealistic expectations of lesser players as it does about the demands of Leadbetter's time.

attention was not forthcoming, he began a slow slide into oblivion.

Leadbetter's explanation is that he hadn't yet set up his European division, with Europe-based teachers to monitor the progress of players like Sellberg. 'It was unfortunate because he was one of those guys who really needs to be constantly fortified as far as confidence goes. He's a little up and down mentally, Ove. He needs a guy to give him a sort of pat on the back. He played well when we started off but he lost some confidence and then it was a case of, he tried this, that and the other and he obviously hasn't played well at all in the last three or four years. We still speak and we're still on good terms and what have you. It's just the nature of the business. You can't be successful with 100 per cent of the people you work with, there's just no way.'

Mark O'Meara, with whom I eventually found Leadbetter, was not among the discontented minority. He stood on the range beneath the vast canopy of blue sky and hit balls with a balanced, beautiful swing. Leadbetter hovered nearby in traditional pose, legs spread, arms folded, expression obscured by dark glasses. 'Does that feel any better?' he enquired of the thirty-eight-year-old Ryder Cup player.

'It really does,' admitted O'Meara, as contented as a cat on that balmy Florida day.

Applause crackled like rifle-fire in the distance. The war being waged between golfing nations amid the pines and jade valleys of Lake Nona seemed as remote as the moon. Hendersen rolled up in a buggy. 'Are those guys doing any good out there?' O'Meara asked, referring to the US team of Couples and Love, who had led by five strokes from the Zimbabweans at the start of the final round. 'Freddie and Davis ripping it out there?'

'Freddie holed his sandwedge at the first hole,' Hendersen told him.

'Come on!' exclaimed O'Meara, his open, friendly face expressing frank amazement. 'Unbelievable. For eagle?'

'Unreal,' agreed Leadbetter.

As if inspired, O'Meara resumed practice with renewed vigour.

'Well, the pattern is there,' Leadbetter said, studying the flight of the balls. 'I mean, I know not everything's perfect yet but . . .'

'No, that feels good,' O'Meara assured him. 'If I can keep hitting it like that . . .'

A pleased smile played around Leadbetter's lips. 'I like the height on those shots, too,' he said. 'You're really starting to show the true loft of the club.'

Even Leadbetter's detractors agree that this is his forte, his ability to communicate – to relax, reassure and instil perfect confidence in a way that makes his lessons less like those of a maths teacher, dispensing complex and indigestible theories, than a sort of intravenous transfusion of technique and positive thinking.

'I'm not saying there aren't people who know more than I do as far as mechanics are concerned,' said Leadbetter. 'I mean, I can speak physics and theory with the best of them, but there are people out there who can cite *The Golf Machine*, which to me is like the most boring book ever. There's some good stuff in there, but people can't relate to: "Your right arm is four degrees out and you've got the blade two degrees above parallel." I'm such a non-technical person . . . I've always maintained that it's not what you know as a teacher, it's how you say it. It's 25 per cent knowledge and 75 per cent communication, no doubt about it.'

There are two major criticisms of Leadbetter's teaching. One is the complexity of the method. 'It seems very simple in its most basic form, but when things start to go wrong, it gets very complicated,' the English professional Roger Chapman said. 'You go to the first tee with two or three different swing thoughts when you should only be going with one.'

'I would tend to disagree,' said Leadbetter when I challenged him on this. 'I mean, yes, I'm known as being analytical because a lot of the players that I teach are that way. But as a teacher you've got to be like a chameleon. You've got to change according to who you work with, which I do – I change hats. My philosophy is, hey, the more versatile I am, the more I can teach any type of player. Because everybody's mind-set is different. With Ian Woosnam, it's very simple, you just stand up there and whack it. With David Frost we also have to keep it unbelievably simple – a lot different to players like Faldo or O'Meara who understand the technical aspects.'

The other criticism is that Leadbetter tends to impose his method on players, rather than working with what they have.

'I would say that when you work with a person for a period of time, that just happens naturally,' Leadbetter said. 'Yes, there probably is a degree of imposition there, if you will. But not to start off with. I mean, I'm careful with that. I never go out to solicit business, I promise. I'll never go up to someone like Olazabal and say, "Hey, Ollie, I can really help you." I mean, Bernhard Langer's asked me to work full time with him now. Bernhard's won two majors and he's had a great year, but he's a bit like Nick in that he wants to be the best he can be. And what we do is we sit down and we discuss things. I mean, my biggest thing working with players is to make sure they understand what they're trying to do and why they're trying to do it. I don't say: "You *have* to do this." I say: "With your build, this is what I suggest." And if you listen to me teach different players, my approach is totally different. That's what's fun to me, that's what's enjoyable. That's what enables me to come back and give clinics to high handicappers, because it's fun, it gets my mind working.'

Nobody can argue that, complicated or not, golf's favourite guru has a winning formula. Yet despite his illustrious stable, his million-pound product endorsements and his global reach, all is not rosy in the Leadbetter camp. A year or two ago, when the classroom of indigents and unknowns Leadbetter had nurtured into the game's top ranks expanded into a multi-million dollar teaching industry, his self-confessed weaknesses as a businessman had begun to show. In December 1992, he did the sensible thing and put his financial affairs into the hands of International Management Group. Not every-one saw this as a positive move. Almost immediately, three of Leadbetter's right-hand men – Simon Holmes, Denis Pugh and Gary Smith, close friends as well as assistants – turned their backs on him. For a man who values friendship and loyalty above all else, it came as a devastating blow.

'He was absolutely shattered,' said Sheehy who, along with Mitchell Spearman, chose to stay. 'I've never seen him so upset about anything. You put your complete trust in somebody like that and basically [they throw it back at you]. You know, money was the governing factor in their decision, it's quite simple.'

'You feel a sense of disappointment,' Leadbetter admitted. 'But, as I say, ego's a big thing in this day and age and people think they can make more money. Somebody asked me the other day: "What do you think about Simon Holmes going?" And I said: "Well, I'll tell you. Without being egotistical, I might have taught him all he knows but I haven't taught him all I know." ' He gave a dry laugh. 'Simon Holmes first came to me as a very so-so player . . . and he learnt everything he knows about anything, I feel, from me . . . I was sad in Simon's case because you think that there's some sort of loyalty factor. I mean, [he and Denis] were earning good salaries and they had the potential to earn a lot of money. They used the excuse: "Oh, with IMG involved you're cutting us out." Which is bullshit because I run this place . . . and I make sure that the good people who work with me do fine. And I'm thinking in the long term, because in two or three years' time we'll probably have ten or twelve academies around the world which will be generating a lot of income. When you're one person, it doesn't take long for Seve to say, "Oh, I'm not working with Simon any more," or Bernhard to say, "I'm working with David and not Simon now," and your popularity goes bump.'

I put it to him that there was a clause in the IMG contract that amounted to restriction of trade, to which Simon and Denis objected. Pugh said that although IMG had 'managed to turn the David Leadbetter disorganization into an organization, the IMG contract wasn't any good for anyone but David Leadbetter. I was changing status from being in partnership with David to being an employee, and I didn't want that.'

Leadbetter's eyes widened. 'That's absolute bull,' he said succinctly. 'I could even show you the contract. All we said was that they couldn't use the David Leadbetter name to promote themselves. There was nothing more sinister than that. They've used a number of excuses for why they left, but to me, it was just a case of feeling that a big organization would cramp their style. They'd lose their individuality . . . But I just let people do their own thing, and maybe that was the problem with Simon who, when he started with us, was just picking up balls and earning a few dollars an hour in order to support himself in the odd mini-tour event. And then he went onto a pretty huge salary for such a young guy, earning more than a lot of Tour players, and sometimes you can lose touch with reality. But life's like that.'

'I think there's a tendency at times for David to think, "I made them and therefore they should appreciate it," ' Pugh said, 'but in my case that wasn't true. There was a lot of dialogue and I would say that I had a lot of input into what he did.' He considered the current lukewarm state of their relationship. 'I think we're still friends,' he said without conviction. 'We're just not very good friends. But in the end, the only reason for signing would have been not to upset David, and that's the wrong reason. The negative side of it has been the politics and backbiting of coaching on Tour, but my biggest regret is just on a personal basis, that we don't phone each other up every week any more just to discuss the weather.'

Sheehy found the whole business nothing short of incredible. 'For me, a big part of why David is the best is because he's such a good guy. That is the bottom line. He's not up in the clouds, he's not pretentious, he's not egotistical. Obviously, his family keep his feet on the ground, but I think it's just being a decent, everyday, down-to-earth, normal person that is the key to him being a good communicator. There are no airs and graces; he just empathizes with people.'

It is perhaps because Leadbetter is so well-meaning and sincere that he feels betrayed by people when they fail to credit him. Other teachers chalk it up to experience; Leadbetter seems to take it personally.

'I'll remember till the day I die Seve coming back here at the start of '92,' Leadbetter began. 'We worked on some things and he left here hitting it really well. He went to New Orleans the next week – that was the week before Augusta – and finished twelfth. I went up to Augusta on the Monday and Billy [Foster, Ballesteros's caddie] said: "I tell you what, Seve could win this week, the way he's hitting it. It's unbelievable." I thought: "Jeez, this is great. I can't wait till this guy plays." I get there Tuesday morning, walk onto the practice tee and Billy comes over and [rolls his eyes.] I said: "What's the matter?" He said: "Watch." '

According to Leadbetter, it wasn't so much that Ballesteros was cutting the odd ball or hitting one fat; it's that they were flying so far out of bounds they were in danger of breaching air-traffic control regulations. Leadbetter didn't need to look far to find the probable cause. In between shots, Ballesteros was engaged in a passionate argument with his brother and sometime teacher, Manuel, with whom he was plainly at odds. Like a man in a dream, Leadbetter walked towards the Spaniards. He took a deep breath. 'What's going on?' he asked.

Ballesteros looked carefully past him. 'Manuel is here,' he said flatly.

'And from that point on, I promise – you look back at the records – from that point on, he has not played well,' said Leadbetter. 'I'm not talking about Switzerland [Ballesteros's best finish in 1993, second at the European Masters] – that was probably a fluke. I mean, he was very sheepish at the Masters. He sort of avoided me. He finished tied fifty-ninth. I saw him in Japan and he said: "David, what we did last year was good but it wasn't natural. I want to go back to my natural swing." I said: "Fine." And you just think, that's strange to do that. I mean, he's wasted the last eighteen months of his golfing career.'

What hurt Leadbetter most is that by denying that his teacher played any real role in the achievements of 1991, his great comeback season, Ballesteros also denied Leadbetter the source of his satisfaction as a teacher – 'feeling what a player would feel for that one moment in time.

'When you say: "Is there an ego involved?" I suppose maybe there is an ego because you say, "Well, Jeez, maybe I did do something to help that person get to that point," ' Leadbetter confessed. 'On the other hand, you also get slapped in the face because sometimes you can help somebody who you've worked really hard with and you don't get any sort of credit whatsoever. But you know yourself personally that you did. But that's the nature of the business. I've come to realize that now. I realized that, hey, these aren't people you can control. Golf is an individual sport and the reason these guys are great is because they're different. They're selfish, to a certain extent. You have to be. But, for the most part, they're a really good bunch of guys.'

The door of Leadbetter's office crashes open and his young son bursts in. He wants to take his golf clubs to show his friends. 'There's too many people around, Andy,' Leadbetter says indulgently, shooing him out. Returning to his chair, he remarked: 'He's really getting into the game. He's just turned nine and he shot 43 off the ladies' tees the other day.'

These are the positives: his wife Kelly, a professional on the LPGA Tour, and their two children, heirs to an awesome golfing heritage. When he's not helping Faldo or Price to victories in major championships, Leadbetter coaches his wife, does an aerobic activity four times a week, pushes weights and stretches three times a week, fishes, skis, plays golf and updates his instruction book collection. He also obsesses about his diet. When he travels to Japan, a suitcase full of bread, cereals and soya milk goes, too. Chicken is on the Leadbetter menu, but not red meat, not junk food, not alcohol.

If his fitness fanaticism is mirrored in his strong, pale face and spare, sinewy frame, then his lackadaisical approach to time-keeping and business management ('My organizational abilities leave a lot to be desired') are reflected in his tiny and chaotic office, with its autographed photographs, framed magazine covers, scattered golf clubs, and desk piled high with contracts, newspaper cuttings, golf balls, swing aids, instruction books, player files and crumpled correspondence.

Following my gaze, Leadbetter grinned. 'I didn't plan this success,' he said, in case I was wondering how it could possibly have come about. 'I consider myself fortunate, I really do. I've never been one of these guys that's been goal-oriented. You get these psychologists that say, you've got to have a one-year plan, a three-year plan, a five-year plan. It's like, hey, whatever happens, happens. I couldn't tell you how much money I've got. I mean, I have no clue. I never sign a cheque. Kelly signs some and IMG do some. I'm not trying to sound big-headed. What I'm trying to say is that because I enjoy it and I get so wrapped up in what I do, I sort of lose touch. Over here, everything is so fast – wham, bam, keep up with the Jones's. You're going at 150 mph. There's nothing better that I can do than to sit in front of the TV and watch cricket. To me, that's totally relaxing. I sit there with my dad and we discuss things.'

In the early hours of the morning, before his one-year-old daughter gets up and starts demanding attention, Leadbetter will often lie awake and reflect upon the extraordinary chain of events that led him to become the most successful teacher in the history of the game. 'It is amazing what's happened. I sometimes actually think: "How come I got so lucky? Do I deserve all this?" Because a lot of it has been through what other people have done. It's not as if I've gone out and won the British Open. I don't know. I guess I just happened to be in the right place at the right time. A bit of luck, a bit of skill, mix it all together and' – Leadbetter laughs, swings back in his chair and raises his hands in a toast to the portrait gallery of champions – 'you've got this.'

3

NOTES FROM DOWN UNDER

'If you want to know what it is to feel the "correct" social world fizzle to nothing, you should come to Australia. It is a weird place. In the established sense it is socially nil. Happy-go-lucky, don't you bother, we're in Australia. But also there seems to be no inside life of any sort; just a long lapse and drift. A rather fascinating indifference. A physical indifference to what we call soul or spirit. It's a really weird show.'

D.H. LAWRENCE, 1922

THE AUSTRALIAN OPEN, MELBOURNE. In sympathy with the outside temperature, the needle on Greg Norman's personal barometer was into the red and rising. Slow play had pushed it there. Instead of taking advantage of the brief respite offered by Trish Hogan of Darwin's do-it-yourself stomach virus cure (a concoction of solidified brandy, sugar and gelatine), he had chosen to deplete his energy reserves still further, and was vigorously bemoaning the fact that his round had taken five hours and forty minutes to complete, including a twenty-minute wait at the seventh.

'Play in Australia is slower than any other nation in the world,' he barked. 'Something has to be done. We have an image problem. Players go home to the US, Britain, Japan or wherever, and say, "Hey, Australia has great golf courses but it takes *forever* to play." It's a joke. What I don't think [the Tour officials] understand is that the golf courses in Melbourne are tougher by far than 90 per cent of the golf courses in the world. And when you come out here and get a hot northerly blowing at thirty or forty mph, it compounds the problem. Maybe we should have a two-tee start. Just because the US Open and the British Open don't have a two-tee start, doesn't mean that the Australian Open shouldn't have a two-tee start.'

He glowered at the contingent of sportswriters over an elaborate display of flowers. They in their turn looked sheepish. They shifted in their chairs. It was almost as if there was a tacit understanding that the media were in some way responsible for slow play. I began to feel guilty myself.

I had arrived in Melbourne from New York. Robinson and I had driven to Manhattan after a surreal final night at the World Cup in Florida, during which we had sat in the darkness at Lake Nona, beneath a vast canopy of stars, waiting for a tow-truck to bring us a new tyre. Alone but for a couple of kitchen staff, we had stationed ourselves between the ghostly columns of the clubhouse and listened to a young American tell us that there wasn't a member at Lake Nona who didn't think that Nick Price was a beautiful human being. Later, in a New York agog with the Bobbitt story, we had done a comprehensive tour of all the boot shops in Greenwich Village.

At Metropolitan Golf Club, the first stop on my planned, four-week sojourn on the Australasian Tour, a statement had been issued by Norman. 'I was halfway to the course when I started to have stomach cramps,' he said. 'I needed to go home and lie down. One minute I am fine, the next minute terrible . . . But no matter what, I'll be on the tee at 8.36 a.m. tomorrow.'

That had been on Wednesday. On Thursday morning, soon after the 'VIRUS HITS GREG' headlines hit the newsstands, Norman was on the first tee, his eyes closed against the cool grey day, his arms wrapped around himself, shivering and in obvious distress. Raymond Floyd, who had flown in with Norman, could hardly believe he was playing at all. For the duration of the twenty-one-hour journey from Los Angeles via Hawaii and Pago Pago, his friend had been running a high fever, huddling in blankets and breaking out in cold sweats, and he had been ill several times. Norman suspected food-poisoning; Floyd was certain it was exhaustion. 'I think Greg is just run down. He's been doing so many things in such a short period without time even to take a breath.'

There was plenty of evidence to support this theory. Beginning in October, Norman had flown from Florida to Japan for a tournament, and then from Japan to the United States, where he finished second in the Tour Championship. From San Francisco, he had gone to Cairns for a fishing holiday, before flying from Australia to Japan on 7 November. There, he holed an eagle putt at the last to win the Taiheiyo Masters by a stroke. He flew back to the US the same night to play in the Grand Slam of Golf, won that event, flew straight to California to play in his own tournament, the A$1.67m Shark Shootout, and was on the plane to Melbourne for the Australian Open within an hour of finishing. And that doesn't take into account the fact that he had already won the Doral-Ryder Open, the Open Championship and A$3 million during the course of the season.

Frank Williams, IMG's man in Melbourne, was full of admiration for his client. 'How he is able to play golf at his level is beyond me. He gets up at the crack of dawn and keeps going till he flops into bed at ten or eleven at night, and then he gets up and does the same thing again.'

Sick and tired and eight pounds lighter, Norman was still determined to play. 'If I was in America I would have pulled out, no question about it. But down here it would have hurt everybody, and I just figured I'd rather hurt myself .'

On Friday, a hot north wind, laden with dust and pollen, slowed play to the six-hour crawl that had infuriated Norman. 'It'll only last for a day,' Peter Thomson predicted. 'There'll be a storm this afternoon and then it will change and blow from the south-west. You can bet on it.'

Grant Waite, winner of the Kemper Open in the US, could see no justification whatsoever for the pace of play. 'It's absolutely ridiculous,' he fumed. 'Whoever it is, the tournament organizers or the rules committee, is doing an absolutely pathetic job.'

The tournament chairman, Jim Barr, was stung. 'We know it is slow but it is the players themselves who should get a move on,' he snapped.

Sandy Lyle couldn't have moved faster if he tried. So painful was the progress of the erstwhile Masters Champion (he took three hours to play nine holes), that even the *Herald Sun* could not remain unmoved. 'As the predictable northerly unleashed its full fury upon the afternoon players . . . Lyle's brittle mind cracked wide open,' it reported, 'and what emerged was a professional in total disarray, a once-fine professional tormented by the enormous disparity between his past achievements and present form.'

Golf is not a gentle killer. First, it seeps into the blood, warm and exhilarating, like the heady rush of some designer drug. Later, it operates a system of reward: the greater a player's gift, the sweeter the adrenalin rush; the harder he tries, the richer the prize. For a while it had seemed to Lyle that every stairway led to heaven. He was childlike in his simple delight in his own ability. When he won the 1985 Open Championship at Royal St Georges and was asked whether this was all he had ever dreamed of, he replied humbly, naïvely almost: 'Well, it's a step in the right direction.' It seemed such a simple game, golf. There were victories on the Continent, in Australia, in Japan and the United States, and all of them were effortless and part of the natural order of things. One afternoon he found himself poised on the brink of winning the 1988 US Masters. His approach shot to the last ended in a bunker. The obvious occurred to everyone but Lyle – that it was virtually impossible for him to reach the green; that even then they were unpicking his name from the winner's jacket. But Lyle simply scooped the ball out of the white sand with a seven-iron and rolled in a snaking, downhill putt for victory. And that's when it happened. Golf, the fickle comforter, turned her back on him. After that, no amount of practising, counselling or coaching could help. As suddenly as it had come, the magic was gone.

Lyle had not lost the ability to win tournaments. After a slump lasting for the best part of three years, he had come back to win the 1991 BMW International, and in 1992 he had won the Italian Open and the Volvo Masters, one of the most prestigious events in Europe. But he had lost that inner belief that separates the good player from the great; he had lost the ability to perform at the highest level. Lyle should have been the twelfth man in the team at the 1989 Ryder Cup, but he asked Jacklin to leave him out. He should have been at Kiawah Island, but his form was still suspect. And he should definitely have been at the Belfry in 1993.

'One of the reasons Sandy Lyle didn't play much in early '93 was because he was hoping to get appearance money,' Mark James said. 'He had 170,000 Ryder Cup points at the end of the '92 season, and he hardly played at the beginning of the '93 season. He should have been able to walk into the team. I'm not saying he was playing well enough, but he should certainly have got another 130,000 points and got into the top ten and then he would have been hard to leave out. Whoever was advising him not to play was making a big mistake.'

Now Lyle was struggling to get to grips with Metropolitan. 'He actually has no idea what he's going to do and then he gets a panic attack,' said Max Cunningham, Lyle's caddie, adding that the Scot had visited places on the golf course where 'elephants go to die . . . He's too inside on the downswing, so he either snap-hooks or blocks it right. He can't stand on any tee and know where it's going to go, and what it's done is just erode his confidence.'

Noel Blundell, the Australian sports psychologist who had helped Lyle recover from his slump the first time round, shook his head sadly. 'He took one bad shot in the pro-am and it affected him for the next seven holes. The frustration levels crept up and snowballed and snowballed.' He said it was almost as if Lyle, runner-up to Norman in the 1987 Australian Open (when the Shark won by 10 strokes with a score of 273), was 'going around with blinkers and earplugs on. All his skills have been slipping because he's so focused on technique.'

Lyle had made five bogeys in six holes in his first round 72, two strokes better than Norman who only just scraped through Friday's cut. 'That tells you something about where he is emotionally,' Blundell said. He compared Lyle's slump to losing a family member. 'It's not realistic to put a time limit on [his recovery],' he added. 'He's just got to concentrate on keeping the anxiety levels down.'

Beside him, Lyle said with a hopeful air: 'It's just a matter of getting myself involved in each shot – which is not easy.'

The Australian Open was not the only show in town. More impressive still was the Van Gogh exhibition, although it was the Madonna concert, with its dazzling sexual effects and attendant controversy that seemed to attract most players; Faxon, the third-round leader, and the Australian Bradley Hughes both went to see *The Girlie Show*. Oddly enough, it had a golf link. Among Madonna's dancers was Jill Nicklaus, daughter-in-law of Jack. She is married to Jack's son Gary and, according to those who saw the show, revealed almost as many charms as the superstar.

This night of revelry had no adverse effects on Faxon. Long, lean and as loose-limbed and friendly as a Labrador puppy, he went out in the final round at Metropolitan and putted the spots off the ball for an easy victory.

I sat in the shade and talked to Peter Thomson, five times winner of the Open Championship, about a bygone era. In Europe, in the 1950s, when Thomson was great, multi-million pound cherries had not yet been added to the top of the professional cake. Some weeks, impecunious golfers travelled the length and breadth of a nobly decaying Continent in worn-out caravans and cars; in others, eccentric British proprietors threw open the doors of musty boarding houses to them and let in the pale yellow summer. But everywhere, golfers played the wild, uncultivated links for the love of the game because there was little or nothing else to play for. There were no swing gurus; no personal fitness trainers; no physiotherapists; no sports psychologists; no equipment vans with computers to test shaft frequency, videos to break the swing down into minuscule fragments, or racks of gleaming titanium, graphite, beryllium and tempered-steel clubs; no courtesy cars; no hawkers of putting-aids or back-supports; and no management companies mutating and spreading poison through the game like an uncontrollable form of cancer.

'Now there are all sorts of fringe dwellers on the golf scene,' Thomson observed, in much the same way one would say that one's neighbourhood was being infiltrated by a bad element. 'There were none of those when we played in the fifties and sixties in Britain. They're hangers-on, most of them. That's probably a sorry aspect of the modern game. People are hanging on, trying to suck a living out of the professional game when they're really not playing professional golf.'

It so happened that there had been an article by Richard Hinds in a local newspaper that very morning, documenting an alarming new trend in the game: that of the entourage. Entitled 'TEAM NORMAN', it dwelled upon a number of people who appeared to be indispensable to the Shark's success. Among them were Butch Harmon, Norman's Texan coach, recommended to him by his former mentor Charlie Earp, his caddie Tony Navarro, his Irish chauffeur John Cott, his then manager Hughes Norton and his personal trainer Peter.

'I'm sorry to see somebody using someone else's brain,' Thomson said, 'because I admired Hogan and Locke and Cotton, people of my era, because they did it all themselves. When you see somebody perform now, there's five brains around him. So I don't give that person the same respect as I would if he had done it himself.'

I pointed out that the golfer still had to hit the shot.

'There's a difference between doing it on your own and having someone to turn to all the time and say, "What shall I do?" ' said Thomson a trifle impatiently. 'None of us had coaches. We were our own coaches, every one of us.'

'But do you not think that the money in the game now is such that a player can't afford not to take advantage of anyone and everything possible if they want to get to the top?'

'The amount of money in the game doesn't make the slightest difference,' Thomson said. 'It's beating other people. And in the end it's a clash of personalities, it's a clash of minds. What I'm suggesting is that the self-taught, self-reliant person will always end up on top.'

'But what about an instance like Faldo's? Faldo says that if he hadn't gone to Leadbetter and rebuilt his swing, he couldn't have won five major championships.'

'Well, that's why you can't give him credit,' Thomson said triumphantly, pleased to have proved his point. 'He's *admitting* that he couldn't do it. He's lacking. He's deficient. Somebody else has done it. Now. Would you ever suggest that somebody did that for Locke? or Cotton? or Hogan?'

Nothing illustrates the echoing void between the golden era of golf and the modern game as clearly as a comparison beween Thomson and the contemporary major champions, players like Faldo, who has won an equivalent number of major titles, or Norman, who has won only two. Everything about Thomson is refined and understated. His dress is simple and immaculate, his manner courteous, his conversation wide-ranging and full of obser- vation and anecdote.

'Peter Thomson . . . has joined the immortals of golf,' *Golf Illustrated* reported in 1956. 'Indeed, it would be accurate to say he has placed himself at the head of the immortals for no man has ever succeeded in winning the Open Championship three times in succession . . . Thomson's feat at Hoylake shines through as one of the greatest sporting achievements of all time and one in golf that perhaps none of us will ever see again.'

'In my day, we worked collectively hard to get a circuit going at all,' Thomson was saying. 'And we all gave our participation – we gave it. And then once it was established and beginning to blossom, it was really offensive that people came along and demanded money before they would play, as if it had been there for all time and it was their right that they should plunder it. Very few of the modern players have given anything to the circuit. They've all taken. And when I hear people say that they're putting something back into the game, it makes me sick.'

GREG NORMAN'S HOLDEN CLASSIC, SYDNEY. It is the sound of the bush that you first notice at Australian golf tournaments. The spine-chilling screeches of wild parrots, kookaburras and cicadas, and rustles suggesting nests of King Browns in the undergrowth, add a primitive and unpredictable element to the garden-party stateliness usually associated with golf events. Then you breathe in the dust and the barbecue smoke and the sharp, minty smell of eucalyptus leaves, and you're surprised by the languid pace of play and the way the galleries look like extras from a XXXX advertisement, and you can't help but be aware of the acute sensitivity of Greg Norman – the way he flinches in expectation of a blow which seldom comes.

A curious relationship exists between the Australasian Tour, press and public and Norman. To describe it as one of love and hate would be over-simplifying a complex set of emotions. It stretches back to the earliest days of his career and has to do with that urge that makes some nations want to tear down their heroes – the same one that makes the South Africans find fault with Ernie Els, the British tear down Faldo, and the Spanish hound Ballesteros. As an amateur, Norman had run straight into controversy. Having taken up golf at sixteen and gone from 27 to scratch in twenty months, he had had a brief and unimpressive amateur career representing Queensland and being beaten in the quarter-finals of the Australian Amateur before deciding to turn professional at twenty. In Queensland, a trainee pro had to wait three years before playing in a tournament, but in New South Wales, all that was required was for him to pass a full examination course.

'So I went down to Sydney,' Norman recalled. 'I passed all the exams in six months – that was the quickest on record – and then I went along and won my player's card. I was ready to try and get an invitation as a national trainee but they bluntly told me: "We're not going to let you play." They didn't give a reason.'

Furious, Norman telephoned Charlie Earp, his teacher, to ask for advice. Earp told him to come and work for him and he would do what he could. Within two months, Norman had received six invitations to national events. He finished equal fourth, third and thirteenth in his first three tournaments, and won the next one, the West Lakes Classic. The press began comparing him to Jack Nicklaus. The draw was fixed at the Australian Open so that the Shark and the Golden Bear would meet. Norman shot 80. Afterwards, Nicklaus told him he thought he was good enough to play on the US Tour. The following season, 1977, he won in Japan and Scotland, and by the time he became the World Match Play Champion in 1981, he had sixteen titles and a fourth place at the Masters under his belt.

'I knew then that there was only one target – to be the best,' Norman said. 'I was certain that I had the ability to be the No.1 golfer in the world – and that is what I'm going to be.'

Like most people, Australians don't like their countrymen getting too far from their roots, nor do they like them getting above themselves. Consequently, Norman's perceived arrogance, his rapid Americanization, and his Hollywood-type celebrity, which very quickly outstripped his achievements, caused cracks to appear in his relationship with the golf world Down Under. A classic example of this was to come later in 1994 when Tom Ramsey, Australia's most influential and widely-read golf columnist, suggested that Norman's 'cranky behaviour' at a Skins game at Laguna Quays, the superb David Graham resort in the Whitsundays – was due to 'a chemical imbalance in the body which can hopefully be rectified.'

Even the Australian players were ambivalent.

'He's a really good bloke,' insisted Mike Harwood.

'Great player, good as there is,' Max Cunningham, a former professional, agreed. 'He's a pretty good guy but as hard as nails, hard *as* nails. I think he values his privacy. It's hard to get to know him well. He's like Seve. He's suspicious of people. Why do they want to talk to him? What do they want?'

'His life must be so strange because he's so recognizable,' observed Mike Clayton, a player, golf historian and columnist. 'I often wonder what it must be like to have people staring at you all the time. I think it must be such a strange existence to be fawned over and worshipped all over the world. Because golfers are normal people. They're not royalty. It's not like Prince Charles or whoever, who's grown up with it. They're just normal kids who have been thrust into the limelight. You finish up like Michael Jackson. I'm sure you must learn to put your shutters up, and then people criticize you for that. But short of locking yourself up, it's all you can do to survive.'

It was not so much the headline 'TRAGEDY' as the picture that chilled. It showed Norman crouched, drawn and helpless, on the fourteenth fairway, as paramedics worked frantically to revive his pro-am playing partner, the fifty-two-year-old managing director of Woolworths. The wife of the man, Marlene Watts, looked on.

It was a terrible blow for Norman, casting a blight over his first major tournament in Australia. Immediately Harry Watts had collapsed, Norman had called for aid on his mobile phone. The paramedics were there within minutes but they were unable to resuscitate Mr Watts, who died from a massive heart attack. 'Of course something like that affects you,' Norman said miserably when asked how he felt. 'You're there on the scene, you see what happens and you're kind of confused about why it happens, why nature is that way. You're with his wife and she doesn't understand what's happening either. It's really sad.'

And with that Greg Norman's Holden Classic was underway. But the pro-am tragedy was only one of a series of misfortunes to befall Norman in Australia. First had come the virus that ruined his week in Melbourne, and on Wednesday there was news of a fresh drama: someone had been stealing Greg Norman's balls. In broad daylight, they had walked, or been carried, off the practice ground, and he intended to pursue the matter with certain players. 'I'm very meticulous about people taking range balls because you don't take other people's property,' Norman told the amused media. 'These are the things that really irk me about running a golf tournament . . . and I'm going to make an issue out of it.'

Unsurprisingly, Norman didn't play well the next day. He shot a 75 in high winds, 8 strokes worse than the tournament leader, Steve Elkington.

'That's the frustration of being a golf writer,' said Mike Gibson, a feature writer. 'The day you decide to go around with Greg Norman, he shoots a 75 and some kid no-one's ever heard of is leading the tournament with a 67 and you haven't seen him play a shot. So golf writers travel around the world to places like St Andrews and Augusta, where they meet up with each other and eat tired salad and cheese plates and sit in tents and watch golf on television.'

This is all perfectly true. Golf writers do travel around the world to places like St Andrews and Augusta, and for the most part we do eat uniformly bad food supplied by vindictive catering companies and sit in tents and watch golf on scoreboards and television monitors. But we also, contrary to popular belief, watch golf on the golf course, deadlines allowing. At least, we do in Europe and we're forced to in America. In Australia, they're more relaxed about it. Time is on their side, but they use it to interview, research features and socialize. There is a warmth and camaraderie on the Australian Tour – a willingness to help outsiders – not found on any other circuit.

On Friday, Norman announced that he was launching a multi-million-pound boat company, to be known as Norman's Yachts International, Inc. of Palm Beach. The Shark, who had flown to Australia in his customized, fourteen-seater Aerospace Gulfsteam III jet (estimated cost A$15–$18 million) said that the new business was expected to earn A$15 million in exports in its first year.

'How much money is too much?' I asked Bruce Critchley, the Sky commentator, as I left the interview room clutching my Norman's Yachts International baseball cap.

'In golf,' said Critchley, 'there's no such thing as too much.'

But to a degree, the amount of money Norman generates is offset by the good he does, most of which goes unpublicized, for worthy causes. Williams insisted that Norman gave all the money from the Holden Classic to charity, and that the Shark Shootout in the States had raised US$3.5 million over four years for charity. In addition, Greg and Laura had spent five years hosting an event which raised US$2 million for the Arnold Palmer Children's Hospital in Florida. And Norman had made a large, undisclosed donation towards cancer research at the Royal Children's Hospital in Melbourne.

On the course, Norman had not contributed a great deal to his own tournament, shooting 75,72,68 to fall 11 strokes short of Curtis Strange, the former US Open Champion, who had not won a tournament since 1989. Like Lyle, Strange had slipped deeper and deeper into a slump from which there seemed no escape.

'Whether we know it or not, most of us are capable of gearing up for one big battle,' Frank Beard, now on the US Seniors Tour, told the *Daily Telegraph Mirror*. 'Whether we're golfers, writers, pharmacists or whatever, we have a certain amount of fight in us to get somewhere, somehow . . . The goal might be your house in a good neighbourhood and a good car. Once you achieve it, you subconsciously become satisfied. You feel you have proved yourself, and when that happens it's difficult to go any further. You've geared yourself for the battle and you have won.'

'There is no simple answer,' said Strange wearily. 'From 1985 through the US Open in 1989, man, I was bullet-proof. Guys who haven't been there cannot imagine what that feels like. Everything I did turned to gold. I thought it would just build up from there. And then – pfff.'

The next day, Strange won Greg Norman's Holden Classic.

THE SUNSHINE CIRCUIT, QUEENSLAND. 'I was driving the bus, but I wasn't naked,' Wayne (Radar) Riley said. 'Only Finchy and Wayne Grady were naked.'

This is how one is initiated to Queensland or, more particularly, to the Sunshine circuit, also known as the Dreamer's Tour, the WAFWOTAM (What a frigging waste of time and money) Tour, or the Tropo Tour. In Australia, when the heat addles your brain to the point where a kind of lunacy sets in, it is known as going 'Tropo'.

In the grand scheme of things, the Sunshine circuit is not particularly important. It consists of a series of pro-ams, mainly played in small mining communities for negligible sums of money, and one could dismiss it in an instant – the baking towns and half-baked locals, the red dust boiling under the wheels of decrepit pick-up trucks, the egg-throwing fights, the long, hot drunken nights – if it wasn't for this: not only has virtually every good player to emerge from Australia in the last two decades cut their teeth on the Sunshine Tour, but it has produced three major champions – Norman, Wayne Grady and Ian Baker-Finch.

'You never played a circuit that did your head in so much,' said Riley, winner of the 1991 Australian Open. 'It really got to you. It would get to the stage where you'd played every day for three and a half months, in these little mining towns, and you'd been asked the same questions every day by your amateur partners, and you'd just go mad. And that's when the fun started.'

The naked bus journey, which is too libellous to be told in anything more than tantalizing fragments ('Do you remember when we pulled over to buy a hamburger? That bird behind the counter, I'll never forget her face'), is probably the most infamous and, by natural extension, the most cherished of the Tropo Tour stories. The most hair-raising is Riley's journey to Weipa, which lies on the Gulf of Carpentaria. That had begun when Riley, flush after winning the Cairns Pro-am and finishing runner-up in Townsville, had decided that he could save the $1,500 he had earned by driving to the Red North with his friend, Robbie Stephens, rather than wasting money on the one-and-a-half-hour flight. The other Tropo Tour pros thought he had had too much sun. 'But it's a twelve-hour drive and there aren't any roads,' they cried in unison. Riley took no notice. He thought they were being unnecessarily alarmist.

The following day, Riley and Stephens climbed into a battered 1964 VW station wagon, and set off into the red haze. At the first garage they came to, the attendant asked them what four-wheel drive they planned on taking to Weipa. 'This is it,' Riley told him. The attendant thought he was kidding. 'But there are no roads,' he squeaked, realizing that they were serious. Riley and Stephens refused to be discouraged. They plunged gamely off the highway into the bush. The road slimmed, it deteriorated, it vanished altogether. Like a demented kangaroo, the VW sprung from one pot-hole to the next, shuddering and groaning and hiccupping. After six hellish hours, they came to an Aboriginal settlement called Coen, where they stopped to get petrol. It was a ghost town. There was a police station, but no garage. They padded around in the eerie silence, puffs of dust dissipating like paprika behind them. Behind the police station, an Aboriginal clung wearily to the bars of a cage.

They left in a hurry, dust uncoiling in a fiery tube from the wheels of the broken-spirited VW. Oil dripped from the undercarriage. They stopped at the next settlement they came to, an encampment of telecommunications workers, and tried to buy more. The answer was a firm no. It occurred to Riley and Stephens that 'borrowing' the oil was an option. So, they drove back along the track, waited until nightfall, swam back to the camp – along a stream that may or may not have been infested with crocodiles – and stole a jerry can. This bought a further three hours of service from the VW, which veered drunkenly between the rocks and puddles, before it collapsed altogether.

At this stage, they were still 240 miles from their destination. Eight hours later, a landrover came bounding along the track. The driver said that he would take them as far as Weipa if they were prepared to sit in the dinghy he had tied to the back. With their permission, he then stripped the VW of its few working parts. Finally, they were on their way. By now, the track had become an obstacle course out of *Deliverance*. They ricocheted from boulder to crater. Riley closed his eyes and tried to get some rest. When he opened them again, his friend was gone. Riley stared around in disbelief. He banged frantically on the roof of the cab. The driver turned back. Several miles down the road, they found a disorientated Stephens. He had been flung over the side when the landrover hit a rock.

Forty-eight hours after leaving Townsville, the two friends crawled into Weipa, grizzled and exhausted. 'The whole town was waiting for us,' Riley said. 'The other guys on the Tropo circuit thought we were dead.'

Not that they learned from experience. No sooner had they recovered from that journey than they had bought a $250, 1967 Holden with which to drive across the Nullabor Plain to Perth, wedged it across a railway track trying to take a short cut to the golf course, and been pulled off the rails by an irrate tractor driver only three minutes before the train arrived. Undeterred, they insisted on driving the car across the desert and all around Perth – despite the fact that the exhaust pipe lay on the back seat, and the Holden roared like an overwrought motorbike and was patently unroad-worthy. It attracted the notice of the police who, after warning them not to continue driving it, arrested them at Kalgoorlie on suspicion of trying to rob a bank. Unwashed, unshaven and rather the worse for drink, they had been found banging on the door of the bank five minutes after closing time. They were jailed for twenty-four hours, whereupon the police sergeant fined them $750 each and bought the car off them for $50.

The journeys between pro-ams were enlivened with egg fights. The Tropo Tour pros would load up their cars with dozens of eggs, and then they would tear along the empty outback roads, hurling these missiles at one another's windscreens. Those with the fastest cars usually won. Harwood and Baker-Finch, who drove, and destroyed, a red Gemini belonging to Harwood's father, were the acknowledged egg-fighting kings.

It was not all fun and games, however. It was in a bar on the Tropo Tour that Mike Ferguson, who was travelling with Norman, turned to the then unknown youngster and said: 'And what do you want to do with your career, Greg?' And Norman replied: 'I'm going to be the best golfer in the world.' And it was in Queensland that Peter Senior went on a drinking binge for the first and last time in his career, fell asleep in the bath on his return, and was unconscious by the time a friend found him and pulled him out.

Alcohol was an integral part of Tropo Tour life, being both the preserver of a player's sanity and the cause of his manic highs. 'Sometimes players would go missing for a week,' Riley recalled. 'Finchy used to go missing. They'd turn up one day and you'd say, "Where've you been?" And they'd just shrug, "Dunno." '

'The goal was to make enough money to pay the major tour at the end of the year,' Harwood explained. 'Then you'd be broke and you'd have to start all over again the next year. And it toughened you up. If you could survive playing with amateurs every day and drinking with them every night – and you did drink a lot, no question about it – if you could come out of that and still manage to do well, it was an achievement.'

'The strange thing is, the guys that didn't play that tour haven't done nearly as well as the guys that did,' Riley said. 'I go home now and I can tell the guys that have been on the Sunshine circuit. They've got this look about them. They're like . . . slightly ragged around the edges.'

COOLUM CLASSIC, NOOSA. It's a belief widely held that the most popular and respected person in Australian golf is Greg Norman. Not true. It is Kathie Shearer, Londoner, wife of Bob, press officer, confidante of golfers' wives around the globe, and the darling of every golf pro, journalist and Tour official Down Under. She is also the author of a book about wives on Tour, which she plans to call *She Didn't Stand Over the Three-Foot Putts* after a story told at the Australian Golf Club in Sydney.

According to Tour lore, an American pro by the name of Jerry was standing at the bar of that club one day, bemoaning the fact that his soon-to-be ex-wife was departing with half his worldly wealth. 'But let me tell you,' he assured his sympathetic Australian listeners, 'she didn't stand over the three-foot putts.'

Soon afterwards, Bob Shearer was relaying this tale to some friends in his own bar when Kathie walked in. 'What did you say?' demanded his wife.

'Well,' Shearer said, 'he's right. She didn't stand over the three-foot putts.'

Kathie gave him a withering look. 'Who got his clothes to the dry-cleaners? Who picked up the newspaper? Who picked up his socks? Who did everything? He wouldn't *be there* without his wife.'

Later, to satisfy her curiosity, she looked up Jerry's record in the Tour handbook. It may, of course, be coincidence, but he had won around $15,000 prior to walking down the aisle, had seen his earnings shoot up to $135,000 and maintain a similar level for the three-year duration of their marriage, and then watched them plummet to $22,000 subsequent to his divorce. 'I documented all this on a piece of paper,' Kathie said. 'I thought: "People should take note." '

This afternoon golfers' wives were again the subject of debate, one wife having been in and regaled us with the news that she had recently been to Greece on one of those courses where you do things with brooms and baskets of fruit in an effort to 'reclaim your inner child'. I said nothing. I was in the midst of reading *Backlash: the Undeclared War Against Women*, in which courses that encourage grown women to return to their girlhood are presented in a very poor light.

'None of the wives are feminists,' Kathie was saying. 'They don't last. When a wife said, "I want to be known as Polly, not Polly Crenshaw," you knew she was on her way out. Then she wanted to take up photography. They were divorced within a year. There's no chance of doing what you want to do on Tour. Forget that, it doesn't work. If they [the wives] start a mini-rebellion, they are exchanged [in the off-season], and often they are exchanged for the same look. I remember one guy who got divorced and remarried and I thought it was the same girl. Only the name changed. She was exactly the same – only two years younger. I remember we used to say goodbye to the US Tour in November, come home to Australia and then we'd go out again in February and I'd say to them: "How's the family?" You dared not say, "How's Susie or Mary?" because they'd say, "Oh, I'm with such and such now." Forget feminism on the Tour. There can only be one star in the family and it's not you.'

Kathie met her own husband, a mild-mannered Australian with kind brown eyes, at a party given by Jack and Jackie Newton in Bournemouth in 1975. 'I remember my first date with Bob,' Kathie said, gurgling with laughter. 'He walked towards me and the girl beside me gasped and said: "He's a great fellow but you're going to have to do something about the way he dresses." And I saw this apparition. He had a pink shirt on, black-watch check trousers, an orange sweater with blue stripes, and blue and white shoes with high heels. He looked like a pimp. I thought: "Oh, my God." I was in basic black. And later I found out that whenever anybody went on a date they always got the clean clothes.'

It's a curious thing but nearly every tournament professional, regardless of age, nationality or prospects, gets married, engaged or embarks on a long-term relationship very shortly after setting out on Tour. Kathie says it's because they need someone to commiserate with them after a bad day on the golf course and none of the other players will oblige. My own theory is that they very quickly realize that (a) they need someone to do their washing and ironing and to carry their golf bag if their earnings don't justify a caddie; (b) the longer they're on Tour, the harder it will be to meet prospective spouses and the more effort romancing them will become; and (c) there's nothing worse than returning home on a Friday night, having missed the cut by a stroke, to a dark house and a cold bed. At any rate, it would be interesting to make a study of how the numbers of unattached players dwindle six months, a year and two years after winning their playing cards. I would hazard a guess that less than 10 per cent make it into the third year.

Bob Shearer was in the minority. He and Kathie were married in 1975, five seasons after he turned professional. Soon afterwards, Bob announced that he was going to try for his US Tour card. 'But that wasn't the plan!' said Kathie despairingly. 'The plan was that you were going to play in England.' Pleas and entreaties proved fruitless, however, and before too many months had passed she found herself rushing frantically through London's Heathrow airport, with her mother running behind her crying 'Take care of her, take care of her!' to the red-faced porter as he whisked her bags away to the US check-in.

Twenty years on, Kathie laughs gaily at the memory; at the time, it was not so easy. 'I had a baby strapped to the front of me and a knapsack on my back, and we went on Tour, and we never came off the Tour until he was seven years old.'

In America, Kathie had to adjust to a unique phenomenon: couple hierarchy on the US Tour. There were the major winners' wives and the tournament winners' wives and there were the others, and the class barriers were well-defined and unassailable. Kathie, with her down-to-earth manner and infectious *joie de vivre,* was consigned to the fringes, a spectator at a designer-label tea-party. 'I knew there was a hierarchy, but I couldn't fathom out why the wives all seemed to know each other so well. Then, of course, it occurred to me that they all went to these special [limited field] events, while the rest of us just muddled in a lump together. Then Bob won the Tallahassee Classic and was invited to the Tournament of Champions, which was at La Costa, the spa. Wherever you looked at La Costa there were wives being pampered, me included. And everybody who was at the Tournament of Champions year after year knew the drill. You know, they'd all have the new tracksuits, the new baby suits with matching coats. I wasn't ready for La Costa, and by the time I was ready for it we never went back again, so that was the end of that.'

Only Linda Watson stood apart from the social-climbing crowd. 'I never saw her with a name on her handbag,' Kathie said. 'I never saw her with a Hermes or a Louis Vuitton – and it was a time when everybody had designer everything. I mean, if you had a designer bed, you had designer sheets on your bed. This was when Tom was the No.1 player in the world and I read a marvellous article where he said: "You've got to keep part of yourself secret in case they realize you're only human." And Linda was very clever. She was there all the time, every week.'

The qualities of women like Linda Watson were overlooked by the American Dave Hill in his book, *Teed Off* (1977), which showcases so accurately the smallmindedness and prejudice rife in pro golf. 'I suppose Tour wives are no worse than any other wives,' he wrote, 'but too many of them second-guess their husband's golf and spend the day gossiping with each other around the swimming pool. Naturally, there are some good wives, but they're in the minority . . . A couple of pros' wives have put them smack into bankruptcy in recent years. Some of these wives travel from one swish country club to another and decide they need to lead that kind of life. The pros have a good year and their wives immediately want to move out of a $40,000 house into a $175,000 house. They want new wardrobes and new cars and maids and first-class airfares to all the tournaments. Those wives don't realize that one good year doesn't make you rich. Next year you might not make the top sixty . . . Travelling with your wife can take the chanciness out of your sex life, but you're going to spend a lot of money on her.'

Contrary to what Hill would have one believe, most golfers' wives did not, and still do not, travel around like the Queen of Sheba. For the Shearers, babysitters were an unaffordable luxury, so Kathie and Margie Caldwell, Rex Caldwell's wife, used to stay at the same hotels and do what was known as 'phone shifts'. One wife would dial the other's room number, place the phone on the table beside the baby's cot and dash downstairs for a meal with her husband, while the other sat with the phone to her ear and listened for the baby's cries. Linda Watson and Susie Pate, who had more money to spend, would book three rooms with interconnecting doors and put the children of both families and a babysitter in the middle.

Gloria Devlin told Kathie she had it easy. Gloria came from an era where the wives had travelled about with electric frying pans and cooking utensils and had teamed up to cook chops and rice after play.

'They never earned enough to go out and eat,' Kathie explained. 'Our generation, at least, could eat in the hotel, but we never had crèches. The next generation have all got crèches and probably the one after that will have aeroplanes. It's all relative, though.' She considered the differences between her life and that of Gloria Devlin in days gone by. 'I mean, we stayed at some joints. We stayed at a place where Almost Elvis was appearing in cabaret. *Almost Elvis.* We walked in the door and there was all this crushed velvet everywhere. And it was a brothel, I'm sure it was a brothel.'

In retrospect, the Coolum Classic was memorable for a number of things: (1) the Hyatt resort, (2) the sensational disqualification of the American, Mike Colandro, and (3) the row at the pro-am pool party – which started when Tom Ramsey suggested that my desert boots and khaki shorts were singularly inappropriate for the occasion, and ended with Debbie Clayton, an image consultant, throwing her champagne at him, except that she missed and drenched Bob Shearer instead.

By coincidence, Colandro had caught my attention at the Australian Open, where he was wearing an outfit of unparalleled hideousness. This is no mean feat. The reason the comedienne Ruby Wax described golf as 'Men in ugly pants, walking,' is that most golfers believe that lambswool sweaters and polyester trousers in primary colours are the cutting edge of fashion. Clothes that a normal, seeing-eye person wouldn't be seen dead in are common-place in our world. Still, Colandro had decided to kick even the generous boundaries of golf tournament fashion to the four winds and had embraced a stiff-collared golf shirt, several sizes too large, and billowing plus-fours. From head to toe, he was resplendent in pink. Not a normal pink, mind you, but a sort of cross between puce pink, day-glo pink, cup-cake pink and newly-born piglet pink. The overall effect was striking and quite horrific.

Incredibly, this did not seem to make any difference to his golf. After three rounds of the tournament, Colandro, who had consistently failed to win friends and influence the open, hospitable players, caddies and journalists of the Australasian Tour since arriving in the country in 1981, was in the lead and looking forward to the Polynesian Beach party (at Coolum there is a party every night of the week). There, he delivered a tedious rendition of *Kansas City*, mockingly applauded, and recited a poem, which if my memory serves me right was about etiquette.

The following afternoon found Ramsey, Peter Stone and a couple of other journalists cruising about like sharks outside the tournament office. Earlier, we had seen a red-faced Colandro being marched into the inner sanctum after allegedly violating the rules, and we were now awaiting the verdict of Trevor Herden, the Australasian PGA Tour's operations manager. At length, Herden emerged from the tournament office. Colandro, who had been two strokes behind the leaders when he was hauled off the course, had been disqualified after confessing to rules officials that he had bent his putter in anger on Friday and continued to use it. He had smashed the club against a sprinkler head and then on the path after leaving the tenth green. According to Herden: 'The caddie had a look at it and said he would have had to alter the angle of his grip on the putter some three inches. So for the next six holes Colandro putted with the toe of the putter. He admitted he had changed the characteristics of the putter but did not think it had been enough to get disqualified.'

Colandro, who had also marked the ball wrongly on the thirteenth green, had been disqualified at Palm Meadows two years previously after a similar incident. Nevertheless, he was still protesting his innocence when David Diaz won the Coolum Classic with a 15-foot birdie putt at the last.

'The issue is, why did he putt with a changed putting action when leading the tournament?' Herden said. 'He admitted he altered the lie of the putter, so he is disqualified. He is not a happy man and I don't think we will see him back in this country. We should leave it at that.'

'Andrew,' Ramsey said teasingly to his son, an efficient and strikingly well-turned-out Tour official, 'we need a quote. Why don't you go and knock on Colandro's door?'

'If he's still got a door,' said Peter Stone with a grin.

Incredibly, Andrew did exactly that, providing us with the pay-off line of the season. 'It was a one-man court,' a bitter Colandro told him. 'Trevor Herden could have given me the benefit of the doubt. My caddie dobbed me in. It looks as if someone is out to get me. I'm not welcome in Australia any more. What more can I say? Merry Christmas.'

TOM RAMSEY'S NEW YEAR AWARDS (selected)

Best tournament: Australian Open
Best round world-wide: 64 by Greg Norman in the final round of the British Open
Worst putt: Greg Norman in the US PGA play-off
Best quote: Rocky Thomson: 'I'd like to have Fred Couples's face, Fred Couples's body, Fred Couples's swing . . . and Fred Couples's ex-wife's bank account.'
Perry Mason award for catching range ball thieves: Greg Norman
Best press officer: Kathie Shearer
Worst champagne throwing arm: Debbie Clayton
Most helpful golfer: Nick Price
Most unhelpful golfer: Greg Norman
Pain in the neck award: Colin Montgomerie
Fading into the West award: Seve Ballesteros who, for the first time in seventeen years, did not win a tournament

4

FLEA-CIRCUS

'The only place I can find him is on the sports pages.'

EDNA HAGEN,

Walter's second wife, explaining her divorce action

It all started in 1980, when a friend of Gordon J. Brand, the normally imperturbable Yorkshireman, asked him to post him some ganja seeds from the Jamaican Open.

'Ganja seeds?' repeated Brand. He thought they were something for the garden.

'No, no, no,' said his friend with some amusement. 'You don't plant them, you smoke them.'

Immediately, Brand was in a quandary. On the one hand, he relished the opportunity for intrigue – Dirk Pitt, the James Bond-type adventurer in Clive Cussler novels, was the hero he most identified with – but on the other, he broke out in hives at the mere thought of doing anything illegal. The vision of himself as Dirk Pitt won over. Despite being convinced that, ere the Jamaican Open ended, he would have descended without trace into a labyrinth of criminals and drug barons, he was determined to track the ganja seeds down. It was easier than expected. Every caddie that leaned drowsily up against the clubhouse wall was enveloped in a haze of marijuana smoke. There was no need to go looking for ganja in Jamaica, it came looking for you. Soon Brand was the proud, albeit terrified, owner of a handful of minute seeds. These his caddie demonstrated for his satisfaction, wrapped deftly in brown paper and tucked away in the golf bag.

That evening, Brand arrived at the hotel shuttle to find a policeman and a large Alsatian standing guard. His blood turned colder than a Saskatchewan winter. 'Oh my God,' he thought in panic. 'The dog's going to jump all over me. It's going to smell the ganja seeds.'

'Never mind,' Brand adds now, 'that the dog was probably higher than the caddies.'

With a supreme effort, he prevented himself from turning himself in to the policeman and, circumnavigating the bus, leapt in the front door. Back in his hotel room, he removed the seeds from their hiding place in his golf bag and popped them into an envelope. Disaster! When he held them to the light, the seeds were clearly visible. For a moment, Brand despaired. Then he did what he always does in times of crisis and invoked his favourite action hero. 'What would Dirk Pitt do?' he asked himself. 'Scissors!' was the answer, and he rushed downstairs to obtain a pair. In the privacy of his room, he cut six pages out of a magazine, making holes for the seeds in the centre of three of them. This done, he sealed the envelope and printed the address in anonymous block capitals so that his handwriting couldn't be traced. He had the letter weighed at reception.

'Airmail to Africa,' he said to the woman behind the counter, thinking: 'She knows what I'm up to.'

In an effort to stave off the moment when the police came to read him his rights, Brand returned to his room for the sixth time and polished the envelope furiously in order to remove any fingerprints. Finally, he took the guilty package carefully by one corner and despatched it in the hotel post-box.

In Africa, Brand's friend smoked the contents of the envelope and enjoyed them enormously. 'Well worth the effort,' he told Brand cheerfully. Recounting the story on the flight from London to Dubai, for the first big tournament of 1994, Brand shuddered. Dirk Pitt or not, he felt he really didn't have the nerve to make crime pay.

Like a cuckoo, Norman Dabell, the golf circuit's Inspector Clouseau, began the new season. 'We hadn't even seen him,' Mark Garrod of the Press Association said. 'He'd been playing in the pro-am. And the first thing we heard was: "Ahhhh!!!" Norman had burnt himself fixing coffee at the back of the press room.'

That had been at the weather-blighted Madeira Island Open, the first tournament of the year. Fog and inclement weather had disrupted every one of the three rounds and left the press and most of the field stranded in Madeira for three days when high winds prevented their flight from taking off. Norman had not reached Morocco, the next venue, until late in the week, and had left almost immediately, telling UPI, the Irish agency he freelances for, to 'take in agency', and making a break for the airport.

Norman is one of those men whom people unkindly describe as 'an accident waiting to happen'. Rarely does he wait very long. In Norman's hands, the most ordinary journey, the most innocuous hotel room, the most unadventurous evening out becomes fraught with peril. He has stepped out of a taxi cab in Nottingham, slipped on a cheese sandwich and broken his coccyx; he has rounded a corner at speed, collided with the chairman of the Caddies' Association, Martin Rowley, taken off over a fire hydrant and cracked several ribs; he has thrown his shoe at a mosquito circling a bulb and fused an entire hotel; he has screamed at a barman for refusing to serve him, only to realize that he was shouting at his own reflection; he has informed Kent Radio listeners that a player 'shit six soxes', instead of 'shot six sixes'; and he has leapt from the taxi in which he was attempting to catch a plane, in order to make an hysterical appeal to traffic exiting the golf club, jumped back into the wrong car and shouted: 'Drive on!' imperiously to an astounded local.

Like Joseph Conrad, Norman began life as a seaman, although there the similarity ends. Conrad would not have crouched down over a sprinkler-head to examine his putt at the very moment that the greenkeeper switched on the irrigation. He would not have turned up at the Italian Open with no trousers. He definitely wouldn't have fallen off his chair during a live radio report and carried on discussing the leaders while lying on his back amid the wreckage. Once, during a round of golf in Sweden, Norman saw his partner's last ball fly (as if directed by radar) into the muddy puddle which was all that remained of a dried-up pond. 'I can get that,' Norman declared, before setting out across the cracked expanse. Soon it became evident that a thin outer crust disguised a treacherous bed of quicksand. Norman could not have cared less. His only concern was the golf ball. He floundered on, wrenching one foot from the mire and squelching in the next. Finally, he drew near to his ball. He reached for it. Then he took a step closer. He reached again. Then it happened. Like an old sea-dog robbed of his wooden leg, Norman toppled head first into the mud. 'Arghhh!!!' he wailed as he fell. Above him, two faces appeared on the bank. 'EXCUSE ME,' came a fruity cry. 'ARE YOU ENGLISH AND CAN WE PLAY THROUGH?'

Golf journalism has a long tradition of characters and eccentrics. Bernard Darwin, the father of golf writing, was, by all accounts, an upstanding citizen, but thereafter it has all been downhill. Take, for example, Jack Statter, the late *Sun* reporter. Statter had been stationed in North Africa during the war, and it had left a lasting impression on him. Upon meeting Bernhard Langer for the first time, he eyed the German quizzically and queried: 'Do you know that your dad bombed our fish and chip shop?' He wasn't to know that Langer's father had been locked away in a Russian prisoner-of-war camp in Czechoslovakia.

Being the *Sun* golf correspondent, he was seldom over-endowed with column inches. It was not unusual for him to be informed: 'Your space for tomorrow is forty-eight words – and that includes your byline.' This left him plenty of free time, which he employed to useful effect. He became Eddie Pollen's mentor when the former Ryder Cup player, not known for his IQ, started out on Tour, explaining to interested parties: 'I help him with his personal problems. For instance, when it's raining I tell him to put up his umbrella.' He spent hours assembling a DIY telescope in his bedroom so that he could see the time on the town clock-tower, only to discover that the clock had stopped ten years earlier. He puzzled for a period over the appearance of a different electrical appliance – now a toaster, now a kettle – on the back seat of his Beetle after late nights at the *Sun*, until he found that burglars had been using the vehicle to go on raids and were leaving him a tip. Mostly, however, he simply thought of Rommel, whom he idolized, and allowed his imagination to roam unchecked across the landscape of tournament golf.

Statter's most notorious exploit came at the Jersey Open in the early 80s. After an afternoon spent imbibing life-giving waters in the ambulance tent, he emerged blinking and befuddled and was struck by the sight of a squadron of army cadets, who had inadvertently wandered onto the course during a map-reading exercise, proceeding along the cliffs. Immediately, his imagination went to work. Rushing back to the press tent, he dashed off a few hundred words on the Channel Islands being reinvaded and golfers having to dive into bunkers to escape a hail of bullets. He then filed the story and retired for the day.

In due course, the *Sun* sports desk rang. 'We've had rather a good story from Jack,' they told Peter Dobereiner, the esteemed *Observer* correspondent, 'and we, er, wanted to check that it was true.' Dobereiner put them on to the tournament organizer who was even drunker than Statter. Asked to confirm the veracity of the report, he gushed, 'Absholutely. Every word.'

'The War Office went bananas,' recalled Dobereiner. 'They sent a colonel over to find out what was going on.' He and Renton Laidlaw were summoned to the tournament organizer's office, where they had to explain several times to an excited military man that the invaders in question had only been cadets and that they had not actually been carrying guns at all. 'He was shell-shocked, that was the trouble,' Dobereiner said of Statter. 'But he was a genius, no doubt about that. He was flawed.'

In the 'chalk and string' days of the European Tour, golf writing was a more precarious business than it is now. These days, whether one is in Birmingham or Berlin, the press centre operates at a sublime level of efficiency, mainly due to the efforts of the Sanderson family who run an up-to-the-minute scoring system. Dobereiner survived bus journeys through the tropics, Moroccan Opens where telephones were installed for decorative rather than functional reasons (nothing new there), and a *coup* in Nigeria where the President was killed on practice day. 'What *was* dangerous was that all the troops seemed to be on pot and they were sleepy and firing at random,' said Dobereiner, who took it all in his stride. Rather disturbingly, the military headquarters was sited alongside the eleventh hole and the golf club committee was composed almost entirely of senior officers from the Army. Dobereiner spent the best part of five days playing cards with Harry Bannerman and pitch and putt with the neighbours, until eventually the rebels were arrested.

Dobereiner is unusual in that he is as wry and well-spoken as his prose suggests; more often than not writers are the antithesis of how one imagines them to be. Pat Ward-Thomas, described by Alastair Cooke as resembling a Mexican farmer with five acres of beans which weren't doing well, used to dazzle his readers with lyrical and considered pieces in the *Guardian* each week, but in person was a walking keg of dynamite. In *Golf À La Carte,* Dobereiner recalls how 'Pat's famous temper could be detonated by the slightest incident, such as the frustration of American hotel breakfasts which required him to unwrap butter pats, pierce milk cartons and open plastic marmalade pots. He was never at his best in the early morning . . . and his electrifying roar of "Damn these bloody parcels" caused waitresses to drop trays and strong men to slop their coffee . . . Once embarked on a tirade, Pat would warm to his theme, laying about him with increasingly extravagant language until what began as a small mishap with a sugar sachet developed into a wish that the entire blank country should blow itself into oblivion with its own blank bombs.'

According to Dobereiner, Ward-Thomas had spent the war in a prison camp and this had 'soured him to a degree and drastically shortened his temper.' He remembered standing behind the eighteenth green at the Masters with his colleague, watching the leader take an interminable age to putt out. Ward-Thomas, who was on deadline, bristled with impatience. Finally, he was unable to contain himself any longer. In a stage whisper that could be heard three fairways away, he burst out: 'DOESN'T THIS MAN REALIZE MY *LIFE* IS EBBING AWAY?'

Apart from the time when he ripped off his blazer and challenged the Reuters correspondent to a duel at the World Match Play, Norman has rarely been known to become violent. He did almost throttle Frank Clough with a telephone cord, but that was purely accidental. Indeed, even when the incident on the Costa Brava degenerated into complete mayhem, Norman managed to refrain from lashing out. Of course, that evening had begun like all the rest: with a deceptive calm. Shortly before midnight, Norman, enjoying the balmy air, had stepped out onto his hotel balcony with a glass of red wine, unaware that the modesty rail concealed his boxer shorts and made him appear naked. When he eventually turned in, he found he couldn't sleep. He was kept awake by the cistern, hissing and gurgling incessantly. When he could stand it no longer, Norman flew out of bed and began plucking aggressively at sundry fittings behind the toilet. One came off in his hand. Even as he was pondering this development, the bathroom flooded to a depth of two feet. 'No!!' cried Norman and plunged his arm into the hole in a desperate attempt to stop the flow.

But already the water had slipped under the bedroom door and set off down the marble passage. Downstairs, the night porter was buried in his newspaper when the switchboard began to chirrup furiously. '*Agua* gone *loco, Agua* gone *loco*!' screamed Norman down the line. All hell broke loose. After an initial crisis period – during which the night porter, misunderstanding Norman's frantic cries for aid, had raced to his door with a tray and two bottles of Perrier only to discover Norman crouching, like the boy and the dyke, over the toilet bowl – the maintenance man had to be uncovered, which was no easy task at 3.00 a.m. When he eventually returned to his post, the night porter was shaken and dishevelled, a shadow of his former self. It had been a long and extremely trying evening. Earlier on, he had had to deal with the arrival of the police. A woman in the block of flats opposite had seen a naked man parading up and down on the hotel balcony. She wanted him arrested for indecent exposure.

Every circuit has its own unique ambience. The Australasian Tour is like an extended package holiday, all beaches and barbecues, oddballs and children, and an easy-like-a-Sunday-morning atmosphere prevails at all times. The US PGA Tour is rather more clinical. Players, officials, caddies and journalists don't just stay in different hotels and receive vastly differing privileges, they move in different time zones altogether. The European Tour is like a family – everyone looks out for everyone else. We stay in the same hotels, eat in the same restaurants and, after all these years and with all the added millions, our tournament venues are still suspended somewhere between gypsy encampments and sophisticated travelling circuses.

Each Tour stop has its accompanying rituals and we cling to them tenaciously, serial nomads in search of stability in a fluid and unreliable world. In Dubai, there is the market with its fake designer T-shirts, cassettes and watches, there's the Gold Souk, and there's breakfast overlooking the Emirates putting green in the cool marble splendour of the clubhouse.

One morning, while we were tucking into croissants, scrambled eggs and pineapple, Ian Wood of the *Scotsman* announced, somewhat melodramatically, that he might be tempted to do something drastic if another Faldo press conference contained the words, 'Fine-tuning with Lead.'

'Why don't you pre-empt him?' the *Guardian*'s Dai Davies

suggested. 'Say to him: "Nick, have you been doing any fine-tuning with David Leadbetter recently?"'

'Fine-tuning with Lead, perchance?' experimented Woody.

We moved on to a discussion of press conference banalities, of which there are many. 'The most fatuous must be, "I'm just going to take it one day at a time,"' Davies said. 'How the hell else can you take it?' The same applies to one game at a time, one step at a time, one decade at a time . . .

In post-round press conferences, Phil Mickelson, the gifted American, addresses every reporter as 'sir' or 'ma'am', and his interviews are filled with sycophantic references to his parents, his caddie, his manager, his great-aunt Bertha and his playing partners, Mr Watson, Mr Crenshaw, etc., all of whom were a pleasure to play with and an inspiration to him as a toddler. Fred Couples's interviews are frank and rambling, Ballesteros's are witty and self-deprecating, David Gilford's are spoken almost entirely in a whisper, and every second sentence Greg Norman utters is followed by the words: 'No question about it.'

'Don't you think that there's such a thing as too much?' I asked the assembled group, still thinking about the Shark, who was playing in the Desert Classic and the Asian Classic the following week. 'I mean, Norman has an Aerospace Gulfstream III jet, worth £10 million, a Rolls Royce, a Range Rover, seven Ferraris, a couple of ordinary cars, an 85-foot custom-made fishing boat and a mansion in Palm Beach.'

'Ah,' said Woody, 'but does he have a Swiss pen-knife?'

When Dale Hayes, the South African, won the Order of Merit in 1975, there were seventeen events with a total prize fund of £427,917. Eighteen years on, Colin Montgomerie earned over £700,000 when he become the European No.1 after playing twenty-four events. In 1994, the prize fund for the season was £24.5 million, and there were thirty-seven events taking place in eighteen countries.

Nowadays, nothing is left to chance. Endorsements, win bonuses, and prizes for everything from low round of the week and golfer of the month, to most improved player and winner of the egg and spoon race, are so abundant in tournament golf that all aids, assistants and advisers are considered grist to the mill. Each January there is something called the Apollo Week, at San Roque in Spain, which is effectively a marketing opportunity for manufacturers and a survival guide for aspiring professionals. There, mock press conferences are staged and golfers are introduced to the gurus, clubmakers, psychologists and fitness experts that are indispensable to the modern player. As a consequence, the gauche rookie, with his empty bank account, ill-fitting clothes and little-boy-lost air is a rare sight on Tour now. Instead, these new kids on the block sport the latest haircuts and strut about cockily in their Titleist visors, Ashworth shirts and Dockers khakis – their caddies scurrying after them bearing king-size Mizuno golf bags – secure in the belief that anyone talented enough to survive the hell that is the Qualifying School is owed a living by everyone else. More often than not, you'll see them six months later, limping along like pricked balloons, but at the start of the season their heads are in the clouds and nothing and nobody can keep them down.

Jonathan Lomas was the first of these young guns to stroll into the Desert Classic press room. Nicknamed Johnny Cash because of his alleged reluctance to part with money, he had more reason than most to feel confident, having had nine top-ten finishes and two victories on the Challenge Tour (the European satellite circuit) the previous season. He had shot a first round 66. A fresh-faced twenty-five-year-old, he rattled off his birdies and bogeys like a veteran.

On the whole, golfers are ten times more articulate than, say, footballers or British Rail platform announcers, but that doesn't make them all politicians. For every David Feherty there are twenty players who think that sparkling repartee is an inexpensive brand of champagne, and Dobereiner's imaginary interview with David Graham is not too wide of the mark.

Dobereiner: 'What went wrong?'

Graham: 'Tripled five.'

Dobereiner: 'I can now go straight to the typewriter and begin: "David Graham's challenge faltered with a third round 76. An otherwise solid performance was marred by a torrid seven at the innocuous 370-yard fifth hole, where the players enjoyed a light following breeze. Graham reeled from the course ashen-faced and groaned: 'I played that hole like an arthritic granny . . .' " '

Lomas's press conference did not require any embellishment. With little prompting, he reeled off a breezy commentary on his week so far. He was staying at the house of a former Miss Trinidad & Tobago, his caddie was a South African woman, and he was concentrating on blocking out the pressure. There was no trace of shyness or hesitancy in his speech, and no false modesty whatsoever. His whole demeanour conveyed an unmistakable message. It was: 'I'm here to stay; get used to it.'

It is perhaps because this 'What do you mean, you haven't heard of me?' attitude has become the norm among young players, that Ernie Els stands apart from the crowd. He is twenty-four-years-old, his achievements are enormous, and yet there is not an arrogant bone in his body. He does not go in for macho posturing or philosophizing, and there is nothing affected about his manner. There is just a sleepy calm, a half-smile that lights up clear, dreamy eyes, and a breathtakingly beautiful golf swing – long, smooth and rhythmical. The fire burns very deeply in Els but no less brightly for all that.

At the Emirates course in Dubai, the young South African shot a record-breaking 61, nine under par, to take a five-stroke lead in the first round. Afterwards, he waved away compliments good-naturedly. Born and raised in Johannesburg, he has a typically Southern African reticence and dislike of self-promotion, and a habit of talking down his accomplishments. He had telephoned his dad, who, he said, thought he was joking. When he was asked the next day how he had celebrated, Els replied: 'I had dinner and one beer. I guess that was my celebration.'

The only time Els betrayed the slightest irritation was when he was compared to Gary Player, whose consecutive victories in the SA Open, Masters and PGA Championships he matched at the age of twenty-two. 'Like Gary says, "Can we compare wallets?" ' was his sardonic response. 'No, it's nice in a way but we're totally different, we've got totally different golf games. Gary always had to work his way around and fight it out. I try and enjoy the game, at least. It's hard to do sometimes, but I try. It's nice when people say that but I don't care about it, believe me.'

Even more impressive than his wins in South Africa or Japan was Els's ability to deal with his success equivocally and with the minimum of fuss. 'That's his personality,' said Sam Feldman, his manager, proudly. 'You're never going to change him.'

Wherever Els was, Feldman could be seen running around like an Afrikaans uncle, benevolent and excitable. 'Ernie's very laid-back in a lot of things and he lets a lot of things go,' Feldman said. 'He doesn't like confrontation. But he's very strong-willed. If he doesn't want to play somewhere he'll say so and that, quite honestly, is the end of the story. He's not as easy to do business with as he is with everything else. He's quite adamant about what he wants. He's stubborn. I'm not saying that's bad, but there is a different side to him. I've stopped nagging him because he says: "You're like my father now. Don't nag me." But I got to a point where I understood what I was dealing with. Some people are highly motivated by training fourteen hours a week and eating the correct foods. Ernie's not like that. Maybe if he was, he'd go backwards.'

As a boy, Els won the World Junior in the United States at the age of thirteen, became a scratch golfer the following year, was Eastern Transvaal's senior tennis champion and a first-class cricketer and rugby player.

'I also did athletics,' Els added rather more quietly.

Feldman burst out laughing. His charge is not known for being overly energetic off the course. 'The only place he runs to now is the bathroom,' he teased.

Nevertheless, he admitted that Els had not been wholly unaffected by fame. 'The notoriety did get to him. One moment he was just somebody playing golf in South Africa, and the next everybody knew him. I think that put pressure on him because all of a sudden he realized that every week he's got to perform. For whom? In our discussions, I've always said to him, "You must do what you want to do. The people that care about you will always be there for you whether you shoot 86 or 66." There's always next week. It's a thirty-year career. It's not going to be done in a week.'

On Thursday, we were invited to an event billed as an 'Arabian evening', although the two Irish musicians rather clouded the issue. Seemingly intent on massacring the most beloved of Irish folk tunes, they stood on the stage where we had expected to see *Arabian Nights* unfold and wailed to an unappreciative audience. To begin with, there were no belly-dancers in sight. Indeed, at the outset there had not even been a bus. We had waited on the steps of our hotel, a hungry posse of journalists, while eight o'clock came and went and a chill desert wind blew ice into our veins. Tempers quickly frayed.

'Do you think we might need another coat?' I asked vaguely, when headlights finally shone and a bus came roaring up the drive.

Gordon Richardson lost his temper. 'How can you say, you think we need another coach? I mean, *really*. You'll just have to make do with this one.' And ignoring my spluttered protests, he climbed on board.

Norman was the last of our company to arrive, wearing a silk jacket with multi-coloured triangles that would have been the clothing of choice for jugglers in the last century. We were relieved to see that he had come without his razor. The previous year, travelling in a similar bus, he had turned up late, flustered and unshaven. Midway to our destination he had produced a battery-operated razor, switched it on and proceeded to saw away at his jaw. The driver cocked an ear in alarm. 'A slow puncture,' he decided and, slamming on brakes so hard that we all almost flew through the window, he leapt from the the vehicle with his spanners and began hammering at the tyres and poking irritably at the undercarriage. Norman kept quiet. Slowly and surreptitiously, he put away his shaving kit and sat looking about him in wide-eyed innocence.

Tonight, fortunately, all was peaceful. We sped through the night on the wide, smooth roads of Dubai, passing the broad, dark humps of camels and shaggy silver-topped palms. A large yellow moon climbed ponderously up the sky. At last, we turned off the main highway and onto a desert road designed to forcibly extract every tooth from one's head. We travelled like this for some time until blazing lights indicated that we had arrived at the beach home of our host, Mohammed Al Abbar, Director General of the Dubai Economic Department.

Everybody who was anybody appeared to be there. They were drinking champagne amid the silk carpets, Arabic coffee pots and lace-covered four-poster beds, or gazing into roaring fires on the beachfront – oil sheikhs, men of Bedouin extraction, scores of expatriates and professional golfers. Greg Norman sat gingerly in a chair, with a plate of tandoori prawns, attempting to combat a severe bout of hayfever. Darren Clarke and Eoghan O'Connell, the Irish players, were alternately tossing back cans of Heineken, gnawing at giant drumsticks and sucking on a hubbly-bubbly. Norman (Officer Dibell) Dabell, who works for Irish regional papers like the *Cork Examiner* and is fiercely protective of his subjects, informed us that Clarke was on a diet. This news was greeted with derision. Based on the evidence before us, we decided that Clarke was of the eating-Kelloggs-branflakes-while-wearing-trainers school of fitness. Later in the season, he was to prove us wrong.

We departed for the culinary village, where a feast fit for kings lay smoking on the dunes, and piled our plates high with snowy rice, barbecued lobster, sweet and sour prawns and stuffed peppers. All was delicious. Expatriates and pro golfers, having eaten their fill early on, lolled about on cushions with hookahs. The Irish musicians lent a surreal element to the proceedings.

The seasonal passage of a golf writer is, it has to be said, accompanied by the not infrequent dispensation of what is collectively known as 'bung' – i.e. logoed shirts, dinners and golf games. For no other reason than the fact I write about golf, I have shaken hands with the Royal family in Monaco, watched Shirley Bassey sing beneath the stars in Dubai, been to Disneyworld in Florida and received enough sweat-shirts to clothe a small football team. Most free gifts are sent the way of charity, but *Golf World*'s Gary van Sickle does a humorous impression of a greedy journalist: 'Thank you very much for my complimentary gift. Please may I have two more.'

Not all journalists are greedy and not all expense accounts are generous, as Ron Wills might have testified. Eating with several of his fellow golf writers one evening, Wills was overcome with dizziness and stepped outside for a breath of fresh air. Minutes later he passed out. In the meanwhile, a large bill arrived at the table. Since there was not enough money to cover it, Mark Wilson went in search of Wills, finding him prone in the gutter. Wills recovered consciousness to find the man from the *Daily Express* emptying his pockets without the slightest concern for his well-being.

The highlight of this particular evening was the appearance of the belly-dancer who, it transpired, was Canadian. She was practised at her art none the less, and a great believer in audience participation. On several occasions, she gyrated her way into the crowd and urged men to dance. Many expatriates seemed to be old hands at belly-dancing and cheerfully obliged. Mike Britten, a diminutive British freelance, turned her down. I think he was afraid that Norman, who has not spoken to him since threatening to drive him into the ground in the summer of '93, would make cruel jibes at his expense.

Somewhere near midnight we decided to call it a day. Mike led the way across the desert to the car-park.

'Lawrence of Arabia,' someone said.

'Lawrencette of Arabia,' Gordon joked.

We piled into the bus, cold and tired, our breath making cartoon bubbles on the window. We steeled ourselves for the bone-shaking ride across the desert. The engine started – one bump, two bumps, three . . . clatter! A knife bounced out of a coat pocket and fell guiltily to the floor. Ten pairs of eyes stared accusingly at the offender. Jock McVicar blushed scarlet to the roots of his hair.

'Well, well, well,' cried Mark, in the tone of a policeman apprehending a criminal. 'What's all this, then? Stealing the sheikh's silver?'

'No, I was just . . .'

'Go on, spit it out.'

'Well, it was just that I had my glass in one hand and my plate in the other and I had nowhere to put my knife and fork . . .'

'A fork, too! What else have you taken? The crystal wineglasses? The salt and pepper?'

And for the remainder of that one-hour journey poor Jock had to endure our taunts, and explain over and over exactly how he had ended up with the silverware of his host in the top pocket of his tweed coat.

In every respect, it resembled a badly acted scene from *Carry on, Cleopatra*. *Arabian Nights* it was not.

On the final day of the Desert Classic, I went out with Norman Dabell to watch Norman, the golfer, play. With his taut, sinewy frame, capped teeth and shock of yellow hair, the Shark resembled nothing so much as Ken, Barbie's companion. 'He doesn't look real, does he?' I remarked to Dabell.

'He probably isn't,' Norman said. 'It's probably a stand-in.'

Greg Norman's usual war-cry had been rather muted after the third day of play. 'It just seems that Ernie blitzed us in the first round,' he admitted, looking with awe at Els's eight-stroke lead. 'If I shot 62 tomorrow, maybe . . .' His voice trailed off. 'I'd like to see it blow really hard tomorrow,' he began again, knowing full well that we knew that he knew he was just whistling in the wind.

But experience is a powerful asset. Els was nervous, he was unsure of himself. He didn't know whether to target the pins or play conservatively. Norman watched him hawk-eyed. 'He hooked off the tee on five,' he told us later, 'and I said to myself, "If you can get a two-shot swing early on, it might make all the difference." Because I could see he wasn't in sync.'

On the front nine, Els drove out of bounds, he three-putted, he took an unplayable from a bush. He opened the door wide enough to drive a bus through and none of his pursuers took advantage of it. 'I felt edgy,' he said after signing for a 71 and his first European Tour victory. 'I've never felt that way before. I was scared of making big numbers instead of just going out there to attack the golf course like I did the first three days. It was funny.'

Norman was impressed. He had been astounded to hear that Els had never won in Europe before. 'He's a lot calmer than I was fourteen years ago,' the Shark admitted. 'He's got more of an even keel about him . . . I just hope he keeps his long, flowing swing. If Ernie tried to shorten his swing, it would hurt him a lot.'

'Is he capable of winning a major championship?' a reporter asked.

Norman pursed his lips. 'Anybody can be a major winner if you've got it in your heart,' he said. 'But a lot of outside agencies come into effect when you get to that level. I've seen a lot of guys get to that level and then back-pedal. But he's good enough to do it, no question about it.'

5

COUPLES THERAPY

'One description of a peak performer is someone who is mentally engaged and physically relaxed. Freddie has taken it to an art form . . .'

CHUCK HOGAN, sports psychologist

On the steps of the Emirates clubhouse, Fred Couples and I were discussing the catastrophic effects of divorce – his, not ours.

'How does the law work in the US?' I queried. 'Is there a fifty-fifty division of property?'

'Pretty much,' admitted Couples. 'In Florida, yeah.' He stopped. As always, his brown, wholesome face, with its soft eyes and easy smile, mirrored the conflict between the two sides of his character – one, shy and intensely private, the other, naturally open.

'The way I look at it is . . .' Couples began. He gave a short laugh. 'I don't know,' he said, shrugging his shoulders. 'I look at it now and it's just frustrating. I'm just glad it's over with. I never thought any of it was very funny at all. You know, to give someone $52,000 a month – I think that's ridiculous. I mean, that was a tough thing to swallow. You try to play golf and earn a living, and you win, and you're giving something to someone, when everyone around you knows that you did *everything*. I mean, I *played* the game. I did it all on my own. I just happened to be married. And I don't blame her at all. You know, she had her lawyers and they did their thing. But it was frustrating. I wouldn't want anyone to get divorced if they didn't need to. And I *needed* to. I needed to have someone travelling and to have fun. It just happened to be the best three years of my life playing golf, and really it wasn't much fun because she was very rarely around. So, you know, you'd win the tournament and go and sit in your hotel room or fly home. I think it was very frustrating to be put through that, and everywhere you went people would say things. The bottom line was that it took a lot longer than I thought, but once it was over with then I just felt good about everything and I got to go and play golf.'

It has taken almost two years of legal wrangles, emotional upsets and unwanted media attention for Fred to get to the point where he can just be Fred again. Which is all he ever wanted to be. Before he won the 1992 US Masters in customary Couples fashion – the gallery exploding and having heart attacks among the azaleas all around him, while Fred, only a degree away from a whistle, wandered happily up the fairway, hitting the odd shot into the water and then saving himself with some belief-beggaring chip or putt just to keep everyone on their toes – he had been perfectly content with his general position in life. In between watching soap operas, cartoons and ball games on television, he had won a few tournaments, scored some top tens and just enjoyed himself. Once he had even had the nerve to say that he was pleased with third place. 'I don't understand that,' Nicklaus said, appalled. Tom Weiskopf accused him of having no goals.

And perhaps Couples did lack focus. In his university days, when his effortless talent and prodigious length off the tee had resulted in him finishing low amateur at the 1979 US Open and twice being named All-American, he caught rides with his Houston Cougars team-mates, Jim Nantz, the CBS announcer, and Blaine McAllister. 'Hey, Fred, why don't you drive?' they would ask. Couples would shake his head. Eventually, they found out he didn't have a driver's licence. He didn't think he needed one.

Couples applied this same, slightly fuzzy logic to his career. Until the 1989 Ryder Cup, he had been largely untouched by the crueller, more capricious side of golf. Then his slow, lazy swing propelled a nine-iron shot past the final green at the Belfry, handing the match to Christy O'Connor Jnr and leaving the Ryder Cup tied and the trophy on European shores. Couples cried as though his heart would break. All of a sudden his happy-go-lucky attitude had cost him more than a place or two in a tournament and a bit of criticism from the Golden Bear. It had hurt his country; it had hurt his team. He took a long hard look at himself. Once he had said that golf was about the fifth priority in his life – 'I don't know what the other four are.' Now, with pride's fire beginning to stir reluctantly in his belly, he decided it was high time he reprioritized.

In 1991, Couples finished third in the US Open, triggering an astonishing streak of form, which brought him five victories and twenty top-six places in twenty-five starts worldwide. Among them were the Los Angeles Open in March 1992 and, three weeks later, the Nestle Invitational, which he won by nine strokes. In between, he finished runner-up twice. In April, he arrived at Augusta as the world's No.1, becoming the first US player to top the rankings since they were launched in 1986. When he won the Masters, beating Raymond Floyd by two strokes, it was no surprise to anyone except perhaps Fred.

What nobody predicted was the resulting Fred mania. No-one could have foreseen that the golfing public, desperate for a genuine, down-to-earth, American-as-apple-pie hero, would take Couples to their hearts in such a way that he became an overnight icon, a symbol of all that was truly good about sport and American life.

'I got to be, not like a rockstar but . . . they wanted more out of you,' said Couples, who has a habit of referring to himself in the second person. 'They thought their time and your time should kind of mix more . . . I mean, I was on Tour for eleven years, and then I finally won a major tournament and it was like a bomb went off.'

The problem was Couples's accessibility. Other top players, particularly on the US circuit, were screened from the travails of everyday Tour life. They were the 'Air People' Jonathan Raban talked of in his American Odyssey, *Hunting Mister Heartbreak*. They occupied a rarefied stratosphere and came and went as secretively and expensively as Hollywood stars. But Fred was like your brother or your cousin. He was the guy at the corner store, the friend you sat next to in school. Women either wanted to mother him or marry him. 'I don't usually do this . . .' their notes would begin, before they invited him out to dinner, to the pictures, back to their apartments. 'He's just so normal,' Tawnya Dodd, Couples's soon-to-be wife, told John Barton of *Golf Digest*. 'He's the boy next door. He's not at all intimidating. It's hilarious at tournaments listening to people in the gallery talk as if they know him. You hear them discussing what Fred probably had for breakfast, or what he's thinking, as though they are personally very good friends with him.'

That had never happened with Norman or Langer or Faldo. For all his attempts to market himself as a regular guy, as likely to enjoy a simple beach barbecue as a ride in a Ferrari, Norman remains a remote figure, while Langer's Christianity has never melted his thick layer of German reserve. And as for Faldo – well, Faldo's just Faldo. But Couples couldn't see why he should be more appealing than they were. He thought it had to do with erratic play. 'Faldo walks down the middle of every fairway and he hits every green, so people don't ever get to see him,' Couples explained ingenuously. 'He's boring because he's so good. I'm not boring because I can drive the ball three hundred yards dead straight and I can hit one in the flowers. So people are going to maybe finally get to see me.'

Shy and retiring, Couples was overwhelmed by his sudden celebrity status. At Greensboro, his first Tour stop after the Masters, he had six security guards escorting him down the fairway. 'It was pretty exciting on the golf course,' Couples said, generously looking at the positive side of the autograph hounds, the banners and the mistimed yells of 'You the man' that accompanied him. 'Off the course, I like to be away from golf so that was a struggle . . . I don't know if it's the way I play, or that I'm easy to get around or get to talk to, but people would just come up out of the blue. So that was difficult. And I had a tough time accepting the fact that all of a sudden people thought I was going to win every tournament. It didn't happen before the Masters and I don't know why because I won the Masters it got in people's minds.'

It was around that time that he made his never-to-be-forgotten remark about not answering the phone 'in case there's someone on the other end.'

In Dubai, he said: 'I'm getting better, I'm getting better,' meaning that he will at least consider answering it now. 'I made that comment a couple of years ago because it got to the point where I was picking up the phone and talking to people I'd never even met before,' Couples explained.

But there was more to it than that. Less than a year after his victory at Augusta, Fred and Debbie Couples were given the tabloid treatment by the American news programme, *Hard Copy*. The subject was their fast disintegrating marriage. Always something of a kingfisher-and-sparrow couple, the gulf between them was growing by the day. Deborah's definition of fun was the antithesis of Fred's.

She liked playing polo, meeting people and wearing exotic, eye-catching mini-skirts. He was reserved and ordinary. His only interests were sport, more sport and watching TV. They had met at a baseball game during Fred's junior year at the University of Houston, where Debbie had been on a tennis scholarship. It was a marriage of opposites but they lost all common ground.

At the 1992 British Open, Debbie was rumoured to have performed a partial strip-tease on a table in a pub near Muirfield. In October, she filed for divorce. When they met in court the following February for a preliminary hearing, she asked him for $168,000 a month to get her through the polo season. The circuit judge awarded her a temporary settlement of $52,000. By now Debbie had decided she didn't really want a divorce, she wanted a reconciliation. She bought Fred a boat and had it painted Masters green. Fred was way past the point of no return. Miserably, he channelled what little energy he had left into his golf, winning the Honda Classic in March. But his heart wasn't in it. The season stretched leadenly before him. Any elation he might have felt after winning at Augusta had been crushed under the weight of his worries. He said that the end of his marriage, finalized a fortnight after the Ryder Cup on 8 October, felt 'like a death in the family'.

The impressive thing was, apart from becoming moody, Couples remained as good-natured and gentle as ever throughout this bleak period in his life. He even tried to give every reporter who interviewed him something fresh and original because 'I hate reading the same thing about myself in Chicago one week and Boston the next, and you get a little embarrassed when other Tour players do it, too.'

Through no obvious means, he had cornered the market on the kind of laid-back approach to life, love and the universe that, every day, people across the US were paying fortunes to psychiatrists to achieve.

'Actually, you know, I get really edgy,' Couples confessed unconvincingly. 'I think if I was as outgoing off the course as I am on it – if I see a little kid watching I like to go and have fun with him – then I wouldn't be so edgy. I get edgy because I think people kind of invade my space. I don't think there's anything wrong with that, but I get scared to be around a lot of people every single day. I like to stay with my friends . . . As far as people finding out about your private life goes, sometimes you might say something you wish you hadn't but there's so many questions being asked that things come out. If you say that you never go out to eat, then they think you're a recluse, and if you say that you like going out to party, then they think you're a drunk. I don't go out much and I don't drink, so there's not a whole lot to talk about except that I like all sports and I like to hang out at home.'

'Do you think a lot came out that was untrue about your divorce?' I asked.

'You know what?' Fred said. 'I don't know what came out that was true or untrue. All I can say is I'm about as happy as can be that it's all over, and things are going great.'

Frederick Stephen Couples was born in Seattle on 3 October 1959. The son of a minor league baseball player, he took up golf at nine, cycling to the local municipal course and hitting balls until it was dark. He never had a lesson, but he did have a temper. He threw clubs on every other shot until the day he rammed a club in his bag at a tournament and broke three others. In the eighth grade, he decided to concentrate on golf, and when he won the Washington State Open at the age of eighteen, he knew it was going to be his career. In 1980, while holidaying in Los Angeles, he went to watch the Queen Mary Open in Longbeach. 'Can I play?' Fred asked the club pro. 'If you turn pro, sure you can play,' was the response. So Fred played, tied sixth and won $3,000.

Mark O'Meara recalled meeting Couples, nicknamed Boom Boom because of his formidable length, at the 1980 Tour School. 'We went through both Schools together,' he said, meaning the pre-qualifying tournament and the qualifying. 'One just outside LA where Freddie had no money. He had to sleep in his car. I didn't have any money either but I was sharing with this buddy of mine who was a landscape gardener. He was trying to qualify but he didn't make it, so Freddie stayed with me. Then we went to the final School at Fort Washington – that was in the Fall of '80 – and we played together the last day. And he's out there just, you know . . .' O'Meara mimicked Couples strolling down the fairway without a care in the world. 'We've got two holes to go and I'm going to make it. I can bogey in and make it. But Freddie's got to struggle. On the last hole, he stands on the tee and he says, "You know, I don't know about all this pressure." He says, "This is like standing on the eighteenth tee at my home course and having to make a par to make it. It's just the same. It's not that bad." And he hit a one-iron off the tee, thinned a wedge over the back of the green, chipped to about eight feet and made it. He was the last guy to make it through the Qualifying School.'

O'Meara pondered this for a moment. 'And you know, a couple of years ago, in about '86, he was miserable. He was ready to quit. I mean, he was on the point of telling his caddie to go and work for someone else. And it turned around.'

Couples hadn't forgotten those days. In the summer of 1985 he played only one tournament in eight weeks – the US PGA Championship, where he finished equal sixth. The following season, he fell to seventy-sixth on the money list. He didn't like to practise; he didn't want to play. It was only when he went to Houston in 1987, and began working with Paul Marchand and Dick Harmon that his game began to turn around. He became better under pressure and more motivated, although he never lost the youthful fervour that had been with him from the outset.

Couples approaches the game with a kind of joyous anticipation, like a natural coming to it for the first time. With Fred, golf is not a life and death business; it's about as much fun as you can have with your clothes on. He doesn't stride down the fairway, he ambles gracefully, plucking at his shirt, stretching to the heavens, talking to the kids in the crowd; and then he takes the club in his hands in an untutored yet familiar way, like a boy in the West Indies discovering cricket on a beach, and holes a full seven-iron from the fairway or propels a drive 300 yards. 'My body swings to where the pin is,' is the extent of his technical theory. When he's playing well, he doesn't even take aim. Only Ernie Els moves as languidly as Couples does on the course, but with Els there are discernible signs of tension in situations of extreme pressure. He chews gum, he bites his lip, anxiety scrunches his brow. Fred might fidget a little more, but his aspect never changes. Nor does his golf swing. 'Beautifully un-schooled, Couples swings a golf stick exactly the way Trevino would if Trevino had a better body,' observed Tom Callahan of *Golf Digest*. 'Aiming his feet far to the left, Couples raises the club high, torques his shoulders without strain, and drops the clubhead on the ball with half the anxiety of Julius Boros. A high handicapper who tried this could put an eye out.'

That's why it seemed so incomprehensible to Couples that Bernhard Langer, having won his second Masters, plus the PGA

Championship and German Open in 1993, could turn up at the first big event of '94 and inform us that he was rebuilding his swing with the help of David Leadbetter.

'That's amazing to me,' Couples said with awe. 'I think the guy's the greatest. I was playing with him the other day and he said: "I don't feel comfortable, so I'm going to use my old swing." You know, you sit there and you think, Why would a guy do that? Everyone says, well, you need to get to the next level. Well, there's only one level. If your name is up there with Payne Stewart, Greg Norman, Nick Faldo, Paul Azinger and Bernhard Langer, that *is* the level. I mean, if I had won the Masters this year and I was now saying, "I want to go to another level," if I was someone out there, I'd probably laugh at me. You know, Michael Jordan won three NBA Championships and quit. He said: "What more can I do?" Well, in golf you can continue to play better and you can shoot better scores and you can maybe break a record at a US Open. But you can't win a major and then say: "Now I want to change my swing and go to the next level." But Bernhard Langer knows what he's doing.'

So does Fred. His goal for the new season was to be more focused and prepared, and to pick up Ryder Cup points. 'Last year is behind me and I should be able to play well and have fun. But really, if I don't play well, I don't have fun. That's the bottom line. It's not much fun to do something you want to do and not play well.'

It helps a great deal that his private life is now so happy. In February 1992, while playing in the Bob Hope Classic, Fred met Tawnya Dodd at a restaurant. 'I was not dressed in golf clothing and she didn't have any idea who I was,' Couples told *Digest*. 'We were just sitting around talking. Then I gave her a call and that's pretty much how it all started. It was good. Obviously, I was married. I felt awkward about it. Certainly it was no fling or anything like that. But it was fun to be around her. I started having fun.'

The word fun has always cropped up a lot in Couples's vocabulary, but now at least he's not talking about its absence. Last Fall, Fred, Tawnya and her twelve-year-old son, Derek, moved into a big white house in Dallas. They plan to marry and start a family of their own. When he's not playing golf, Fred spends his time flicking through the channels, attending upwards of twenty-five football, baseball, hockey and basketball games a year and pottering around the yard

('I don't try to ruin too much, I'm not a big flower planter, I'm just out there chopping trees') or polishing his Mustangs.

He's so settled that when his mother said that she wished he could just make $50,000 a year and stay at home, he said: 'Mom, don't you think I'd like the same thing.' And he's so content that it's hard to imagine that an emotion like anger ever makes a blip on the Couples graph of goodwill. Yet it seems it does.

'Actually . . .' Fred gave a slightly embarrassed laugh. 'I'm no politician but what really makes me angry is when people hurt other people. I think it's ridiculous. Or when people steal things. Sometimes when you play, you hear somebody took some guy's putter or some guy stole something out of someone's house. Nick Faldo had some jewellery stolen. Things like that make me angry. Because I don't think there's any reason for me to ever harm anybody and I don't ever want to be harmed.'

He considers his professional and personal frailties as the world might see them. 'My golf strengths are my distance and my putting. My weakness is that in big tournaments I don't really drive the ball as well as I should. You're never going to win a major tournament by a lot of strokes, especially US Opens, but you do need to hit fairways. But that's just the way I play. I know that and I accept that. So what I need to do is to play a lot smarter.

'As a person, I'm kind of soft,' Couples admitted. 'But I enjoy being that way. Other people might say, to be the best, he's got to be more tough or mean or whatever. But if I'm the best player in the world, I want to have fun and be jovial and say "Hi" to everyone. And if I'm the worst player, I want to be the same way.'

6

ON THE ROAD

'What are these people up to?'

JACK KEROUAC, *On the Road*

HONDA CLASSIC, WESTON HILLS, FLORIDA. In Fort Lauderdale, I checked into the Paradise Club or Motel Heaven or some such place near Weston Hills Country Club, which wore a fresh lick of paint but in all other respects was just the same as it had been the previous year. In the mornings, stolid waitpersons served cold, dry bagels, squalid coffee and jam in pots, and in the evenings, prostitutes and pretzel machines murmured in the corridors. Courtesy cars were parked bumper to bumper in the courtyard.

The first thing I did was turn on the Weather Channel. If there was to be a repeat of the Storm of the Century, I wanted to be prepared for it. The last Honda Classic had been hit by a hurricane on the eve of the third round. I'd been woken at around 4.00 a.m. by a terrible roaring noise and had been confronted, when I peered out into the darkness, by what appeared to be the onset of Armageddon or a scene from *Hawaii Five-O*. Vast oaks thrashed and moaned like madwomen beneath the onslaught of a gale made white and supernaturally visible by the rain. Palm trees lay helplessly on the ground. On the television, hysterical anchorpeople took calls from hysterical citizens and delivered stern warnings: 'Do not, repeat, *not*, leave your home unless it is absolutely necessary.'

It was then that I made the mistake of getting up. I was standing

84

at the wash-basin, nervously watching the light fittings shivering in the mirror, when, without warning, a great pipe burst and scalding water spewed forth. With a cry of pain, I leapt onto the bed. Beneath the chipboard counter, a small dam had come into being and was operating at an impressive level of efficiency. Within minutes, the room resembled a heated swimming pool. Articles of clothing orbited the furniture on a brisk current. Steam rose from the carpet. Then I discovered that the telephone had ceased functioning. At that point, waves began to lick the edge of the bedspread and it became obvious that I was either going to be boiled alive or drowned, so I jumped onto the other bed, then onto a chair, wrenched open the door and vaulted into the corridor. Outside, the wind banged and whined, and pushed and pummelled. It was like being trapped inside a giant spin-dryer. Later that day, after the receptionist had shut down the water supply and helped me into a new room, and I had been down to the golf course to review the wholesale devastation of the tented village, I found that, in the full fury of the storm, gales of up to 80 mph had been recorded. An estimated $500,000 of damage had been caused to the tournament site and nearly $100,000 lost at the gate.

This time, the sky was a guileless egg-shell blue. Robinson picked me up from Miami airport in a car that had evidently seen more than its fair share of tournaments. Dog-eared science fiction novels, histories of the Middle Ages, golf magazines and *People* magazine shared the crowded confines of the Toyota with lottery tickets, loud jackets, country music cassettes, crumbs and sticky canisters; Robinson's diet consists largely of Frosted Mini Wheats, Graham Crackers and Slurpees, a kind of syrupy soft drink combination whipped up with crushed ice, which she purchases at the 7-Eleven.

Like me, Robinson spends her days dreaming of ways in which to cure herself of her golf addiction. While still studying history at college, she used to pour over the reports of Gordon S. White Jnr, the former *New York Times* golf correspondent. 'I'd think: "I can do that. What a cool job." But it never really seemed like a reality.' Then she won $9,000 on the gameshow *Jeopardy* in 1987, spent $200 on a 1970 Dodge Dart Swinger named Minerva, was somehow credentialled for the 1987 Ryder Cup and took off on a three-year experiment. She's been trying to give it up ever since. Her longest ever drive was twenty-seven hours, from New York to Houston for the Nabisco, and her favourite anecdote is the time she was caught speeding and jailed in Nowhere, Kansas, on her way to the Senior Skins Game in Hawaii.

'I was not treated as a dangerous criminal,' Robinson insisted.

It used to be that the European Tour started in April and ended in October. After that, the top players would depart for warmer climes, participating in a couple of events in Japan, a couple in Australia and either the World Cup or the Million Dollar in Sun City, and then everyone would retire until springtime for a well-earned rest. Now it is long and straggly and occupies every week between mid-January and mid-November, after which invitational events such as the 'World' Championship keep us busy until the week before Christmas. There is neither enough money nor enough top players to pad out the extra weeks in the schedule, but IMG hit upon the bright idea of spreading their big names thinly through the season, rather than putting them all in the same events, thereby ensuring that the appearance money cup keeps brimming over and justifying their 'phony' rankings, which are boosted by the presence of IMG players in the field. You are now left with two choices: either you can work yourself to a frazzle chasing solitary stars to places like Czechoslovakia, or you can cover the events with the strongest entries. Hence, the golf media tend to go to the Desert and Asian Classics at the end of January, one Spanish event in March, and then head over to America for three or four weeks for the Florida swing and the Masters.

Our main interest at the Honda Classic was not, however, Faldo or Lyle, nor even the extraordinary series of coincidences which had seen Fred Couples suffer a serious back injury while practising at Doral the previous week, Phil Mickelson break the femur in his left leg and suffer a hairline fracture in his right ankle in a skiing accident, Mark Weibe break his shoulder on the ski slopes in Colorado, and Larry Mize undergo arthroscopic knee surgery in Columbus. We were there for the long-awaited return of John Daly. The 1991 US PGA Champion was playing in his first event since being suspended – it almost goes without saying – in November for picking up his ball during the Kapalua International pro-am. He had begun the '93 season in an alcoholic rehabilitation centre.

'I think the incident at Kapalua was telling me that I needed to take some time off,' Daly confessed, after describing this latest recess as the proverbial blessing in disguise. 'I'd been running myself

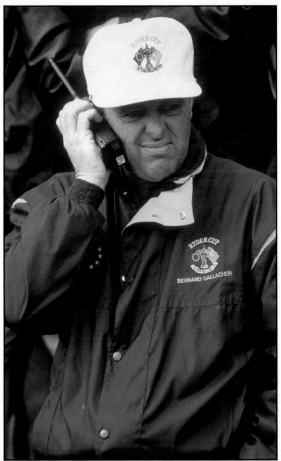

WATERLOO: European Ryder Cup captain Bernard Gallacher contemplates the spectre of defeat.
Phil Sheldon Golf Picture Library

THE DECISION-MAKERS: *(from left to right)* John O'Leary, then Tour chairman; Emma Villacieros, head of the Spanish Golf Federation; Ken Schofield, executive director of the European Tour; Sandy Jones, PGA supremo; and Andrew Morgan and Phillip Weaver of Johnnie Walker, umbrella sponsor of the Ryder Cup. *Phil Sheldon Golf Picture Library*

In a now infamous portrayal of the American Dream, Fred and Debbie Couples celebrate his victory on the 18th green at Augusta. Within months, they announced their plans for divorce.
Allsport/Stephen Munday

THE BIG THREE: US Open Champion Ernie Els and British Open and US PGA Champion Nick Price – the most successful players in the world in 1994 – share a joke with World No.2 Greg Norman.
Phil Sheldon
Golf Picture Library

David Feherty and Sam Torrance kiss the blarney stone at Mount Juliet.
Allsport/Stephen Munday

FAIRY-TALE ENDING: Carl Mason, who became a double winner on the European Tour for the first time at the age of 40, sees out the year in style with his wife, Beryl, and son, Andrew, at the World Championship in Jamaica.
Phil Sheldon Golf Picture Library

Ernie Els takes time off from winning the World Championship to play beach
cricket at Montego Bay, Jamaica. *Allsport*

MAN OF THE PEOPLE: Nick Faldo does his bit for Anglo-Carribean relations.
Phil Sheldon Golf Picture Library

The strain shows as Greg Norman tries to prevent yet another one from getting away. *Yours In Sport/Lawrence N. Levy*

ARABIAN NIGHTS: Ireland's Eoghan O'Connell and Darren Clarke participate vicariously in a spot of pipe smoking during the Desert Classic in Dubai. *Lauren St John*

AFTER THE GRAIL: Tom Watson puts heart and soul into overcoming Turnberry and achieving his final dream – to equal Harry Vardon's record of six Open titles.
Phil Sheldon Golf Picture Library

A minor detour for Jose Maria Olazabal *en route* to victory in the 1994 Masters.
Phil Sheldon Golf Picture Library

Hot and weary, Colin Montgomerie and Loren Roberts prepare to bow to the inevitable as Ernie Els, the man Curtis Strange described as 'the next God', takes control at Oakmount. *Phil Sheldon Golf Picture Library*

INSTRUMENT OF TORTURE: Greg Norman jettisons the putter that cost him victory in the 1993 US PGA playoff against Paul Azinger. *Phil Sheldon Golf Picture Library*

John 'Wild Thing' Daly, a volcano just waiting to erupt.
Phil Sheldon Golf Picture Library

ragged . . . Hell, for two years, I never even worked on my game for a good solid week, much less two and a half months.'

Attending a Daly press conference is much the same as watching the *700 Club* or even *The Oprah Winfrey Show*. He's very earnest and very frank and he unburdens himself in such a way that one keeps expecting a caption to appear beneath him: 'John – recovering alcoholic, alleged wife batterer, rebel without a cause.'

'Last year, I cried a lot,' Daly, who has lived fast for most of his twenty-seven years, told the *New York Times*. 'You go through some things that some of us have had to go through and you've got to cry. But I think I handled it a lot better last year than I did when I didn't think I had problems. It was actually a good year for maturity. I didn't trash anything. I think I handled it really well.' Now he said: 'Last season I didn't play well, but I achieved one goal. Being sober felt like winning a major.'

It had been fourteen months since the last drop of Jack Daniels had passed Daly's lips. Since then he had shed 25 lbs, although it was hard to see how when his other addictions had tripled. In a normal day, he consumed up to sixteen Diet Cokes, a bag or two of M&Ms, a pint of chocolate yoghurt and four packs of Marlboro Mediums. Asked why he smoked so much, Daly glowered and retorted: 'You quit drinking and you'll find out. It's hard. You smell it, you see it.' The previous season, a spectator had shouted to him: 'Why don't you start drinking again? You'll play better.'

However, that was all behind him now. He was healthy, he was focused, he had purchased a 40-foot bus to live in on the road, and he planned to spend the new season playing good golf and practising 'Stairway to Heaven' and other standards on his new Fender Stratocaster. Larry Rinker, another US player, had suggested he learn to play guitar as a distraction from the temptation of drink. 'You know, when you give up drinking cold turkey like he did, all of a sudden there can be forty-eight hours in the day instead of twenty-four. I saw it as a way for him to occupy some of that time, as an outlet for him.'

If he felt himself weakening, Daly had former Dallas Cowboy, Thomas (Hollywood) Henderson, standing by to counsel him. He avoided Alcoholics Anonymous meetings. 'I'm sure they do a good job for some people,' Daly said, 'but I find them too negative. I don't want to hear somebody else's sob story.'

*　　*　　*

With the eyes of the golf world on him, Daly went out in the first round of the Honda Classic and shot a two under par 69. At the eighteenth hole, a 585-yard par five, he pulled the cover off his Killer Whale driver, threw his cigarette to the ground, and despatched a 320-yard tee shot, outstripping his playing partner Nick Faldo by some 70 yards. He then squinted over the lake at the distant green, took out his two-iron and hit it 265 yards, setting up a 30-foot eagle chance which yielded a birdie. The gallery were beside themselves with joy.

'John certainly gives it a good hit,' remarked Faldo. 'My Sunday best is a Wednesday afternoon compared to his. Luckily, there's more to the game.'

But it was Daly's time to shine. The following day, he shot 70 in a fresh, swirling wind, so strong that the sixteenth tee was moved forward 55 yards, and on Sunday, he made three birdies on the front nine to draw within a shot of the lead, eventually finishing equal fourth. 'I'm really happy,' Daly said afterwards. 'I didn't know what to expect. I'm real proud that I finished in the top ten. I've already tied my top-ten finishes for last year. I worked hard. If I had a hat, I'd take it off to myself.'

All of this detracted somewhat from the triumph of the real hero, Nick Price. The Zimbabwean came back from a wrist injury and a lay-off to shoot a final round 66 and win by a stroke from Craig Parry and Brandel Chamblee. It was his tenth US Tour victory and it lifted him into twelfth place on the all-time money list with $5.4 million.

'Last year fuelled my desire,' Price said. 'It's a result of the 80s when I was practising hard and playing hard and just couldn't win. That hardened me. I don't want to back off now. I want very, very badly to win more majors. I've just got to make up for lost time.'

THE NESTLE INVITATIONAL, BAY HILL, ORLANDO. It had to happen sooner or later. Anyone who persists in staying in $28 motels, where squad cars are permanent fixtures in the parking lot, can take it as a given that criminals stalk the corridors and that before long, oneself or one's neighbours will appear as an item on the local news. Thus, Robinson and I, having elected to stay in the cheapest, most convenient accommodation in Orlando, were sitting in the press centre at the Nestle Invitational (otherwise known as the Candy Bar Classic) when a disturbing picture popped onto the television screen. Squadrons of police cars, an ambulance, and several crying guests were milling around outside our motel. An anchorwoman informed us that an intruder had obtained a pass key, and had been rushing from room to room, terrorizing their occupants and making off with their possessions. Robinson and I were aghast but our colleagues were unsympathetic. They seemed to feel that any assailant coming across either of us on a dark night would get far more than he bargained for.

The best thing about life on the road is that each Tour stop presents an opportunity to renew old friendships, catch up on the latest gossip and revisit favourite haunts. In November, whilst in Orlando for the World Cup, we had been invited to the Peabody Hotel to see the 'world famous' duck ceremony. Every morning, hordes of adoring tourists gather to witness the Peabody ducks climb out of their pond, traverse the lobby by way of a red carpet, take the lift to the top floor, and waddle into a different pond on the roof. In the evening, they return to their original watering hole. They are guided there by an Australian woman known as the Duck Master.

'That's a highly specialized field,' I remarked to Robinson. 'I wonder what you'd do after that.'

'Who knows?' Robinson said. 'Become a golf writer, probably.'

In essence, Bay Hill is Arnold Palmer's week. He is attached to the club and everywhere you turn you see his influence on the game that he made great. Nearly four decades have passed since Palmer, the son of a club professional, left Latrobe, Pennsylvania in a trailer with his new wife Winnie, returning as a national hero, a swash-buckling genius whose magnetic personality and exuberant game were to change the face of golf for ever. 'Arnold is the King,' Chi Chi Rodriguez said.

Even now, at sixty-three, Palmer still has more charisma in his little finger than Faldo and the rest have displayed in their entire careers. At the 1987 British Open, he put his approach shot in a greenside bunker on a par four. He had no shot. With the ball below his feet in an evil lie, his safest option was to play out sideways. Palmer refused to waste a stroke. It took him five attempts to escape from the trap, and he chalked up a ten.

'I was going to stay in there until it came out the way I wanted it to,' Palmer said stubbornly. 'I'm not saying God couldn't have got it out but he'd have had to throw it out.'

Hale Irwin smiled. 'There's still a lot of game left in that old boy,' he said affectionately. 'There's still a lot of tiger in his tank.'

There was still a lot of competitive fire as well, as we saw when Palmer and Nicklaus came in for a joint interview. 'There have been times when we've fought each other so hard that we've let others go by us,' Palmer admitted to one reporter. 'But frankly, I think our rivalry, if that's what you want to call it, would have been even more intense if we were the same age.'

Nicklaus said that Arnie was the only player he had ever played for more than $10 in a practice round. They always put down $20. Arnie was ahead on the lifetime stakes. Palmer laughed. 'But it doesn't matter because Jack never pays me anyway.'

'I'd rather owe it to you and then beat you out of it,' Nicklaus told him.

The talk at Bay Hill centred around Vijay Singh, the rangy Fijian whose game is ideally suited to US conditions. There was a story going around (which may be apocryphal) that Bob Torrance, Sam's teacher father, had been walking across the range one evening when he spotted Singh practising. He stopped to watch. Singh ignored him. Finally, Bob said: 'Vijay, you're laying it off at the top. Ben Hogan never laid it off at the top.'

'Yes,' said Singh, 'but Ben Hogan wasn't black.'

Singh and Tiger Woods, the eighteen-year-old Calfornian prodigy, represent the new generation of black players. As Jim Thorpe told *Golf World* (US), a few years ago there was a lot of black talent – Calvin Peete, Jim Dent, Lee Elder and Charlie Sifford – but 'most of us didn't manage ourselves well. We didn't get the most out of our games . . . I had years where I made $500,000, $600,000. And I bought $100,000 race horses and Corvettes. Man, it was stupid . . . I'll never forget Milwaukee in 1985. After my round Friday, I drove to Chicago, went to the track and the Playboy Club. The next day I got back to Milwaukee ninety minutes before my tee time – and shot 62. That helped me win the tournament. I was lucky. I knew it was the wrong thing to do but somehow I got away with it.'

These days, Thorpe is a model of decorum, hanging out with Vijay at the practice ground and working to bring golf to underprivileged kids. Singh just practises. 'Vijay Singh is known far and wide as the hardest practising player since Ben Hogan,' Rick Reilly reported in *Sports Illustrated*. 'He is the sort who would like nothing more out of life than a very nice villa on the range, overlooking the 200-yard sign.'

Dedication pays. In 1993, Singh notched up top-three finishes on six tours and won $1,183,000. At Bay Hill, he led Nick Price, Tom Watson and Andrew Magee by a stroke going into the final round, before surrendering to a 65 from Loren Roberts. It was Roberts's first win in thirteen years on the US PGA Tour.

Twilight was throwing a purple cloak over Bay Hill when Curtis Strange, who had finished a distant twenty-fourth, made his way unmolested through the dispersing crowds to the locker-room. There, his arrival went unnoticed. He sat down in a quiet corner, laced up his street shoes and absorbed the atmosphere: the grainy posters of Fat Jack and a youthful Arnold Palmer; the bantering players; the pungent aroma of polished wood and linseed oil; the tradition.

Outside, his good friend Peter Jacobsen leaned against the door jamb and talked of the days before the dream turned sour for the thirty-nine-year-old Virginian. 'Emotionally and physically, it took a lot out of him,' Jacobsen said, recalling how Strange had writhed and fretted under the unrelenting glare of publicity. 'He's a very private person and he was under the microscope. He won two US Opens and he tried and failed to win a third, and afterwards I remember him saying: "Thank God the speculation is finally over. Now I can go back to being a normal person again."'

Statistically, Strange had suffered a great deal since then, free-falling from the state of grace which saw him top the money list three times between 1985 and 1988, and become, in 1989, the first player since Hogan to win back to back US Opens, to the humble status he now occupied after finishing fifty-third, forty-eighth, ninetieth and sixty-third in the last four rankings.

Paradoxically, he had seldom been happier. 'I think I'm easier on myself,' Strange admitted. 'I'm not torturing myself. I think the pressures that I put on myself kind of drove me a little bit. Right from when I was ten years old, I always practised harder than the next guy, I always cared more. I always got more upset. It made me feel so good to play well; it made me hurt so much to play bad. The only time it changed was in 1990. I'd never done anything except go forward, climb the ladder, but in 1990 I went backwards.'

In explaining the reason why a major champion slumps, Sandy

Lyle once said that the difference between winning and contending was infinitesimal, as subtle and elusive as the fractions of seconds separating the world's top runners. It has to do with talent and it has to do with raw ambition.

Strange agreed. 'Look at Greg Norman, Nick Faldo and Nick Price,' he said. 'They all have an inner licence to kill. They want to go at it and they want to beat your brains out, and that's the way you have to be.'

Golf is a game of extremes, of excruciating lows and champagne highs, all bridged and disguised by etiquette and sportsmanship. One morning, Strange woke up and found he no longer had the stomach for the fight. 'You have to be very self-centred and the older I got, the more I didn't want to be that way because it's not a nice way to be. But that's the way to play good golf. It's not an ugly thing. You try to be a gentleman about it, but you have to be very, very focused. You have to be hard. You're not an egomaniac by any means, but you have to put yourself first. Your golf has to be No.1 and everything else takes a back seat.'

In the early years, when he was oblivious to everything except the craving for glory, Strange had a reputation for having a shorter fuse than a stick of dynamite. Once, he threw a club on every hole and still shot 68. Another time, he tossed all but five of his clubs into a ditch mid-round and returned a sub-par score. At a tournament in Las Vegas, he was so angry with himself for losing that he punched the bonnet of a Cadillac, breaking a bone in his hand. In 1982, Arnold Palmer singled him out as the epitome of all that was wrong with modern golf – an example of 'discourteous and ungentlemanly behaviour and thoughtlessness which is despicable to me.'

The result of it all was burnout. In 1990, he was forced to pause and re-evaluate his life. He took things easy for two years. He straightened out his priorities, becoming in the process 'a better husband, a better father and a better person.' Soon, quicker than he ever dreamt possible, he stopped hurting. In 1993, he had four consecutive top-ten finishes and in the winter he won the Holden Classic. Gradually, he discovered that even those small achievements meant little to him. 'These days, I think, I wouldn't struggle out here but as long as I can contend on somewhat of a regular basis, I'll play for ever. I enjoy it.'

In retrospect, Strange finds it curious that contentment was the commodity he found least of during the seasons when everything he touched turned to gold. 'After I won the US Open, the one thing people kept saying to me was, "Enjoy it." Well, you don't take time to enjoy it because you don't want to stop. When you try to get back up the second time, you know what's there. But to me, all of the fun was spitting and clawing and grinding and doing everything you had to do to get there in the first place. You know, watching your pennies, travelling in cars – that was all fun when you look back on it. But being there – being one of the best or the best – it's OK but I don't think it's everything it's cracked up to be. When you get there, you think: "Is that it?" '

THE PLAYERS CHAMPIONSHIP, SAWGRASS. Sometimes it seems like the loneliest place on earth is a hotel room. You unpack, you take a shower, you try to frighten away the silence by locating MTV or phoning home, but the slow-moving clock drowns out all of these. I've spent nights without end in windowless boxes in red-light districts in Spain, in airless mausoleums from Dubai to Miami, and in spacious coffins in the north of England, rank with the lingering smells of bad cooking and other people's holidays. But I had never really known what motel misery was until I arrived in Jacksonville, Florida for the Players Championship.

The nightmare began when I tried judging prospective motels by their façades. The Sea Turtle looked like a tenement block, the Holiday Inn could only be recognized as such by the black outline left by its long-departed neon sign, and the Comfort Inn was bleak and uninviting. By contrast, the Ramada appeared quite respectable. It was only after I had checked in, hauled my luggage into a construction-site-type lift and prised open the door of my room that I smelt a rat – or, to be more accurate – mould, disinfectant, stale cigarette smoke and moth balls. Damp stains crept across the ceiling; shoes were required for the smallest journey across the carpet. And there was hardly a spare inch of wall space, mirror space, window space or door space that was not hung with a sign warning you to guard your valuables, quadruple lock yourself in and never, never open the door – not even to housekeeping (assuming there was such a beast). I sat down on the bed and cried. The next morning, the taxi driver who carried me away to the relative sanctuary of the Sea Turtle told me the Ramada was a known den of iniquity – drugs, gangsters, etc. – but at the time all I knew was that there was no room service, the TV didn't work and you couldn't make outside calls. It's not always fun being a woman alone on the road.

In the spring of '88, when I first started covering golf on the European Tour, the myth that prevails in virtually all male bastions where women are seen as bimbos, tray-carriers or insurgents, was alive and well – i.e. any woman wishing to work in a man's world has to accept that sexual harassment, obscene jokes, bad language and suggestive remarks go with the territory. This comes under the heading: Equal Opportunity – the opportunity to hear how men talk and women are discussed in locker-rooms across the globe.

I was twenty years old and I was very naïve. Outcast by the golf writers (not for personal reasons but because a kind of mafia existed among the media élite at that time that closed ranks against all newcomers for anything from a month to four years), I turned to the players and caddies and spent every hour of every day out on the course, the practice range or socializing with them. Almost immediately, I started being harassed. Indoctrinated with the belief that this kind of treatment went with the turf, I just smiled and shrugged it off. Inwardly, I fumed, but all I could think was: if I want to make golf writing my life, I'm going to have to just ignore it or get used to it. If I start to make waves, I'll be out.

It wasn't that simple. If the harassment had been limited to lewd comments, it might have been, but a number of men took it much further. One player thought it an enormous joke to grab me from behind in public places – once in a restaurant where his wife was present. A series of people pounced on me in unexpected situations. Another player, also married, who was a virtual stranger to me but was generally regarded as quiet and well-mannered, persuaded me to interview him for an instruction series in his hotel room because his schedule was too full to do it anywhere else at any other time. Reluctantly, I agreed. It was one of my first assignments and I didn't want to blow it. Midway through the interview, he disappeared into the bathroom. When I heard the taps running, I became alarmed. I was hastily gathering my notebook and tape-recorder when he leapt on me, naked except for a tiny towel, only allowing me to struggle free when I lied, pretended I liked him and promised to come back later.

One man propositioned me so crudely and so often, that I decided that unless something was done about him, I would have to give up golf. I went to Ken Schofield, the Tour supremo. In an agony of embarrassment, I started to outline the situation to him. Schofield blanched. Scurrying away through the Wentworth car-park in an effort to escape from a situation that might bode ill for his everyday paradise – heaven forbid there should be a serpent in the Garden of Eden that is the Tour – he said that he was far too busy to look into it and that I was to make an official report to John Paramor, the tournament director. This I duly did. Nothing was ever done about it and I never followed it up. Prior to the ground-breaking Anita Hill trial, sexual harassment was viewed as a menace, largely imagined, that was supposed to be suffered in silence.

Obviously, I'm not the only woman to have encountered these problems on the Tour. Melanie Simmons of *Golf World* was attempting to ask Gordon Brand Jnr some innocuous survey questions at the European Masters a few years ago, when, for no reason at all, he hit her on the shin with his putter. He thought this was hilarious. Melanie, strangely enough, didn't. When she expressed her dissatisfaction, Brand Jnr called her a bitch. 'Look,' Melanie said, 'I'm just trying to do my job. Why don't you give me a break?' Whereupon, Brand Jnr launched into a vitriolic attack on the media in general and women journalists in particular. He has been similarly abusive to me. The incident involving Melanie was reported to the Tour, but to her knowledge it was never taken any further.

Discrimination is also a factor. Liz Kahn of the *Mail on Sunday* has spent years campaigning for equal access for women journalists into areas such as the clubhouse at St Andrews and the men's locker-room, one of the main story sources for our male colleagues at the Open. In 1970, she stormed into the Home of Golf, making it as far as the trophy room before being forcibly halted by a club steward. He told her that she wasn't allowed in the clubhouse. 'How extraordinary,' Liz Kahn said, 'all my colleagues are.'

'No, madam,' the steward assured her, 'no ladies are allowed in. Not even the Queen.'

When the Open returned to St Andrews in 1978, she tried again. This time she was confronted by the then Secretary of the Royal & Ancient, Keith McKenzie. 'You're not allowed in here,' he screamed.

'My badge says I am,' Liz told him.

'Only wives of the players are allowed in,' McKenzie said rudely.

An English player looked up from a nearby chair. 'If she's living in sin with a player, is that OK?' he queried sardonically.

Across the Atlantic, women journalists were winning the battle. Melanie Hauser even managed to gain access to the locker-room at Augusta. In Britain, equality comes slower. In 1990, Liz Kahn was bodily evicted from the locker-room at St Andrews after the Deputy Secretary of the R&A mistakenly told her that women had been allowed in the locker-room for years. It was not until '92 that she finally crossed the threshold legitimately – a privilege that might yet be revoked because Jack Nicklaus complained.

Even the media is not entirely free of sexism. One morning, I was minding my own business in the press centre when a television commentator whom I know walked in.

'Got any stories for my book?' I asked after we had exchanged greetings.

He thought about it. 'Well,' he said, 'do you know how I got my job at the BBC?'

'No, tell me.'

It turned out the audition had been tougher than he expected. He'd decided immediately that the post had already been filled and that the panel of judges were merely going through the motions. Consequently, his attempts at commentary were more flippant than they might otherwise have been. Towards the end of the golf film he was supposed to be bringing to life, a white poodle walked onto the green, rolled on its back and waved its legs in the air.

The would-be commentator laughed. 'That reminds me of some of our lady members,' he said.

The BBC could hardly wait to take him on.

Fortunately, there are a great many liberal and genuinely wonderful men on the European circuit and things are improving. However, there are still a few bad apples. In Spain earlier this year, I was discussing my air ticket with the travel agent in the hotel lounge when a player whom I had never laid eyes on before started hassling me and making suggestive remarks. As I turned to go, he said: 'What's your room number?'

'Don't be ridiculous,' I said, not looking at him, swallowing my drink and fumbling for my key. He persisted. I rejected him in slightly stronger terms.

The leer vanished from his face, to be replaced by a kind of sadistic sneer.

'All right,' he said. 'Don't tell me. I'm going to find out and I'm going to come up anyway.'

Who was I supposed to turn to? Complain to? Ask for help? Nobody. On the European Tour, there *is* no-one to ask.

As always, these fears abated and became manageable within the cosy environs of the press centre and golf club, where there was safety in numbers. Out on the golf course, among the pines, flower-beds and oily green creeks, life was simplified and became sweet again. In the first round of the Players Championship, Greg Norman shattered the course record with a scarcely believable 63, nine under par, on a course that J. C. Snead once described as a cross between a strip mine and *Star Wars,* and Dobereiner called golf's equivalent of the Christians versus the lions.

Afterwards, I watched Norman hit balls. Daly walked across the Shark's line of fire, acknowledging him with a hurried wave of one enormous paw. Brad Faxon caught Norman's eye and grinned. He whispered something in his ear.

'A volcano!' snorted Norman.

'Just waiting to erupt,' laughed Faxon.

Fuzzy Zoeller, who had finished runner-up at the Bob Hope Classic and the Nestle Invitational and was now lying second to Norman after a 66, was practising near by. In 1984, Zoeller, standing on the seventy-second fairway at Winged Foot, saw Norman hole a 44-foot putt for par up ahead and mistakenly thought he had made a birdie to win the US Open by a stroke. So Zoeller did what no other player in the world would have done under similarly devastating circumstances. He took out a white towel and waved it in surrender. On Monday night, when Zoeller had won the US Open by the biggest landslide margin of any eighteen-hole play-off in major championship history – 67, 75 – it was Norman's turn to wave the white flag.

'It wouldn't have mattered who was standing there, I was going to beat 'em,' Zoeller recalled happily. 'I had that much faith in my game at that time. It's crazy how we go through spurts like that, where we feel very good about what's happening and we have control of the golf ball at all times. I don't know why, 'cause we come out here some days and we feel like Sally and Johnny Chop

– hitting it right, hitting it left. Why is that? That's what makes the game so great.'

On the off chance he'd agree, I had asked Zoeller, master of the one-liner, for an interview. 'Sure,' he said affably, dropping everything and heading for a chair in the shade. Not for Zoeller the aloof practice range demeanour of other major champions. 'That's the way I play my best, is being relaxed,' Zoeller said. 'Some guys have to be a little bit more tight, concentrate on every swing, every shot out here. I basically use this practice stuff to kind of get loose, to get a feel for things. I don't care where the ball goes. I'm not here trying to hit the perfect golf shot on this range. The time to be perfect is when you're out there counting.'

'You're everybody's friend, aren't you?' I commented when the umpteenth player had walked past, clapped Zoeller on the shoulder and congratulated him on his form.

'Well, I'm close to a lot of these guys,' he said. 'I don't think that you ever get real close to 'em because of all the travel and everything, but I've been friends with Hubert Green for fifteen years and John Daly and I are very close.'

'Were you as wild as Daly when you were young?' I asked.

'Oh, yeah. Oh, I had the fire lit twenty-four hours a day.'

'Do you think you're a similar personality to Trevino?'

'Lee's very quick-witted,' Zoeller conceded, 'but Lee runs hot and cold. When he's playing bad, he's very cold. I'm very consistent. Whether it's good, whether it's bad, I *enjoy* being out here. I'm very fortunate. I haven't had a job in the forty-two years I've been on this earth.'

'Why do you think you haven't won for so long when you're playing so well?'

'I don't know why that is. My nerves are still good. I'm playing smarter golf. Maybe I'm not playing that stupid golf I was when I was winning – you know, get up, have no fear and let it rip. Soon as I figure out why, we'll get together and we'll write a book and we'll let everybody know.'

'Have you ever been to a sports psychologist?'

'No, I don't believe in all that,' Zoeller said. 'You have a sports psychologist right between your ears. To me, that's like a crutch. It's like trying to straighten your life out with cocaine or saying: "I've found Jesus, he's going to save me." '

'Jesus does save people,' I pointed out.

'Well, let's hope so,' Zoeller said easily. 'Thank God, he's there.'

The next evening, I came across Zoeller fishing in the lake beside the putting green.

'Caught anything?' I asked.

'Caught a few over in the other pond. Nothing here.'

'Let me try,' I suggested.

'Oh, no!' Zoeller said, taking several steps back. 'This is an expensive reel and you're a woman. You'll turn it into a bird's nest.'

'I'll have you know that I happen to have caught one of the biggest tiger fish ever caught in Zimbabwe,' I said indignantly. 'I know all about fishing.'

A small crowd was beginning to gather. 'Trust me,' I coaxed, knowing there's nothing Zoeller likes better than playing to a gallery.

'OK,' Zoeller said magnanimously, surrendering the rod.

With what I hoped was a professional casting action, I flicked the rod in the direction of the water. The reel made a funny, strangulated sound, and the hook landed with a plop a few yards in front of us.

Zoeller let out a shriek. 'You've turned it into a bird's nest,' he cried, grabbing the rod.

I was mortified. The crowd laughed. Zoeller's face lit up. When I last saw him, he was making a great meal out of untangling his line and swopping fishing stories with his fans.

By Saturday night, Norman held a four-stroke advantage over Zoeller, his nearest pursuer, after scoring 63, 67, 67. On Sunday, he birdied three of the first four holes to establish an unassailable lead, scanned the horizon for challengers, and then settled down to eat Zoeller and Sawgrass's Stadium course – the same one Weiskopf likened to Donkey Kong – for breakfast, lunch and dinner. Zoeller made seven birdies on the last day, shot a twenty under par total and never had the ghost of a chance. In what he later described as his best round outside of a major, Norman shattered Nick Price's winning eighteen under par aggregate with a twenty-four under par 264. He had gone ninety-two holes without a bogey when he slipped up at the thirteenth. His first prize of $450,000 took his career earnings to $7 million.

On the seventy-second green, after Norman had lagged his putt up to the hole, Zoeller took out a white towel, walked over to the Shark, removed his hat and wiped his brow.

'I was just trying to cool him off,' he laughed later. Norman had done 'everything he needed to do. In my twenty years out here, I haven't seen a player play as well for seventy-two holes. I got beat by the best player in the world.'

7

THE TALL POPPY SYNDROME

'I have been forced to live a false life . . . People don't relate to you as the person you are but to a myth they think you are, and the myth is always wrong. You are scorned or loved for mythic reasons that, once given a life . . . live forever.'

MARLON BRANDO, *Songs My Mother Taught Me*

If ever a man wished, indeed hoped against all hope, that divine intervention would excuse him from confronting an intolerable situation, then it was Greg Norman at the Players Championship. He may have just scored a record-equalling 63, but his body language did not reflect his good fortune. Angular face pinched and sullen, blue eyes averted, he sat on a bench in the locker-room at Sawgrass, with an empty nylon bag clutched against his chest like a security blanket and one golden leg jogging impatiently up and down. He managed to convey the simultaneous impressions of a spoilt playboy, made to spend five minutes doing an unpleasant chore, and a wounded and unhappy animal, straining at a leash.

I sat at the opposite end of the bench and tried, unsuccessfully, to keep the resentment out of my voice. At that moment, I disliked Greg Norman as much as I have ever disliked anyone. I was convinced that, unless he had completely misled me during the course of a two-and-a-half-hour interview at St Andrews in 1990, one of two things was true: either he was a deeply sensitive, inherently decent man, who had been so injured by the sustained cruelty of his critics that he had built a wall around himself that nobody would ever again penetrate, or he was a Machiavellian egotist who had manipulated us all until he had grown tired of it and then given up the pretence.

Certainly, Norman's actions in recent months had not been those of a sweet-natured athlete, weighed down by the demands of an avaricious media. Ever since he had refused point blank to speak to me in Australia, jerking his head arrogantly towards IMG's Anne Farrow and saying, 'Tell her what my schedule's like, Anne, go on, tell her,' and then had inexplicably changed his mind and agreed to an interview, he had been alternately dismissive, charmingly evasive and downright rude. The final straw had come on the Tuesday of the Players Championship when, having given me his word the previous week that the interview would take place on one of the two practice days, he told me that he had no time to do it then and was unlikely to have any in the future. I was crushed. Three and a half months of phone calls and the combined efforts of Frank Williams and Tom Place, Norman's media co-ordinator, both of whom had made appeals on my behalf, had come to nought. I resorted to begging. '*Please,*' I said plaintively.

'You can say "please," ' Norman said unsympathetically, 'but I've got a Cobra shoot this afternoon, I've got a meeting, I've got to practise . . .'

'I appreciate that,' I said, 'but I'm desperate.'

Norman gave a short, scornful laugh. Like a petulant child, he said: 'Just once, just one week, I wish I could do what *I* want to do.'

I was speechless. As far as I could tell, Norman's entire life was one, long hedonistic journey of self-gratification. But Norman wasn't interested in what I thought. He was interested in the three cameramen who had just rushed spontaneously up to him, and he pushed his lips back into a grimace that passed for a smile and gave an on-the-spot interview. Later, after I had pleaded with him once more, he described me as 'a persistent bitch'.

So here we were, mutual antagonists, Norman having been forced into this position by Williams and an apparently deep-rooted belief – that had belatedly tugged at his conscience – that he should honour his word. My immediate concern being the story I had promised my newspaper, I embarked upon a neutral line of questioning, designed to elicit maximum response in the limited time available. Norman proffered answers in small, reluctant fragments. He hunched forward on the bench, straw-blond hair falling over his brow, and picked irritably at the edges of his orange boxer shorts. Years before he had said that in order to become successful he had had to alter his whole personality. 'I went from being an introvert, a shy guy, to a guy thrust into the world, and I had to adapt very, very quickly, and the only way I could adapt was to teach myself to change.'

'Did you like the person you became?' I asked now.

'Oh yes,' Norman said.

'Liar,' I thought.

'I like my life. It probably took me five or six years to get used to it but, yes, I like my lifestyle. I really wouldn't do much different if I ever did something over again. The only thing I would probably change is I wouldn't be as open, I wouldn't be as honest. Unfortunately, people don't want to hear honesty and it gets you into trouble more often than not.'

I stared at him incredulously. 'You know,' I said, 'I probably shouldn't say this to you because of who you are, but when I interviewed you in 1990 I thought you were one of the most genuine and down-to-earth people I had ever met. You showed so much integrity off the course, and such passion and commitment when it came to the game, that it was easy to see why you had become a champion. Since then, you seem to have undergone a complete character transformation. You're unapproachable and you don't trust anyone. What happened? What changed you?'

For a split second, hurt, shock and anger rippled in seismographic waves across Norman's face. Then he exploded, almost choking on his words as he struggled to get them out fast enough. 'I'll tell you exactly what happened,' he said, pale eyes glittering with emotion. 'You become cynical. Why did Michael Jordan retire? Because of all the badgering. Why do athletes go into a shell after a period of time? Because of all the constant badgering. Unfortunately, that's the nature of the beast. We do it to ourselves and the media is such now that it focuses on whatever it can get its hands on. I was never a cynical person. Never have been. But I am now. Because there've been things written about me that are grossly untrue, and when I give an hour interview on TV, a recorded deal, and [what's broadcast] is five minutes of sex and finance, you become cynical. You say, why should you put yourself through that? We all go into our shells. What happened in Australia was disgraceful. The reporting down there was terrible. I mean, I didn't deserve what happened down there. When I go down to Australia now, I can tell you, my interview time is just about done. *Finished.*'

'That's sad,' I said. 'Your openness was your best quality.'

'Yeah, but my best quality's been chopped down.'

'That's the way the media works. That's what makes news.'

Norman scowled. 'Yeah, well, you just take myself for the last couple of years. When I was up, everybody wanted to chop me down, and when I was down, everybody wanted to get me back up. Now when I'm back up again, all of a sudden the needles will start coming in again. I just know it. And I understand it. That's the sequence of events, that's the way it goes. There's an Australian saying – 'the tall poppy syndrome'. That's why I've become cynical. I know it, I can feel it, and it affects my game because I don't like some of the things said about me because I'm very sensitive. And being sensitive, it hurts me, because I know the type of person I am. I'm a giver, not a taker . . . So that's why I've become cynical. And I felt for Michael Jordan, I really did. I just knew exactly what he was going through.'

There was an uncomfortable silence. 'But don't you think you're in a no-win situation?' I said at last, meaning that the more unpleasant he was to journalists and the more resistant to interviews, the worse the picture the media would paint of him.

'You can win the situation by changing it yourself,' Norman said firmly. 'That means you've got to change your personality. But if that's the way it has to be, that's the way it has to be.'

There is a photograph of Norman in the March 1989 edition of *Golf World*, taken while he was holidaying in Australia. In it, he is wearing a rumpled khaki shirt, a shell necklace and baggy shorts to which a hunting knife is attached, and proudly displaying a small white fish for the camera. His face, beneath a battered, leopard-skin-banded bush hat, is sunburned and unshaven, his hair is stiff with salt water, his smile reaches his eyes.

This is how Greg Norman seemed to us in the early years of his career, a sun god, a gregarious adventurer, a rugged warrior. 'I like everything that goes fast and high,' he would laugh, and prove it by courting danger with an abandon that was strangely life-affirming. Norman was the Camel man before the Camel man smoked too many cigarettes. Other professionals spent their free hours mowing the lawn or watching ball games on television; he went out and wrestled fifty-foot Marlin off the side of bucking fishing boats, swam with sharks, pierced the skies in F16 jets, became a member of a consortium with a Formula 1 team, tore about in Ferraris, jet-skied, surfed and earned scuba-diving certificates on the Great Barrier Reef; and each new exploit was recounted with awe on the Tour. Once, Norman had taken one of his Ferrari out for a spin and had begun to whip it around blind bends on a narrow country road. His wife, Laura, who was pregnant, watched the ascent of the speed-ometer with growing terror. 'Please, Greg, slow down,' she begged when it passed the 140 mph mark. 'OK,' Norman said, foot flat on the accelerator.

Another time, when Norman was playing in the European Open at Walton Heath, Nigel Mansell, a close friend of the Australian's, came to watch him. After his round, Norman bet the racing driver dinner that he could get back to his hotel in a Jaguar (normally a journey of some thirty-five minutes) before Mansell could fly there in his helicopter. 'I had the car off the clock all the way and he landed at the same time as I pulled into the hotel,' Norman recalled. 'That's how we are, both very competitive.'

Nobody who knew Norman was surprised. 'I think he has a death wish,' one friend remarked. Steve Elkington agreed. 'Greg likes to stand right on the edge of the cliff,' he said. Laura, a former airline stewardess, found it disturbing. 'Anything dangerous he likes,' she told *Golf Digest*. 'People used to tell me he'd change. But he never will. He's just that way.'

For years, Norman was the superstar who was always accessible (too accessible in some people's eyes); who never said no because he believed you met the same people going down as you did on the way up; who relished an evening of beer and banter with Fleet Street's hardest; who lived a life of such unabashed extravagance (he once spent £1,100 hiring a taxi to take his and Laura's luggage from Monaco to Milan because it wouldn't fit into their car, then joked that the driver had ripped them off because they were foreigners) that it would have been offensive had it not been tempered by his regular-guy image, who gave and gave and never stopped giving. Charity was his closet enthusiasm. The story of Jamie Hutton, the seventeen-year-old with leukaemia and Crohn's Disease, who stayed with Norman the week of the 1988 Heritage Classic and became the recipient of his trophy, is one of the very few that have been publicized. Less well known is that of Sam, the haemophiliac son of Australian television commentator Sam Roberts, who contracted AIDS through a blood transfusion. What began as a request for a shirt for a dying boy to whom he was a hero, became a friendship lasting several years, so that when Norman was told of the boy's death moments before he teed off in an Australian tournament, he walked down the first fairway with tears coursing down his face. It took him six months to get over it.

Naturally enough, Norman's larger-than-life persona was at its most visible on the course, where it manifested itself in an undeniable arrogance and a flamboyantly aggressive game not seen since Arnold Palmer first hitched up his trousers and let rip. As long ago as 1981, Louis T. Stanley wrote that the 'secret of [Norman's] success is an outsize ego . . . When he arrived in Britain this year he mentioned as an aside that he intended to win three tournaments. Just like that. And the remarkable thing is he almost did so.' More remarkable still, in Stanley's opinion, was IMG's idea that a nickname might enhance the Australian's image. 'It was suggested by Norman's advisers that he might be alluded to as the Great White Shark – a title that does little for Norman or those who put the idea forward. Greg Norman is noticeable enough in his own right without having to dream up a Disney image.' He could not have known then that that Disney image would ultimately become more caricature than character, or that the Great White Shark, far from being a name to conjure with, would merely become a convenient handle on which to hang Norman's major championship disasters, mutating into the Great White Carp, the Great White Minnow or the Great Fishfinger.

In 1981, Norman's youthful boast that he had ambitions to beat Peter Thomson's record in the Open did not seem beyond the bounds of possibility. He had finished fourth in the Masters earlier that season, and his record since turning professional was astonishing. Yet prior to joining the paid ranks in 1976, Norman's future had seemed to lie in an altogether different direction. At nineteen, he had sat with his engineer father before the squadron leader under whom he had trained and prepared for a career in the Australian Air Force and, confronted with the contract that would commit him to fighter pilot training, had balked. 'Nope,' Norman said. The two older men stared at him in bewilderment. 'I looked at that piece of paper and I told myself: "Don't sign it," ' Norman recalled. 'I told myself: "Go and play golf." '

Remembering his boyhood and the choices that have shaped him, Norman said: 'I was never a dreamer, never a dreamer. I never ever knew what I wanted to do until I wanted to do it. You just let life go on. When a situation arises, you better grasp it and take advantage of it.'

The irony of his words did not occur to him. With redemption still fresh in his mind, he was able to stand on the hill of his 1993 Open Championship triumph, and survey the bittersweet path of his career through a rose-coloured haze. To begin with, we had all viewed it in the same light. Apart from the hecklers who called Norman a 'choking bastard' at the US Open, causing him to storm up to the ropes and challenge them to a post-round duel, most golf followers regarded 1986 as the season when a great champion came of age. Norman succeeded in winning ten tournaments worldwide, became the first player to earn more than $1 million in prize money and, in what became known as the Saturday Slam, led all four majors going into the final round, winning the British Open. Reviewing the year, Dan Jenkins came up with a list of ways in which to prevent Norman winning every tournament on the PGA Tour. Among these were: (a) Confuse him mentally by making him have dinner with Mac O'Grady every night; (b) Penalize him two strokes for every time he smiles at a fan, four strokes for every time he squanders more than 30 seconds on a journalist; (c) Sabotage his VCR so that it plays nothing but Bob Tway's sand shot on the seventy-second hole at Inverness.

The moment when the gentle ribbing turned to barbed and vicious criticism is easy to pinpoint. It was the moment when Larry Mize stood over his 40-yard chip shot at Amen Corner, on the second play-off hole of the 1987 Masters. Severiano Ballesteros had already been eliminated, and had begun the lonely walk back to the clubhouse along fairways pooled with shadow. Norman was lining up his putt. He turned to his then caddie, Pete Bender, and said: 'I think if we just cozy this little son down within two feet of the hole, we'll have a two-footer to win the golf tournament.' Feeling the adrenalin rush that accompanies victory begin to flood through his body, he studied the putt again. It was a good 55 feet. He looked over at Mize and felt comforted. 'Seeing where Larry hit it, you know, you have been there, so you know what the circumstances are and the difficulty of the shot. That is what I said to Pete as I looked at the putt. I'm thinking, he will still be putting after he pitches on. It would have gone by, or been short, and I would have cozied it on down and he would have had to make it to force me to make my little one. That is the scenario that goes through your mind. Of course, it didn't happen that way.'

It is strange how the bounce of a ball or the rub of a green have the power to change lives; how a single flash of white against emerald could transform Mize from the boy who had stood with longing in his heart at the locked gates of Augusta National, into a local hero, and his opponent into the man who disproved the law of averages. Afterwards, Norman was shattered. In later years, he would say that it took him seven months to recover from that defeat. Not even his wife believed him. 'Inside,' Laura said, 'he was dying.'

But fate had not done with the Shark yet. By the start of the 1989 season, Norman's record had begun to look like the hamburgers he so proudly advertised: all artificial fillers and no substance. He might have won thirty-four tournaments in Australia and dozens more around the globe, but he had won only five in six seasons on the US Tour. 'There's a close correlation between Greg Norman and Tom Weiskopf,' Johnny Miller said disparagingly. 'Tom should have been the best golfer in the world but he never was.' So Norman teed up in the Open in July, determined to prove his critics wrong. Four days later, he drove into a bunker on Troon's eighteenth hole and handed the claret jug to Mark Calcavecchia. With that, the pattern was set. The following spring, Robert Gamez holed a full seven-iron to beat him on the final hole of the Nestle Invitational, and then David Frost added insult to injury by sinking his bunker shot on the seventy-second hole at New Orleans just as the engravers were adding the last flourish to Norman's name.

There were others. There was the 76 that Norman shot to Faldo's 67 when both men had been contending in the third round of the 1990 Open, for example. But by then the role of the Shark as golf's last action hero had been so indelibly impressed on the public imagination that the illusion was maintained long after it ceased to be a reality. It was only when the weight of circumstance brought about the dissolution of the myth, that the vibrant, laughing star of screen and course that Norman had become was wheeled away, and all that was left behind was a tarnished misrepresentation of the original. 'When you're down and out, everything compounds itself,' Norman said, remembering the years when he seemed shrunken and withdrawn, devoid of his former magnetism. 'You know, you get into problems with a lot of things. And if you're strong enough to stop the slide, it's three times as hard to get up the second time as it is the first time.'

At Sawgrass, I asked him whether or not he felt that he could, in some way, have prevented the unhappy outcome of any of those majors.

'Oh,' Norman said tiredly. 'You're talking about those shots. Well, those shots I had no control over – the shots that Mize hit and Tway hit and Frost hit and Gamez hit. I'm just an innocent bystander. I might as well sit up on the bleachers above the eighteenth hole. You know, I've done my job, I'm finished, over and done with.'

'Did that make it hurt any less, knowing that it wasn't your fault?'

'The back to back ones hurt, yes, because it had never happened to anyone else in a major championship but it happened to me. But from the point of view of being able to control the situation, I never cried over spilt milk. The only thing I didn't do for years was admit that it hurt. I thought I could deal with it. That's the only thing I did wrong. I wish I had talked about it a little easier, earlier, instead of waiting until 1991. But those shots never affected me like everyone thought they did.'

On 17 July 1993, Norman stepped onto the eighteenth tee at Royal St Georges in the final round of the Open Championship. Three years earlier, he had walked away from his disastrous encounter with Faldo at St Andrews like the dazed survivor of an avalanche, having apparently become, at thirty-five, the one major wonder he had vowed he never would. Now he was hardly recognizable as the same man. In the translucent light of that English summer evening, he radiated confidence and a kind of raw, uncontainable energy. He knew his hour had come. In the autumn of 1991 he had gone to see the Texan coach Butch Harmon, on the recommendation of Elkington. By then he was a ghoulish parody of the player he had once been, and Harmon had taken one look at him and decided that if the kernel of greatness that remained was to be saved, they would have to get back to basics. 'Greg's a real, live-on-the-edge person, with his racing cars and his scuba diving. You can't make him a by-the-numbers swinger. It took me a year and a half to get that out of his system.'

With the help of Harmon, his new caddie, Tony Navarro, a practice and exercise regime of labour-camp severity and a copy of

Zen of the Martial Arts, Norman took the first tentative steps towards regaining his position at the pinnacle of world golf. By the following year, he was well on the road to recovery. 'I played great in the British Open at Muirfield,' Norman said, 'even though I didn't score that well because I hadn't been in the hunt for about six or eight months. I came off the seventy-second hole and said to my wife and Butch Harmon: "We're back." I said: "I've just put on a clinic out there for seventy-two holes. Nobody'll know about it but I did." And that was it. Muirfield was the turning point.'

And so it was that after seven barren years Norman's ship finally came in, and it wasn't, as expected, the *Titanic*. Instead, he walked down the final hole at Royal St Georges and into history, his rounds of 66, 68, 69, 64 establishing a new seventy-two-hole record. 'I played the best I have ever played in life,' he said afterwards. 'I never mishit a shot. I hit every drive perfect and I hit every iron perfect . . . I was in awe of myself.'

One afternoon at the Coolum Classic in December, shortly after it had become common knowledge that Norman was leaving IMG, Frank Williams breezed into the media centre. The previous day he had been airlifted off a fishing boat after failing to find his sea-legs ('How anybody can spend that much money to be that sick is beyond me') and being terrified by an over-familiar shark. Even Williams could see the irony in that. Thus, he quickly dispensed with the subject of one great white fish and moved on to another. 'Greg's the best player in the world, the most charismatic and probably the most marketable man on the face of the earth at the moment,' Williams said. But he confessed that it was unlikely Norman was ever going to be worth as much as Arnold Palmer. 'Arnold Palmer's been at it a very long time. Arnold Palmer is a legend. No-one is ever going to fire a legend.'

Williams reclined indolently in a wickerwork chair at Coolum. He was considering the months ahead when he would move to Palm Beach, Florida to become the managing director of Great White Shark Enterprises. There was no doubt that he was apprehensive. An Englishman who grew up on a council estate before he became a wealthy entrepreneur and head of IMG's Australian golf division, he was well aware that Norman did not suffer fools gladly. His most fervent hope (unexpressed) was that their friendship, which stretched back seventeen years, would stand him in good stead. For that reason, he dwelled on the fun-loving, easygoing side of Greg Norman.

It transpired that they loved to play practical jokes on one another, none better than the one which began at the Australian Skins game in 1993 when Norman, autographing visors, programmes and shirts for the television cameras, was asked to sign a glove for Boris Yeltsin.

'Screw Yeltsin,' Norman said with a grin. He thought it was a joke.

Observing this, Williams decided to teach him a lesson. He told the media and various Tour officials to pretend to Norman that his microphone had been on and that his comment had gone out on live television. Then he sat back and waited for Norman to finish his round. The Shark came off the golf course worrying about his performance. 'Oh, Frank,' he fretted, 'I didn't play too well.'

'Greg,' Williams said, in a tone heavy with foreboding, 'that's the least of our worries. We've had to close down the switchboard at Sanctuary Cove because of all the complaints. Why would you say: "Screw the Russian president"?'

'What are you talking about?' Norman asked nervously.

'Look,' Williams snapped, 'how many times have I told you that when you've got your mike on, you must put your hand over it if you don't want to be heard.'

Norman went white. 'Oh my God!' he cried. 'What am I going to do?'

'Well, I can't get you out of this one,' Williams told him heartlessly.

'Oh, come on, Frank,' pleaded Norman.

Williams pretended to mull over the dilemma. Finally, he said: 'I'll tell you what we're going to do. We're going to say that there's a boat builder from Detroit called Yeltsin, and he's been trying to sell you a boat for a month, and you said: "This is the wrong time and place, fuck off!" '

'Fine,' Norman said. 'I can carry that off.'

In the interview room, Tom Ramsey was the first to stand up. 'Greg,' he said, 'Rupert Murdoch has phoned me personally and he wants to know why you said fuck off to the Russian president.'

'You always believe what you want to believe,' Norman told him. 'There's a boat builder in Detroit called Yeltsin and . . .'

He stopped. The journalists were falling off their chairs with laughter. Norman looked over at Williams. 'I'll get you,' he said. 'No matter what, I'll get you.'

A week later, Williams was throwing a party for the golfers in Melbourne when five policemen arrived at the door. They ushered him into a quiet room. 'It's the noise,' Williams thought to himself, but when television cameras appeared from nowhere he began to smell a Great White Shark.

'We've got a warrant for your arrest,' a policeman informed him.

'Oh, yes,' beamed Williams. 'Who's arresting me? Greg Norman?'

The constable gave him a dark stare. 'If you think we've got nothing better to do than to come here on the whim of some adolescent golfer, you're very much mistaken,' he said and handed Williams the warrant. On it was the emblem of New Scotland Yard and a list of charges, including tax evasion and illegal transference of money. Williams began to panic. 'I thought to myself, "No, it's got to be Greg," but I can't see Greg anywhere to pounce on him. And then I look across and I see my wife crying. I thought, "Oh, my God, this could be for real." '

At that point, a policeman grabbed him by the belt and cried: 'OK, I've got him! Let's go.' Like a sheep bound for the meat-market, Williams was loaded into the paddywagon, whisked down to the station, finger-printed and read his rights, and then locked in a cell for the night after first being told to remove his belt and his shoe-laces. 'Jesus Christ,' Williams thought, slumping down on the prison bed. 'My whole life has suddenly fallen apart.' He opened the envelope he'd been told would inform him of his legal position, and unfolded its contents with trembling hands. It read: 'Paybacks are hell, you arsehole!!!'

'Basically, Greg's the same person now as he was when I met him seventeen years ago,' Williams said, after relaying this tale. 'He's a little more wary but underneath it all he's still the same raw kid – still enjoys life, still has a zest for life. I think he's worked very hard for everything he's got. People say he has this enormous natural talent, which he does have, but, God, he's brought the best out of it by sheer guts and determination. I mean, the man is mentally very, very strong. To achieve what he's achieved – to go to the heights and then to the depths and then to the heights again – takes a unique talent and a unique mind. There's very few that have done it . . . And he's very true to himself. When he says he looks in the mirror and talks to himself, he means it. He knows when he's right and he knows when he's wrong. Basically, what you see is what you get.'

'Do you think you're the same person you were twenty years ago?' I asked Norman at Sawgrass. I thought of Williams's comment at Coolum: 'At the end of the day, the things that are important to Greg Norman are the same things that are important to the guy in the council house – that you love your wife and family. It doesn't get any better than that, no matter how many millions you have. And there's the other side of the coin – the amount of nonsense you have to put up with. The price of fame is quite extraordinarily high sometimes.'

'Oh, I'm the same person nature-wise,' Norman replied, 'but as I said, I'm more cynical.'

'But deep down inside?'

'Oh, I'm still the same person. If you saw me at home, away from all this, or on the boat with Nicky Price . . .'

'But if you feel cynical in this environment, doesn't that diminish the pleasure of achievement?'

'No, not at all. No, the greatest reward you can ever give yourself is success. It's not to prove anybody wrong or anybody right, it's to prove that what I did was the right thing. And that's the most satisfying thing you can ever get out of success.'

Times have changed for the man they once called the unluckiest golfer in the world. Off the course, he still lives fast and plays as hard as he ever did, but now it seems that the 'death wish' quotes have joined the rest of the Great White Shark jibes as thorns in his side. 'I don't live on the edge,' he frowned. 'I don't put my life or anybody else's at risk.' On it, he has yet to eradicate that fatal flaw that makes him lose more than he wins. In Australia, Thomson tried to put his finger on it, without success. 'He's a very unusual player. Absolutely brilliant, with a very unique style that is a bit of a mystery. He's not the perfect technician that, say, Hogan, Snead and even Nicklaus were. He's hard to categorize as a player. I mean, there's that streak of brilliance, but there's something missing somewhere.'

These days, Norman is again the great golden force of a man he was before Mize and Tway dealt their double blow. He may suppress any altruistic tendencies he has until he gets home, and he may reserve his carefree, open self for the times he is out fishing with Nick Price, but on the golf course he is as fiery and dominant as he ever was. Nevertheless, as Thomson says, it is difficult now *not* to believe that the indefinable weakness, be it physical or psycho-logical, which has cost him so dearly over the years, is an inherent part of his make-up, and thus will always come into play on the back nine of major championships, regardless of how many times he wins. For instance, no sooner had he played one of the most boldly imagined and exquisitely managed rounds of golf in the history of the game at Royal St Georges, than he had bogeyed two of the last three holes to hand the Tour Championship to Jim Gallagher Jnr, and three-putted the second extra hole of a play-off to lose the US PGA Championship to Paul Azinger.

'Greg Norman reminds me of the movies,' Rick Reilly said. 'Every time you think he's going to get the girl and ride off into the sunset, his horse breaks a leg.'

In the locker-room at the TPC, Norman stretched and sighed. Some of the tension seemed to have drained from his lean, burnished-copper frame, and for a moment it was easy to imagine that he had suspended hostilities with the world at large and resigned himself to a lifelong dance with a whimsical and capricious destiny.

'My negatives and bad times have probably been some of the best things that have happened to me because you learn more from those than you do from the positives,' Norman was saying. He hugged the gym bag tighter to his chest, as if to reassure himself of the truth of his own words. Once he said that nothing frightens him as much as being out of control, but the last few years have mellowed him and made it easier for him to let go. He considered the words of Teddy Roosevelt, which lately have become his mantra. Then he said quietly: 'I'd rather experience the agony of defeat and the ecstasy of victory than experience the great twilight that 99 per cent of this world live in. A lot of people experience the agony, very few people experience the ecstasy, and to experience both of those makes you a better human being.'

8

A HEAVEN OF SORTS

'If there's a golf course like Augusta in heaven, I hope I'm the head greenkeeper.'

GARY PLAYER, 1992

'There are several things you need to know about Augusta,' Robinson said, as we cruised down Washington Road some time after 1.00 a.m. on Tuesday morning. 'The first rule is: never, never lose your badge because you'll never even get onto the premises to get another one. The second is: egg salad is the only edible sandwich and they're gone by ten past eleven. There *are* other sandwiches. There is the hot barbecued pork sandwich, for example. That comes out of a can with a list of ingredients eight hundred words long. Some people claim they've seen a human being eat a pimento cheese; personally I never have. The chocolate milk is the whole reason to go to Augusta, but if there is a rain delay the photographers drink it all. That's all you need to know to survive at Augusta.'

With that, we continued on our journey through the moonlit streets, with the original innocent abroad, Graham Spiers, a sportswriter for *Scotland on Sunday*, wedged in the back of the car. We were headed for the Super 8, a $23 motel that had become an $89 motel for the week of the Masters.

Graham left his badge behind on the first morning. No sooner had we crawled back through the traffic to Augusta National and negotiated our way through five security checkpoints, than Martha

115

Gaye herself had lost Robinson's badge. At Augusta, Martha Gaye has more influence than the Queen. Indeed, the Queen would not even make it through the gate. It matters not a jot to Martha Gaye whether one is an award-winning writer of international repute in the game of golf, whether one works for a publication that reaches two million people, or whether one is a freelance working for three golf magazines, two newspapers and a news agency; if Martha doesn't think you merit accreditation for Augusta, the Pope himself could not persuade her. There are journalists and editors who have spent small fortunes over the years courting her with flowers, trinkets and boxes of chocolates, but Martha Gaye cannot be bought.

Not that that stops the optimistic from trying. On 5 April, Martha's power centre at the entrance of the media room was a positive hothouse of floral tributes and saccharine bribes. Behind them, Martha Gaye was staring about her with murderous eyes for the culprit who had made off with Robinson's badge. A lackey incautiously mentioned to her that Bernhard Langer, the defending champion, was waiting alone in the interview room. 'I'm busy looking for Robinson's badge,' snapped Martha Gaye. As a point of principle, she continued searching for a couple of minutes longer. Then she leant irritably into the microphone on her desk. 'Burn'd Langurr fur interview,' she intoned.

Augusta is golf's nearest realization of heaven. There is nothing to compare with the vision that lies beyond Magnolia Lane: the rich, velvety lustre of the steep emerald fairways; the whispering pines; the vibrant splash of red and white dogwood, fuchsia, azalea, juniper, redbud, wisteria and holly; and the smooth outlines of the traps, as glistening and powdery as fresh-fallen snow. There is no afternoon more enjoyable than to lounge beneath the umbrellas on the clubhouse lawn, where the likes of President Eisenhower and Alastair Cooke have enjoyed clam chowder and peach cobbler, with an eye on the first tee, where Tom Watson is launching his drive, and an ear cocked in the direction of the interviews taking place beneath the old oak tree, where Gary Player is holding court. And there is no feeling sweeter than to lie in the sunshine on the bank above the short sixteenth, drinking pink lemonade and gazing down on the black shining mirror of Rae's Creek as all the greats come walking up to the green – Palmer with his distinctive swagger,

Norman with his long, confident stride, Faldo with his eager, slightly self-conscious march. A mile downtown, there might be joblessness and murder, and in Rwanda there might be genocide, but here at Augusta, time stands still for golf.

'I'll never forget how I was struck by Augusta that first year,' Norman said. 'This was what golf was meant to be, pure golf. This was the purest form of golf tournament. Everything about it was first rate. That drive up Magnolia Lane, with the clubhouse ahead, the practice ranges on either side, it just gets you in the perfect frame of mind for a tournament.'

There is something about Bobby Jones's Cathedral in the Pines, a tangible sense of joys and sorrows past, that makes history as weighty a presence here as it is at St Georges or Muirfield. 'I get so sentimental and starry-eyed when I get here that I can't play,' said Ben Crenshaw, the 1984 Masters Champion. 'Sometimes I wish it all didn't get to me so much.'

Even Palmer wasn't immune. 'I walk this course and suddenly I feel like I'm twenty-three again,' he said, his brown face creasing into a smile. 'Only, I'm walking considerably slower.'

'Augusta,' observed Crenshaw, 'is the most tempting golf course I've every seen. It *goads* you into trying different shots because there's so much to gain. If you're right on your game and you live dangerously for a day and you can just skirt the trouble here and there, you can come off with a brilliant score. But if you're not, that's when it's really punishing.'

Herein lies the secret of Bobby Jones's masterpiece; at Augusta, even disaster comes wrapped in an aesthetically pleasing package. The key to survival is remembering that behind every graceful curve, every sparkling stream and every smiling azalea bush lurks a double-bogey – or worse. The real test is psychological. It's not enough to strike the ball well at Augusta. You have to be calculating enough to outsmart the swirling wind and outwit the enigmatic greens. And even then you might lose. Twenty-five years ago, on his forty-fifth birthday, Roberto De Vicenzo scored a magical 65 for a 277 total, eleven under par. It seemed certain he had won. Pressured by a television crew for an instant interview, the gregarious Argentinian signed his scorecard and departed to the press room just as Bob Goalby, a little known Midwesterner, began eagling and birdying to take the lead. Goalby had three-putted the seventeenth to fall back into a tie when De Vicenzo was told to go back to the scorer's tent. Something was wrong. 'At that moment,' De Vicenzo said, 'my feet went to my head.'

Tommy Aaron, his playing partner, was waiting solemnly by the eighteenth. 'He be very quiet,' De Vicenzo recalled. 'There were so many people around the table and someone said to me, "Roberto, check again. You make a mistake on your scorecard – it's not 65, it's a 66." I told them I think it was 65, but when I check again I saw that for 17, where I made a three, Tommy Aaron had written four.'

When the full horror of what had occurred first hit the Masters committee, they had consulted Jones himself, who was in agony at the time with the degenerative central nervous system disease syringomyelia that eventually took his life. To Jones, who had once called a penalty on himself that cost him the US Open – saying afterwards when his honesty was admired: 'You might as well praise a man for not robbing a bank' – the matter was cut and dried. The rules were unequivocal: if a player signs for a score lower than he shot, then he is automatically disqualified; if, on the other hand, he signs for a higher score, then that is the figure he is stuck with. Thus, the much loved De Vicenzo, who had won two hundred events round the world, including the British Open nine months earlier, had to be told that Goalby was the new Masters Champion.

Under the cruellest of all possible blows, his courage and sportmanship were incredible to behold. He simply said sadly: 'I play golf all over the world for thirty years and all I can think of is what a stupid I am to be wrong in this wonderful tournament.'

We had come to Augusta via New Orleans, where I'd found a different kind of paradise. After the purgatory of Jacksonville, a benign twist of fate had ensured that, along with the other British golf writers, I had ended up in a suite in the divine Windsor Court Hotel. The only drawback was having to cover the New Orleans Classic, which is held at English Turn, half an hour out of town. The press centre is (I suspect) a converted greenkeeper's shed, the scoring is done by quaint old ladies who keep life interesting by making sure that the scores posted on the leaderboard, the scoreboard and the computer bear not the slightest resemblance to one another, and the whole thing is run, if that's not too strong a term, by a press officer who makes one think of a panic-stricken John Major on acid.

Naturally, there was no transport to the course. Michael McDonnell and Michael Williams, respectively of the *Mail* and the *Telegraph*, found themselves being ferried to English Turn one morning by an Eritrean cab driver who told them he was a civil engineer by trade. Presently it became clear that map-reading had not been included in his training. Not only was he unable to find the Mississippi River Bridge, he was unable to cross the river at all. An element of desperation entered his driving. He raced down a motorway slip road, decided he was going in the wrong direction, did a U-turn and went back up again. Beads of sweat broke out on his neck. McDonnell and Williams gripped the seat covers. The final straw came when he took a charge at a red light from 150 metres away. 'Why didn't you say something?' an ashen-faced Williams asked McDonnell after the one-time civil engineer had admitted defeat and, unable to find his way back to the hotel, dropped them at a taxi rank half an hour after they set off. 'I did,' replied McDonnell. 'I said, "Bloody hell!" '

At Augusta, another type of insanity had strolled unmolested up Magnolia Lane. It was currently residing under the bows of the oak tree on the clubhouse lawn. 'There are at least seven players in the world's top thirty, some from Europe, who are taking beta-blockers,' Mac O'Grady, Seve Ballesteros's eccentric coach, was telling reporters. 'By reducing anxiety, which is the effect of these beta-blockers, some players have improved their putting and they have been winning tournaments, including majors. Guys are suddenly making putts they never used to because they're taking the drug. Just look at some players who have been meandering over the past four or five years, not quite making it. All of a sudden their putts are going in and they are making a name for themselves.'

Unsurprisingly, all hell broke loose. At the Ryder Cup and the four majors, when there are a lot of newshounds about, a media silly season tends to result and you have relatively minor incidents, such as the Watson autograph saga, blown completely out of proportion. Now we had the *Star* screaming 'GOLF DRUG STORM!', the *Mirror* wailing 'DRUGS SLUR ROCKS GOLF', and the *Daily Record* revealing, 'I POPPED PILLS SAYS SAM', when anybody could have told you that beta-blockers and pot have been around golf for years, and neither have been shown to improve performance on the course.

When Nick Price was told of O'Grady's claims, he immediately volunteered the information that he had taken beta-blockers for seven years. 'It did more harm to my career than anything else,' he said. 'You don't seem to have any energy. You never seem to get tired and that means you can't sleep at night . . . My family has a long history of high blood pressure. My pressure is so high that without daily drugs I could die from a heart attack. I switched to another drug five years ago because beta-blockers wouldn't let me be myself. It was a terrible time in my life.' Price said that he didn't believe for a minute that what O'Grady said was true. 'We don't have that kind of thing in our sport.'

Sam Torrance admitted he had popped beta-blockers in 1992 after hearing that snooker players found they helped to steady their nerves. When he promptly fell to sixty-second on the money list, his worst position in twenty years, he stopped taking them. 'Last year, drug-free Sam won three times in Europe,' the *Record* reported triumphantly.

Faldo thought O'Grady was talking nonsense. 'The only stuff that goes into me are vitamin pills – and the occasional whisky,' he insisted. Lyle, too, denied any knowledge of drugs in golf. He said the only white powder he sniffed was his baby daughter's talc.

But O'Grady stuck to his story. Beta-blockers are banned by the International Olympic Committee and by the Sports Council, even with a doctor's prescription, but they are not restricted in golf. 'The PGA Tour should introduce random urine testing to check for such substances and other prescription drugs that are used to help putting and any other aspect of the game,' said O'Grady, who claimed that he had taken beta-blockers for six months in 1988 and it had improved his putting. He had stopped for ethical reasons.

But as they say, there's nothing new under the sun. As long ago as 1986, US Tour players were calling for drug-testing. 'I'm all for it,' Hubert Green had told reporters. 'I feel sorry for someone born in Ethiopia but I can't feel sorry for someone who puts a gun to his head by taking drugs.' Mac O'Grady, a self-styled voice of conscience for the narcotically challenged even then, had his own balanced view. 'Whenever you have leisure time there's going to be decadence,' he said. 'Once you become successful it's easy to get involved in negative escapisms. You start to lose your basic chromosomes of integrity. Besides, what do people think this is, the 1950s? *The Donna Reed Show* or "Leave it to Beaver"? We've got to do something.'

* * *

Of the Europeans, Severiano Ballesteros did best in the first round, much to the astonishment of those who had collapsed in hysterics when he announced he was being coached by O'Grady. Prior to arriving at Augusta, he had missed three cuts in four starts, and his path to a 70 was by no means a smooth one. He missed five of the first nine greens and four more on the back nine. He also missed more fairways than he hit.

'His short game is fantastic,' enthused Raymond Floyd, his playing partner. 'There isn't anyone in the world even close to him. He hits a shot and you think, "Boy, that's lucky," but if it's lucky, he's lucky an awful lot.'

At the first hole, Ballesteros missed the green by 20 yards and needed two chips to get to two feet. At the second, he drove into the trees, but got up and down for a birdie. At the third, he missed both fairway and green, but chipped stone dead. At the fourth, his approach finished short of the green and right. He was now faced with a 20-yard shot over a bunker onto a lightning fast downslope. Unfazed, he played a gentle lob to within six feet of the flag and holed his fourth successive single putt for a par.

'That was the most fabulous par I've ever seen,' exclaimed Floyd.

Ballesteros was more reserved. 'You can't win the Masters in the first round, but you can lose it,' he said. He was asked whether he thought he could triumph again in the event he had won in 1980 and '83 and so nearly won in 1985, '86 and '87. 'No, no, I'm just here for fun,' the Spaniard said with an attempt at lightheartedness, but he seemed dispirited and lacking in confidence. Beside him, the press officer had all but nodded off.

Ballesteros's 70 left him two strokes behind the leader, Larry Mize, at the end of the day. Tom Kite, the former US Open Champion, and the South African Fulton Allem were in second place, with Watson, Norman and Tom Lehman a stroke further behind. Elsewhere, the foreign challenge had faltered. Faldo, who had recorded two of the seven European victories at Augusta in ten years, slumped to a four over par 76, as did Woosnam, while Langer, Price and Olazabal all scored 74.

For Mize, who had spent his childhood wishing and dreaming outside the gates of Augusta, it was a poignant homecoming. In 1987, after he had watched Ballesteros three-putt the first extra hole of the play-off and depart in tears along fairways striped with shadow, he and Norman, then world No.1, had continued alone. At the eleventh hole, Mize's approach veered away. Norman waited on the green, fit and dominant, his Masters jacket just a heartbeat or two away. Then Mize had chipped, and the ball had bounced and skipped, checked and gained momentum until finally it toppled into the hole.

'For the most part, people just remember it as a great shot,' Mize said of the 105-foot chip that cut Norman's soul to ribbons. 'I think you have some who remember it as the lucky chip-in or whatever, and I'm sure at times that got under my skin a little bit, but it doesn't any more because I won the tournament and it's as simple as that. It isn't a one-hole golf tournament. I hit a heck of a chip to win.

'I've always felt that the timing of the shot is the incredible thing. If I chip in there on the eleventh hole in regulation and win it by one . . . it's not a big deal. But to be on the second hole of a play-off with one of the best players in the world [Norman], and one of the other best players in the world [Ballesteros] has already been knocked out of the play-off, then to hit that shot to win the Masters – underdog local boy from Augusta – is just incredible.'

In explaining the differences between performing in a major championship and an ordinary event, Bobby Jones once used the analogy of a trapeze artist on a high wire. 'In a major they remove the net,' he said.

Jones, one of only four men to win the Grand Slam of majors, thrived on the electrifying atmosphere, the tension accompanying that live or die gamble. So did the Golden Bear. 'I guess we'll have to handicap Mr Nicklaus like a thoroughbred and put a couple of hundred-pound weights in his pocket,' said Jones after Nicklaus won the 1965 Masters by nine shots. He might have made good his promise had he known then that Nicklaus would win his sixth Green Jacket in 1986, at the age of forty-six, and that by the time he teed up in his thirty-fifth Masters, he'd have accumulated more eagles (18) at Augusta than double bogeys (17), and Sunday would have been his best scoring day (he averaged 70.84).

'Every time I went to Augusta, I played well,' Nicklaus recalled. 'I was the guy to beat. I always enjoyed that. Not only did I know that, the other players knew that. And the writers knew that. That made for a confrontation – me against the rest of them. That was true of a lot of golf tournaments, but really at Augusta more than anywhere else.'

In his heyday, Nicklaus liked to say that the majors were the easiest tournaments to win because everyone is trying so hard they don't play their normal games. Dan Forsman knew what he meant. In 1993, he took a seven on the twelfth in the final round to effectively throw away the title. Walking the high wire between glory and ignominious failure, he had suffered from vertigo. 'I've often tried to describe it to somebody by saying: "Put a two by four plank over a couple of cinder blocks and walk six feet – no problem. Well, put it over the World Trade Centre, and have the wind blowing and people waiting for your demise and roaring here and there, and think about what you've read about the ones that have gone through there and have fallen to their death. That gives you an idea what it's all about." '

This year, Forsman had a chance to relive that experience, to make amends for his mistake. He made seven birdies in a round of 66 to lie a stroke behind Mize on four under par, level with Norman and Lehman. Jose Maria Olazabal, Hale Irwin, Tom Watson, Tom Kite and Ernie Els were in third place on 141. 'Now everyone is telling me if I can just get by twelve on Sunday, I might be able to win the tournament,' Forsman said in annoyance. 'It isn't life and death here, even if some players, including myself, think it is. Other things are far more important than what I did on the twelfth hole here.'

He stopped, realizing he was kidding nobody but himself. A small spasm passed across his face as the agony of that quadruple bogey seeped back into his mind.

'I walk across that bridge [to the green] a little softer,' Forsman admitted. 'I turn the corner on that bridge a little bit quieter. I sort of bow and pay homage to that great hole, the twelfth. It sounds corny but anybody who has been through the same situation would say the same thing.'

On the three practice days preceding the Masters, some 50,000 people poured onto Augusta's sea of green. On Saturday, only the élite and the privileged dared come, and their passes were scrutinized by a scanner as they entered. At Augusta, tournament tickets are not sold, they are handed down like family heirlooms, so ticket touts do a roaring trade. The *Augusta Chronicle* revealed that patrons were asking for as much as $3,200 per badge, with one woman, a Mrs Ezell, buying a Masters badge for her husband for

$600 a day. What's more, the committee had issued a statement to say that, as from next season, practice day passes would no longer be on public sale.

Augusta's rules and regulations are as arcane as the club itself. Along with forged tickets, one is forbidden to bring any drink not transported in a Masters green cup onto the premises (there are no commercial logos other than Augusta's own on the course). Lewine Mair's *Telegraph* diary reported that one spectator, having paid his $20 practice day fee, realized he had forgotten his binoculars. He pointed to a white car in the nearby parking lot, and asked the man at the gate if he might nip back and fetch them. 'Certainly,' said the guard, 'but it will cost you $7 to get back in again.'

Political correctness has never strayed onto the jewel-like turf of Augusta National. It could have held its head high in the days of the Civil War; on its sixtieth anniversary, only one black member among 310 besmirches its reputation as a white stronghold. 'I don't know if they voted on it,' Ron Townsend told a journalist, 'I just know I've become a member. But this is the South here, and let's face that fact.'

'One of the great disillusionments in my life is the way the Masters has become such a revered tournament,' former US Tour player Charlie Sifford said bitterly. 'As far as I'm concerned, it is one of the most racist and hateful spots on golf's globe.'

Nevertheless, African-Americans continued to spear rubbish, serve cocktails and cut sandwiches annually. Until 1975, no black man played at Augusta. Luckily, for the club's regular all-black team of caddies, conditions are improving. The loos in their accommodation now have doors.

In the third round, when a twenty-mile-an-hour wind whistled through the pines and turned the putting surfaces into ice rinks, Tom Lehman took the lead with a 69. 'Who would have thought a kid from Minnesota would be leading the Masters?' Lehman said wryly. It wasn't so long since he had considered abandoning the Tour to coach golf at the University of Minnesota. 'I would have taken the job but I didn't want to have to rent cross-country skis at the pro shop during the winter,' Lehman said.

A stroke behind the American came Olazabal, who had scored 67, 69 in the second and third rounds. Mize was in third place on 211. Norman had fallen away with a 75. For the third time in his career, Augusta, his nemesis, had whipped out her knives and (to quote Rick Reilly) carved him into sushi. He was still in with an outside chance, but it was Lehman whom Olazabal seemed most concerned about. 'I don't know much about him,' he said. 'You don't need to know much about a guy who can shoot seven under round here.'

Jose Maria Olazabal was two years old when he first picked up a golf club. The son of the greenkeeper at Real Golf Club de San Sebastian, he grew up in a stone farmhouse situated behind the ninth green, 35 feet from the putting green and 100 feet from the first tee. Golf was all he ever wanted to play. 'I didn't force him,' recalled Gaspar Olazabal, his father. 'He started himself. When he first began to walk, he picked up a club and began to hit and hit with it. He did it himself. He took to the sport.'

At fifteen, Olazabal was a small, light-boned boy with a delicate touch around the greens, who passed before John Jacobs's gaze as a member of Spain's national squad. At twenty-five, he was the best young player in the world, his inspired performances at the World Series and with Ballesteros in the Ryder Cup indicating that a major victory was only months away. Then came the 1991 Masters. On the final day, Olazabal, within easy grasp of his first Green Jacket, chalked up a record quadruple-bogey seven at the 180-yard sixth, before bogeying the last to lose by a stroke to Ian Woosnam. It precipitated a two-year slump, during which Olazabal, who had always seemed impossibly composed and mature off the course, became obsessive to the point of madness on it. Perfection was what he wanted and the boundaries of that perfection, unobtainable in golf, seldom extended beyond ten feet from the hole. If an approach shot dared to run to 15 feet, he would slam his club down and, hands on hips, stand glowering at the green, steam issuing from his ears.

'He became very, very morose and bad-tempered,' Jacobs recalled. 'Funnily enough, we made an instruction video in May 1991, soon after he had taken five at the last and lost the Masters to Ian Woosnam, and I remember saying to him, "Come on, stop looking so miserable. You didn't play well by your standards and you still got within a shot of the play-off." What had upset him is he'd been such a winner as an amateur, and he had had all these victories as a professional, and that was probably the first time he had failed in the hot seat with a chance to win.'

Sergio Gomez, Olazabal's manager, watching with growing concern, began to feel that the game was destroying the man who is like a son to him, that Olazabal's reaction to less than ideal shots was so disproportionate it was as if he had lost a member of his family. 'I said to him, "If you behave like that when you hit a golf shot to twenty feet, what are you going to do when something really terrible happens. When your father dies, are you going to react the same way?"'

The first thing that had to change was Olazabal's attitude. An astonishing outburst, prompted by Olazabal's appalling behaviour at the Tenerife Open in February, from Maite Gomez, Sergio's wife, for whom he has the utmost regard and who had hitherto shown him nothing but kindness, shook Olazabal profoundly. At the New Orleans Classic, where Olazabal finished runner-up to Ben Crenshaw, Gomez observed with something approaching awe: 'Yesterday he said to me: "Have you seen how beautiful this place is? How lovely the houses are?" Two years ago, he would never have noticed that.'

Next to undergo revision was Olazabal's swing. In March, Jacobs, in Spain on business, bumped into Gomez at the Andalucian Open. Sergio told him that the lesson he had given the young Spaniard at the Ryder Cup had helped, but he still wasn't happy. Jacobs went down to the practice ground to Olazabal. 'He asked me: "How do I draw the ball?"' Jacobs recalled. 'I put him in the right position and I said, "Hit it from here and you'll draw it."' Olazabal went home with second prize and won the Mediterranean Open the following week.

On the morning of the final round at Augusta, Olazabal found a note pinned to his locker. It was signed by Seve Ballesteros and it read: 'Be patient. You know what you have to do. You are the best player in the world.'

For the first time in several years, Olazabal believed it. Sergio compared his mood at breakfast to that of a matador about to enter the bullring. From the opening tee shot, he played to win and he rarely faltered. The pivotal hole was the 500-yard, par five fifteenth. While Olazabal's approach only just cleared the pond, Lehman landed 15 feet from the pin. But Olazabal had been preparing for this moment all his life. Without hesitation, he stroked in a 30-foot putt from the fringe for eagle. 'Great putt,' Lehman said. But he was fired up, not discouraged. 'I thought, "OK, he made his, now

I'm going to make mine right on top of it," ' he recalled. 'I hit a really good putt. It looked perfect all the way. A foot short of the hole, it was dead centre, but right at the very end it seemed to touch the front of the lip and take a ninety degree turn to the right.' Lehman fell to his knees and pounded the ground with his fists. 'It was like a stab in the heart,' he said later.

Back at San Sebastian, club members and friends of the Olazabal family had gathered to witness Jose Maria in his hour of glory. 'Here in the clubhouse,' Ramon Galdos, the club secretary, said, 'there was a crowd of us watching the whole four days. There were twenty-five of us, and of course it was a very lively atmosphere. But when he reached the seventeenth, everyone got worried, very worried.' All except Gaspar, Olazabal's father. 'I was quite serene,' he remembered. 'I felt he was going to win. When he finished, we cracked open the champagne. We had it all ready. And we went on until three in the morning.'

Olazabal, who had just two bogeys in the final fifty-six holes, won by two strokes from Lehman, three from Mize and four from Kite, becoming the sixth European winner in seven years. His score of 69 gave him an aggregate of 279, nine under par. 'You will never know how happy I am,' he said.

Norman did not share his sentiments. His 77 had left him thirteen strokes behind the Spaniard. He strode wearily into the clubhouse bar and leant on the counter. 'Give me a beer for every bogey I've made,' he told the barman.

At San Sebastian, they were already planning the celebrations that would take place when the Masters Champion returned, including 'a dinner, a dance and all the honours that he merits.'

9

THE RAINS IN SPAIN

'One day I'm going to die out there.'
SEVERIANO BALLESTEROS, Volvo Masters, 1992

A decade ago, Seve Ballesteros conquered America; now he had to conquer himself – and it wasn't easy. He set up over the ball and took a last glance down the ninth fairway (his eighteenth) in the second round of the Players Championship. His face was just as intent and revealing as it had been when he took golf by storm at nineteen; his hair, whipped by the wind, was still raven; he still had the same grace and fluidity through the ball and the same high, stylish finish; and he waited to see if he would get the same result. So did the gallery. They held their breath with him as the ball sliced cleanly through the clouds and on towards the lake. Agitation crossed Ballesteros's face. The crowd murmured uneasily. In mid-air, the white sphere slowed, it began its descent, it dropped like a stone into the water. Stunned, Ballesteros drove again, then lashed too hard at his approach. It sailed over the green into a bunker. He tried and failed to get up and down, taking a double-bogey seven to miss the cut by a shot. The new swing, the Sam Snead/Mac O'Grady inspired swing, was still too fragile to be trusted.

Billy Foster, Ballesteros's caddie, was almost in tears. Through suffering and flashes of ecstasy, they are bonded as close as father and son, and there are few people who believe in Ballesteros the way Billy does, or who agonize as much when he doesn't do well. In March, when the Spaniard was struggling painfully towards a 79 in the second round of the Majorcan Open (following an opening 78), Billy had implored him to walk in after nine holes. 'I can't stand to see you suffer like this,' he said. Ballesteros had looked him straight in the eye. 'We are professionals,' he said. 'We *must* keep going.' Now he put his arm around Billy's shoulders. He seemed helpless to know how to console him. 'Don't worry,' he said inadequately. 'It'll be all right.'

It seemed ironic that it should be Ballesteros comforting Billy and not the other way round. 'Look,' I suggested gently, 'we can talk another day.'

'No,' Ballesteros said with a lift of his chin. He once said that when his career is over, his only wish is to be remembered as someone 'who did what he did with honour', and that is the rule by which he governs most of his relationships. 'I promised,' he said proudly.

Later, we sat on a bench in the TPC locker-room, the same place Norman had come to so grudgingly, and talked softly about the past and the small steps he had made towards recovery from the slump many people thought had already ended his career. He confessed that it helped him to lose himself in videos of his major victories. 'Not only to see if I can learn a little bit, but also because it inspires me. Watching the winning moments helps.' He looked away. The double-bogey was still hurting him.

'Did you realize when you were young just how good you were?' I asked.

'Not then, *now*.' Ballesteros gave a short laugh. 'Now, as time goes by, I realize how good I was because things are not going well, so looking back and seeing how much I did is great and very special.'

'You were very, very good, you know. Your talent was completely unique.'

Ballesteros's eyes rimmed with tears. 'Still,' he said urgently. 'Still. It's just a matter of . . . I just feel that in life everything went OK for me, and I just feel that everybody has to pay their duties and it looks like I'm paying that now. Because I really feel that my game is still there and it's coming along. I can feel it. So, it's just a matter of being patient and waiting for my time. My time will come back, I'm sure of it.'

'Can you still feel all your old feelings?'

'Yes,' Ballesteros said wistfully. 'It's just that nothing is going right for me at the moment – golfing-wise. Apart from that, everything is very good, so I don't complain.'

'Do you think the problem is mental or physical?'

'Not mental, physical probably. My back has not been very good lately and it's getting worse and worse. So it could be because of my back. The brain of the body is very smart so it's always looking for the easy way, you know. So that could be it. I don't know, I just don't know.'

It had been a long and terrible fall from the pinnacle Ballesteros had occupied for over a decade, when he won three Open Championships and two Masters and challenged in as many more, to the hellish depths he had reached at the World Match Play in October 1993, when he broke down in tears after being beaten 7 and 6 by David Frost. After that he had disappeared for the season, emerging bright-eyed and bushy-tailed at the Andalucian Open in February as if it had all been a bad dream.

'I was very low,' Ballesteros conceded when he was asked whether, psychologically at least, the World Match Play had seen him at his most desperate.

'You gave us the impression you were thinking of quitting the game.'

'Quit! What? The *game*?' A broad smile broke across Ballesteros's tanned, expressive face. 'No, no, I might have quit for the year, but not for ever. I'm only thirty-six. I'm just a kid.' But he admitted that he had been 'mentally very tired. That's why I didn't play the Volvo Masters.'

But that was all over. That entire season – the fact that he had failed to win a European Tour event for the first time in seventeen years, that he had slumped to forty-second on the money list, his worst position in nineteen years, and that his stroke average of 71.54 was two shots a round more than it was when he last won the Order of Merit in 1991 – had been consigned to the dustbin, along with tousled hair and fatty foods. He wore a smart new military haircut, and new muscles flexed under his red polo-shirt. He had rarely looked happier or healthier. He had, he explained, found salvation. A chance phone call in November to his old friend, the zany Mac O'Grady, had borne unexpected fruit. O'Grady, (whom one cynical observer remarked 'couldn't teach Lassie to bark'), had agreed to look at him and then to help him.

This was not as crazy as it sounded. O'Grady may have needed seventeen attempts to get through the US Tour School, won a few tournaments, been fined $5,000 by Deane Beman and suspended for six weeks for refusing to pay a previous $500 fine, and then retired to Palm Springs to find golf's secret, but his technical knowledge was second to none. At one point in his career, he had even tried playing left-handed. 'You know me,' he said, 'I've got these demons inside me and maybe those left-handed demons are trying to come out . . . No-one's ever tried to develop their golf skills on both sides to the same level of performance. I'm bored with it right-handed. So I said to myself, let's do the impossible.' Another time, he remarked: 'Right now I'm going through a catatonic, neurosomatic disorder. I'm in a total emotional upheaval.'

Presently, he was in the midst of writing a five-volume treatise, following a 'ten-year neuro-biological study of the golf swing' in conjunction with the University of California. Going under the name of MORAD (Mankind's Objective Research and Development), these volumes would each be 250 pages long, with twenty-five pages being devoted to analysing the forces that made Ballesteros hit his five-iron shot into the water to lose the Masters in 1986. O'Grady was now prepared to share these insights with the Spaniard. What is more, he told interested reporters at Augusta, where David Leadbetter had charged Seve $500 an hour, he, O'Grady, was not going to be charging anything. After muttering something about other teachers being 'sycophants looking for a ticket to legitimacy', Mad Mac (as they used to call him on Tour) said benevolently of Ballesteros: 'I am trying to give him an injection of scientific principles.'

Only Ballesteros, the most natural golfer ever born, seemed unworried. 'Mac is a very good player,' he said. 'He probably strikes the ball better than anyone else. He has only one problem: he cannot focus on what he is doing, he is too friendly with people. He has a great heart and a lot of people misunderstand him.'

Outside, O'Grady stood under the oak tree and, in between suggesting that seven of the top thirty players in the world were on beta-blockers, explained that Ballesteros had already assimilated thirty-eight of the forty changes he had recommended into his swing. 'Seve has always had a steep back swing. He tilts and sways, and his genius has been that he made it work, especially from the five-iron to the wedges. He used to try and hit a two-iron like a wedge and that is not easy.' He rolled his eyes. 'I have got him to raise his hands at address, which flattens the backswing and takes the movement out of it.'

In all, Ballesteros had spent eight weeks in the States over the winter, most of them in Scottsdale, Arizona at the Desert Institute of Physical Therapy. Under the guidance of Brett Fischer and Paul Hospindal, he had worked for up to five hours a day to strengthen his back, the root cause of many of his problems. 'Last year it was very bad,' he said. 'I couldn't sleep for the pain. I have been through chiropractors and witches and they haven't helped. The injury is a product of a general wasting away of the spinal column, typical of a person who has undergone a lot of training. I practised a heck of a lot between the ages of ten and twenty-five. The problem with golf is the turn is not natural.'

As a result of his rehabilitation programme, Ballesteros now had 60 per cent less back pain and had lost 30 lbs. He had played little golf, listening instead to O'Grady and reading Sam Snead, whom he said had the best swing in the history of the game. His confidence was slowly returning. 'I am very serious about this year. I have the desire and the determination to regain my position as No.1 ... These things don't happen overnight, so I must be cautious. But I have very good expectations.'

Even after Ballesteros had fallen to pieces at the Majorcan Open and the Masters, and missed the cut at the TPC, Greg Norman had no doubt he would succeed. 'It's like riding a bike,' he said. 'It's always in your heart. If you know how good you are, then you can get back on that bike after fifteen or twenty years and know exactly what you're doing. And Seve's got it in there. He's just a little confused right now.'

But when all was said and done, O'Grady ('I'm not nearly so bingo-bango-bongo as people think I am'), Sam Snead and the Desert Institute were not half as effective in Ballesteros's recovery as the Ryder Cup venue controversy. 'When the tree falls down a lot of people want to take a little cut out of it,' Ballesteros was to say later in the year. 'My feeling is that this is what's happening. I have only one way to go and that's to reach the top again. Then I'll have my power back.'

In February, the lines in the battle for the 1997 Ryder Cup venue were drawn. Ballesteros, a Ryder Cup committee member, was pitching for Novo Sancti Petri, the course he himself had designed. He launched his campaign to win support by declaring that it would be 'fatal' to take the 1997 Ryder Cup match to a private club. 'The Ryder Cup *must* be played on a public course like Novo Sancti Petri,' he said. 'Valderrama and Augusta are the two most exclusive clubs in the world. Turespana has been trying hard to bring tourists into Spain and it would be contradictory if the match goes to a private club. It will go against the principles of the Ryder Cup. My principles are that golf is reachable for everybody. The concept and the philosophy of the Ryder Cup is first to test the power between Europe and the US, and second to spread the game of golf. It would be fatal for Spanish golf and Spanish tourism if the match does not go to a public course, and I will try to persuade my fellow members on the Ryder Cup committee of this.'

Earlier in the week, Ballesteros had attacked the Spanish Golf Federation in the national newspaper *El Pais*, describing it as 'a cancer' which saw its job as 'maintain[ing] a social circle . . . I feel very let down by the Spanish Golf Federation,' he said. 'When, at last, the Ryder Cup was given to Spain in May last year, nobody called me, nobody congratulated me, and nobody asked for my opinion. The most normal thing would have been to consult various people and to present a united candidature. Now we are all in a fight to see who wins. I put myself forward with the course at Novo Sancti Petri before my election as a member of the Ryder Cup committtee, and now it seems incredible to me that these people who have done nothing for golf are wrestling with me, when it is I who have brought the Ryder Cup here.'

It was not the first time that the Ryder Cup had featured as a catalyst in Ballesteros's personal war. In 1981, he had, as we know, resigned from the European Tour following the ban on appearance money and was left out of the Ryder Cup team. Colin Snape, the head of the PGA at that time, was outside the meeting room at Fulford when Jacobs, Coles and Langer filed out and announced that Mark James and Peter Oosterhuis were in and Seve and Jacklin were out. 'All I would say is, I was secretary to the Ryder Cup committee and I had sat in on every meeting since I became secretary in '73, and my predecessors since 1927,' Snape said. 'And the selection committee then was the leader of the Order of Merit, the Chairman of the Tour and Jacobs . . . I had turned up for the meeting, because it was my job to read the team on TV, and Jacobs said, "You won't be needed." I said: "But it's my job . . ." In fairness, Seve was more sinner than sinned against. Seve's Seve. He gets these bees in his bonnet. He was a crusader just like I was, in the context of demolishing the old order. He said, "Why shouldn't I get appearance money – Jacklin did? And he was right." '

All of these things – not to mention the fact that his performances, in and outside the Ryder Cup, had been largely responsible for precipitating the golf boom in Europe – contributed to Ballesteros's feeling that the 1993 Ryder Cup should have been held in Spain. So strongly did he feel about this that, at the behest of the Spanish Golf Federation, he led a delegation to the PGA early in 1990. At the Spanish Open in May of the same year, Faldo was asked which of the favoured Ryder Cup courses, Club de Campo in Madrid, Portmarnock in Ireland or Royal Birkdale, he preferred. After due consideration, he replied that he thought that Birkdale would give the Europeans the best chance at the trophy.

Ballesteros was beside himself when he was told. 'Why should we play in England, why?' he cried passionately. 'Why should we play in Ireland, why? Spanish players have done enough for European golf. We *must* have the Ryder Cup in Spain. I'm not saying I won't play if it doesn't come here, but remember one thing: I would be disappointed. I would lose a little of my desire for the Ryder Cup.'

The press room erupted. There were cries of protest and much wringing of hands as a large contingent of British golf writers and local news reporters not versed in golf's etiquette and decorum, struggled to come to terms with the full impact of what Ballesteros was saying.

'People should remember that, without the European players, there probably would be no Ryder Cup,' Ballesteros said sullenly when order was restored. 'The future of the European Tour is in Spain . . . Golf here needs the push the Ryder Cup would provide. It would be the best thing for the Ryder Cup as a whole. It is what Samuel Ryder would have wanted if he were alive today. To wait until 1997 would be too late.'

He glowered down at the reporters. 'I feel I have played a part in the success of the Ryder Cup,' he said. 'This is the first time I have asked for anything.'

Even supposing that bringing the 1993 Ryder Cup to Spain would have been a good thing for golf – which no rational-minded person could have imagined – the European Tour were in no position to yield to Ballesteros's demands. They were at loggerheads with the PGA and the PGA were calling all the shots. 'They wanted to nominate the venue,' Bernard Gallacher recalled, 'despite the fact that, in our opinion, they already had nominated the venue at the Belfry for the last two Ryder Cups, when it was played there in '85 and '89. And we really felt it was our shout the next time round. We wanted to take it to Spain – providing we could get a good venue and that it made commercial sense. Our second choice was Portmarnock in Ireland. Some of the players felt it was just a bit too early for Spain. And, of course, what's transpired since that time is that we've actually had a problem getting an agreeable venue for Spain in '97, so what would have happened was that we'd have probably gone to Portmarnock . . . The problem was, both sides put Lord Derby on the spot. He had to make a decision between going to Spain and going to the Belfry, and he popped down on the PGA's side partly because he was president of the PGA. Since then, I think he's felt a little bit let down by the PGA officers of that time, for not informing him of the full facts.'

It was because he had lost that particular battle that Ballesteros was so frantic to make up for it in 1994, by making sure that the Ryder Cup didn't just come to Spain but to the golf course he had designed. 'The Federation says it has to remain neutral but in this, as in other matters, there is a lack of dialogue. Novo Sancti Petri is one of the best. The Ryder Cup should be played in a tourist area. It would be a grave error to play it in Madrid. It must go to the South.'

A friend of the Spaniard's once noted that: 'All his professional life he has been inspired to great deeds by his craving to stick it to someone. Go through his record and you can match his triumphs to his mood. Here's where he stuck it to the American pros for calling him lucky. Here's when he stuck it to Deane Beman for not changing the qualification rules . . .' Peter Dobereiner agreed. 'He is hypersensitive to slight or injury, and cherishes his grudges like a miser gloating over his hoard of gold pieces,' he wrote. 'People, places, golf courses, events and even entire nations which incur his displeasure are marked down for vengeance. It may take years but eventually he will stick it to them. He is not content just to even up the score; he needs to win the replay 8 and 10.'

As long ago as June 1985, Dobereiner observed that 'in the case of the Ryder Cup [Ballesteros] might be in for an exciting double thrust. The PGA has it coming to them for their petty-mindedness in not selecting him for the 1981 team. On the other hand, the America team has it coming to them in retribution for Ballesteros's failure to gain a single point in the 1979 match.'

Ballesteros was honest enough to recognize this trait in himself. 'I have a lot of pride and it has been damaged,' he admitted at the Andalucian Open. 'It gives me strength and makes me more aggressive. The last couple of years have confirmed what I already knew. That I have few friends, many acquaintances and very many enemies.'

On 8 May 1994, Ballesteros won the B&H International at St Mellion in Cornwall. It was twenty-six months to the day since he had last won, and in his previous fifty tournaments he had missed seventeen cuts and had just four top-ten finishes. He had been inspired to victory, partly because his struggles to sway opinion in favour of Novo Sancti Petri had resulted in his resignation from the Ryder Cup committee the previous week, and partly because of a letter he had received from the United States Golf Association telling him that unless he played well before the Sunday of the PGA Championship, he wouldn't be receiving an invitation to the US Open. Ballesteros was boiling with rage and indignation. He said he hadn't had to qualify for a tournament since 1974, when he finished last with an 89. 'I took 56 for the back nine,' Ballesteros reported. 'My sponsor Dr Campuzano said: "Don't worry, you are still the best in the world." '

The following week, speaking from a position of strength, Ballesteros walked calmly into the Spanish Open press centre at Club de Campo and, with a few well-chosen remarks, sent shock waves through the golf world.

At first, the journalists were not even sure they had heard right. They stared at Ballesteros uncomprehendingly. Ballesteros stared malevolently back. Moments before he had matter-of-factly alleged that he had been offered $1 million to help ensure that the 1997 match went to Valderrama, venue of the Volvo Masters, the exclusive course owned by the Bolivian millionaire, Jaime Ortiz-Patino. He claimed that the inducement had come from Valderrama – a club he once described as 'the most élitist in the world, even more than Augusta' – in 1993, shortly before his appointment to the

Ryder Cup committee, although he would not reveal who had made it.

'The letter did not actually specify that figure, but that was what it amounted to,' he said. 'I have a letter at home which tells me I would get a percentage of the green fees and the sales of the building plots. It has nothing to do with the work I did in redesigning the seventeenth hole there, because I did that for nothing.'

He was asked whether he regarded the letter as a bribe. 'Take it what way you like,' Ballesteros replied. 'But I don't like to be bought. I have my principles.'

Patino's story was very different. He told Ian Katz of the *Guardian* that in April 1993, a month before the committee announced the 1997 event would be played in Spain, he had decided to seek the support of Ballesteros, who had helped to redesign Valderrama's seventeenth hole but refused to accept a fee. He wrote to him on 30 April, offering him a percentage of Valderrama's green fees for the redesign of the seventeenth, and 'for your . . . agreement to support our candidacy for the Ryder Cup and in particular if you are prepared to publicly communicate your support to the press and the PGA executives at the Volvo PGA at Wentworth on 28 May 1994.'

The green fees alone were worth an estimated £675,000, but Patino insisted that he didn't see the offer as a bribe. 'I felt honestly that, knowing the politics in Spain, it could become very nasty, as it did in the end, and that I could avoid all this nonsense. I knew we had the best course, and if we had Seve on our side there would be no opposition.'

Katz believes that Ballesteros 'was initially of a similar mind. In a letter dated 22 June 1993, he thanks Patino for the "very kind offer to collaborate in your project." He asks for time to consider the offer and signed the letter with the fond Spanish greeting *un fuerte abrazo,* a big hug.' In October, Ballesteros wrote again, explaining that he had received similar offers from the other short-listed Spanish courses. He said he was unwilling to commit himself to any particular one, but concluded his letter: 'I thank you from the bottom of my heart for the interest you have always shown me personally.'

The next Patino heard, Ballesteros was declaring his support for Novo Sancti Petri, and at Club de Campo he told us that the technical committee which advises the Ryder Cup committee had presented them with a report that said that Valderrama did not have the minimum number of necessary facilities to host the event. However, Gallacher had told him that the committee were considering taking the match there.

'So one has to ask whether those gentlemen on the Ryder Cup committee have received similar offers to the one I received,' Ballesteros said darkly.

David Huish, a member of the committee, was incensed. 'If Seve said that to my face I'd punch him on the nose,' he said angrily. 'I can't believe it. If he's suggesting that members of the committee have been offered inducements I'd take it all the way to the courts. It would be like winning the pools.'

There was one other man qualified to speak with authority on the subject of whether or not Novo Sancti Petri was the most suitable Spanish course to host the Ryder Cup – which Ballesteros was still adamantly maintaining much to the incredulity of the Tour players who had played there – and that was Olazabal, Ballesteros's Ryder Cup team-mate and close friend. Between them, they have won nine of the twelve matches they have played and lost only one. Their friendship is founded on respect and mutual admiration. 'There is a special chemistry between us,' Olazabal said. 'Playing together brings out the best in us.'

Nevertheless, it is an attraction of opposites. Where Ballesteros is wilful, dramatic and ultimately very human, Olazabal is a diplomat. In 1990, he took the fire out of what was rapidly developing into an ugly situation, by responding to his compatriot's threat to lose interest and motivation if the Ryder Cup didn't go to Spain with a calm: 'Well, he had to say that, didn't he? When he gets on the golf course, I know he will give 110 per cent. He wants to kill everyone. He won't need any motivation.'

'They are completely different,' Sergio Gomez said. 'Seve's naturally aggressive. In life, he tries to make room for himself with his elbows. That's what we say in Spain about someone who's always pushing ahead and trying to be one step further than the others. Jose is totally different. He feels that he should make his own decisions and take responsibility for them, and if the others, for example the press, don't like those decisions, then it doesn't bother him. You will never see Jose pushing his arguments or pushing a situation to the boundaries. Seve's always on the edge of being impolite, and being so harsh with everyone that everyone is shocked.

When Seve's not happy, he always threatens: "I will lose interest in the Ryder Cup, I will play on the US Tour, I will go to Japan where everybody loves me." If Jose was in the same situation, he would say, "We have to change things." He will not be the guy trying to buck the system. He will be trying to compromise and to talk to the ears that will listen.

'For instance, with the Ryder Cup course. Seve pushed the situation to the absolute limit: "I won't be captain, I don't know if I will play again in Spain." Jose, from the beginning, was favouring Valderrama. But not publicly, because he didn't want to be in that situation. He went to Ken Schofield and he went to George O'Grady and he said: "Don't be stupid. The only place we can play is Valderrama." He came to that decision because he said: "Where can the Ryder Cup work? Valderrama. Why? Because Jaime Patino will make it work." '

Unluckily for Ballesteros, this was the view of the Ryder Cup committee. At the PGA Championship at Wentworth, on 25 May, Ken Schofield announced that the 1997 Ryder Cup match would be staged at Valderrama. It had been chosen from a short-list of five courses, which included La Manga, La Moraleja, Novo Sancti Petri and El Saler.

Tony Jacklin, who served on other Ryder Cup committees, found the politics of the decision laughable. 'Well, you didn't have to be Einstein to figure it out,' he said. 'It was all very obvious what was going on. It's clearly a prize to have the Ryder Cup and people will do almost anything to get it if they've got a vested interest, as Seve had and Patino had. The thing that always amazes me is how these decisions are made. I remember when it was going back to the Belfry in 1993, other courses were mentioned – places like Turnberry, which is a wonderful course. And there were questions like, "Are the equinoxes in?" Lord Derby asked that one. "No? Well, Turnberry's out, then." Boom! It's a joke how things get done.'

On Thursday, Ballesteros strode into the press centre wearing a slightly mischievous smile. He was at his most charming, but he said that there would be 'no questions, only answers' and he reached into his pocket and plucked out a scroll of white paper covered in pink scrawl. 'I wrote this statement last week in Spain,' he said innocently. 'I knew who was going to win so I had plenty of time to write down what I wanted to say so that it would not be misinterpreted.'

As loser's speeches go, it was a masterpiece, both gracious and full of subtle digs at Patino. He began by extending his 'heartfelt best wishes to Valderrama and Mr Patino for winning the right to stage this prestigious event and I am sure that every one of the American team will enjoy Valderrama . . .

'I know that all the other clubs who were hoping to be selected are greatly disappointed. I wanted Novo Sancti Petri, but life sometimes is not so sweet. We do not always get what we want. Everyone must forget any hard feelings and work together in assisting Mr Patino, Valderrama and the Ryder Cup committee, to show the world that Spain is worthy of hosting this magnificent event.'

To crown it all, walking out of the interview room the following day, Ballesteros was confronted by the sight of Patino blocking his path. Without a moment's hesitation, he rushed up to the Bolivian, threw his arms around him and congratulated him on his victory.

Patino confessed to being bewildered by Ballesteros's behaviour. 'When I saw him at Wentworth he grabbed me and gave me a big hug and said, "You won. You were too strong for me," as if nothing had happened. He had a smile from ear to ear. I can't understand how he went off the deep end.'

10

THE DEVIL'S PLAYGROUND

'I will dismiss this harrowing reflection.'
                    BOBBY JONES, on escaping from Oakmont's
                               dreaded Church Pews bunkers

US OPEN, OAKMONT, PENNSYLVANIA. Along the leafy lane outside Oakmont Country Club, a caravan of eccentrics had halted and set up stall. Beneath a vast oak, a sweating Father Christmas was attempting to sell iced sushi to sceptical passers-by, while leggy California girls enticed them away with Frozen Lemonade. Suburban entrepreneurs with homemade parking signs jostled for space at the junction. And near Oakmont's grand entrance, past a red sign advertising the area as a 'Drugs-free School Zone', and makeshift stands offering baseball caps, umbrellas and ball-markers, Old Glory flapped from a zimmerframe.

For the survivors of past Oakmont championships, these carnival surrounds represented a breathing space, the last chance they had to gather their resources and steel themselves for the ultimate golfing war zone. But for Oakmont initiates, the Mardi Gras at the gates was a smokescreen. Amused and slightly bemused by the juxtaposition of gay vendors, fairground trivia, and pensioners tottering in and out of the hospital on golf club grounds, they sailed serenely up the driveway of Oakmont Country Club, blissfully unaware of the fate that lay beyond.

Oakmont may be the hardest course in America. Tommy Armour, the winner here in 1927, described it as 'a cruel and treacherous playground'. Gene Sarazen said it had 'all the charm of a sock to the head'. And even the members, a charmless crew with the sadistic and masochistic tendencies of veteran legionnaires, nicknamed it 'The Hades of Hulton'. Henry C. Fownes, Oakmont's founder, took these epithets as compliments. The pursuit of sublime forms of golfing torture was his life's work. When his doctor made the mistake of telling him to go out and enjoy himself, he turned his family motto – 'a shot poorly played should be a shot irrevocably lost' – into a blueprint for the golf course from hell and, by 1903, had put 150 men and two dozen mule teams to work on a links-style course. With few trees to relieve it, a tortuous lunarscape resulted. 'Like a midnight walk in a graveyard,' one historian shuddered.

H. C. Fownes was puritanical, but his son William was worse. If, while traversing the monstrous creation (which originally featured eight par fives and a par six), he saw an errant shot go unpunished, a bunker was immediately put in its place. Thus, three hundred and fifty traps came into being. These were raked by a 100-lb instrument of torture, which created three-inch furrows in the sand. 'You could have combed North Africa with it and Rommel wouldn't have got past Casablanca,' Jimmy Demaret commented drolly.

Unsurprisingly, when Oakmont hosted the first of six men's US Opens, in 1927 no-one broke 300. Today, the number of bunkers has been reduced to 165, and it is a comparatively tame 6,946 yards, and yet it is still the only course where the United States Golf Association, notorious for the Draconian specifications it imposes on prospective venues, spends months in tense negotiation with intransigent members, pleading with them to widen the fairways, cut the rough and slow down the greens. On the day that the USGA first persuaded Oakmont not to furrow rake the bunkers for a US Open, Richard Fuhrer, the former president, described the club as 'mortally wounded' by the decision.

But the putting surfaces are the most frequent cause of revolt. In 1962, Sam Snead said that negotiating Oakmont's slippery greens was like trying to putt down a marble staircase with the pin on the third step, and in 1973, Charlie Sifford proved it by six-putting the seventh. The USGA thinks itself harsh when it cuts the greens to register 10 on the stimpmeter; Oakmont members consider themselves cheated if the stimpmeter doesn't read 13 at the monthly medal.

The Fownes retained their enthusiasm for a brutal Oakmont until the bitter end. William finally resigned when the members decided they wanted a club swimming pool ('over my dead body'), but he left an awesome legacy. His medieval maxims are still cited today. Notoriously, he had once felt obliged to inform the swine before whom he and his father had cast their redoubtable pearl, that Oakmont was for golfers not posers. 'Let the clumsy, the spineless, the alibi artist stand aside,' he screamed. It was something for the hopeful contender to bear in mind.

In 1973, Johnny Miller, a twenty-six-year-old with flaxen hair and forearms on which the veins interwined like mating snakes, entered the final round of the US Open and single-handedly extended the boundaries of what had hitherto been dreamt possible in golf. He did this by taking on the lions of the game – Palmer, Trevino, Nicklaus and Weiskopf, not to mention Julius Boros and John Schlee – and killing them softly with peerless iron play and a devastating putting stroke. That he also did it from six strokes behind on the last day of a major, makes his achievement all the more remarkable.

'It sort of came out of nowhere,' Miller explained. 'It was one of those rounds you dream about. It was a fantasy round where the moon was aligned with Venus and almost everything went perfectly. It was almost a perfect round of golf. It was the best round of golf I've ever played and the best round I've ever seen played. I shot lower scores in the 1970s during my prime – a lot of 61s and 62s in tournaments. But to shoot 63 on what a lot of people considered the most difficult golf course in America, and to do it on the last day of the Open . . . it was crazy good. It was a once in a lifetime thing.'

Throughout the tournament, a clairvoyant had followed Miller around Oakmont. 'She came up to me Wednesday during a practice round and said: "I predict things, I see things days in advance, and you're going to win the US Open this week," ' Miller recalled. 'I didn't know who she was. I had never seen her before, and I thought she was kind of a kook, maybe a little crazy. But I listened to her. On Thursday after my round, she said: "I'm never wrong, you know. You're going to win the US Open." She was there again Friday and it started to sound a little eerie. I thought maybe I'd mention it to Arnold after our round, but I figured he'd think I was really crazy. I started to believe her a little bit until I shot that 76 Saturday. It was funny, because she didn't show up Saturday. I had to laugh when someone mentioned it that night. Sure, I was going to win the Open now, wasn't I? I was six strokes back with eighteen holes to play.'

It was perhaps with this in mind that *Golf Journal* consulted a professional astrologer on the likely winner of the 1994 US Open. Having glanced at her charts and indicated that, provided he used intuition and visualization techniques, Curtis Strange had the best chance at the title, Sara Hosier turned her attention to Greg Norman. The prognosis was not good. 'Saturn is in his mid-heaven, giving him what we call a Napoleon Conflict, and his cards were pathetic,' she said sorrowfully. 'He has a nervous stomach and is probably downing lots of Maalox these days, but there is a woman in his life who is very supportive of him.'

This analysis turned out to be curiously apt. A doleful and uninspired Norman came into the press centre after his practice round on Wednesday, and informed reporters that he was feeling the middle of the year blues. 'I haven't played well lately,' the Shark said bleakly. 'On a scale of one to ten, I'd put my game at four and a half. I don't know why. I guess you go through little peaks and troughs and I've fallen off the edge a little bit.'

Asked for his opinion on the way in which the USGA had set up the course, something akin to a sneer developed on his face. 'Of all our majors, this is the only one where we might as well not bring our driver,' he complained. 'It seems like it's a redundant deal. If you can't hit your driver it takes away six per cent of your shot-making ability. I don't know why they do it. And every year you say something, and every year it gets worse.'

But most players felt that Oakmont was the major championship layout by which all others could be measured. 'This is the toughest course we play,' Faldo said. '[The greens] are brutal. There's a couple of them out there where you could be thirty feet from the hole and have thirty-one feet of break. I mean, they are quite something.' Arnold Palmer, who had received a special invitation to the event, agreed. 'The greens are about as fast and difficult as I have seen on any golf course, period.'

The most momentous event to have occurred on the PGA Tour since our last visit was the appointment on 1 June of Tim Finchem, Deane Beman's former deputy, as Tour Commissioner. In the two months it took to select a replacement for Beman, few serious candidates emerged. Dan Quayle's name was bandied about for a time, but it turned out that he was saving his energies for the 1996 Presidential race. Jack Prazee, a business tycoon, and David Ogrin, whom *Golf World* described as 'a fringe player with a warped sense of humour', were never realistic contenders. Finchem is a four-handicapper with an impressive background as a lawyer, strategic consultant and White House adviser to President Carter. It was said that he had two goals: to make the players richer and to keep their stainless reputation. But as Peter McCleery pointed out, 'Among a tour of right-wingers, Finchem's liberal bent could be out of step with his constituents.'

At Westchester, Mac O'Grady was asked to comment on the choice of Finchem, who was nicknamed 'Beman's hatchet man' in his role as No.2. 'Well,' said O'Grady consideringly, 'there are two things to remember. Firstly, the guard may have changed but the light is still on in the lighthouse.'

'Oh,' said the journalist, 'and what's the second thing?'

'This,' replied O'Grady, taking a baby's dummy out of his pocket and sucking on it.

On Thursday, when temperatures climbed to 96 degrees and Oakmont became a scenic Turkish bath, a heat emergency was declared by the Allegheny County Board of Commissioners. Chris Patton, the well-built former US Amateur Champion, was the first to suffer the consequences. 'I four-putted the seventh hole, and I think the reason for that was I didn't have the ability to concentrate,' Patton said, looking wan and nauseous after being treated for heat exhaustion. 'I was just dead tired. I felt dizzy and sick to the stomach.' After putting out on the eighth green, Patton told his playing partners that he couldn't take any more. 'I've been on a diet and I've lost thirty-five pounds in about thirty-five days or so. I weighed 352 around Christmas and that's the most I've ever weighed. A while back, a guy wrote an article in *Sports Illustrated* called, "A Giant Disappointment". That really hurt. I've wanted to prove to that guy that, even if I can't play golf, I can do something. I wanted to make him eat his words.'

Out on the course, Jumbo Ozaki had taken the early lead. Asked afterwards what it would mean to him to win the US Open, he replied: 'It would be like becoming President of the United States.' You couldn't imagine him saying that about the British Open. Who in their right mind would want to become Margaret Thatcher or John Major?

The heat was fiery, oppressive. It sucked the life out of the most ambitious heart, it stole the hard edge from skill, and it made sweat collect at the base of every spine in boiling pools of sapped energy and willpower, so that all that was left was experience and imagination.

Watson glanced up at the scoreboard and saw with a start that Nicklaus was scaling it with ease. Earlier in the week, Watson had said that only 5 per cent of the field had a chance to win. Nicklaus had not featured in his calculations. Neither, for that matter, had Watson himself. His ball-striking was the match of any man in the field, but his putting was dangerously unreliable. Still, the sight of his old sparring partner stirred his blood. He remembered that blue-grey day on the cliffs of Pebble Beach in the 1982 US Open, when his recovery chip had bounced airily out of tangled rough and into the hole at the seventeenth, giving him the shot necessary for victory and crushing the Golden Bear. Watson called it 'The Shot . . . the greatest shot of my life, the most meaningful.' Nicklaus saw it differently. 'How would I evaluate that shot? One of the worst that ever happened to me.'

At Oakmont, Watson put to the back of his mind the recollection that he had also had a five-stroke lead in the third round of the 1978 US PGA at this very course, but had been beaten in the play-off by John Mahaffey. Or that he had had a three-stroke lead with nine holes to play in 1983, but had bogeyed the tenth, twelfth and seventeenth to hand the US Open to Larry Nelson. He simply thought: 'If Jack's up there, there's no reason why Watson can't be. It inspired me, no doubt about that.'

The reverse may well have been true. Thirty-two years before, Nicklaus had ushered in golf's new era when he overcame Palmer in the US Open at Oakmont. Now his only wish was to turn the clock back. 'I've played absolute rubbish, with the odd exception, for the past three years,' he admitted wryly, after a 69 gave him a share of second place with Hale Irwin, New Zealand's Frank Nobilo and Ernie Els, one stroke behind Watson. 'This morning, Barbara put a spell on me. She told me I was twenty-two again. I guess it worked because although I always feel like a twenty-two-year-old, I seldom play like one.'

It was with a gasp and a gesture of joyous disbelief that Nicklaus had watched his 60-foot birdie putt drop at the last. 'Power was always my game when I was younger,' he said. 'But I don't have the power to play a golf course the way I used to, so I have to play it differently. Now when I get to a golf course that doesn't require power, then it sort of evens things out.'

In the right hand corner of Friday's *US Open Update*, below the COOK BURNING UP OAKMONT banner, was a box headed: 'O. J. charged', with a Los Angeles dateline. It read: 'Charges were filed today against O. J. Simpson in the slayings of his ex-wife and a male friend . . . The forty-six-year-old Simpson denied any involvement in the slayings. The bodies were found Sunday night outside Mrs Simpson's condominium.'

We had arrived in Pittsburgh to an America reeling from the shock of the Simpson murders. Every other newsworthy event of the day – the war in Bosnia, the crisis in Haiti, the soccer World Cup and even the US Open – had been demoted or rendered insignificant in the face of what was viewed as a uniquely American tragedy. 'To me, this is the equivalent of the Pope showing an act of violence,' Ron Yary, Simpson's team-mate at the University of Southern California, told the *Pittsburgh Post-Gazette*. The LA District Attorney called it 'the fall of an American hero.'

At virtually the same moment that Simpson was plummeting from grace, the nation was paying tribute to another American hero, the footballer's friend and co-Hertz advertisement star, Arnold Palmer. Mercifully, Palmer was unchanged after forty years at the top – untainted by scandal, unaltered by fame. A little broader, a little browner, his flaxen hair a little thinner, he nevertheless retained that indefinable aura of greatness. For a generation, his capacity to inspire love, respect and awe in equal measures had helped him epitomize an entire game. In his thirty-second and final US Open, he three-putted five of the last six greens for an 81 and an aggregate of 158, sixteen over par. No matter. The gallery began applauding when he walked onto the eighteenth tee and they never stopped until his last putt rolled reluctantly into the hole.

'You made all this possible,' Rocco Mediate, his playing partner, whispered to him as they embraced on the green. Palmer, fighting back the tears, was unable to answer. It was the end of a marvellous era, during which he had won four Masters, two Open Championships, one US Open (losing three play-offs), fifty-seven regular

Tour events and ten Seniors. But he hadn't won anywhere since 1988.

In the press centre, he just sat on the platform with his scarlet face buried in a white towel, sobbing quietly and struggling to regain control.

'Could you just tell us what you are feeling right now, and what it has been like the past couple of days?' Les Unger, the press officer, asked gently.

Palmer took a deep breath. He lifted his tear-stained face to the world's media. 'I think you all know pretty much how I feel,' he began raggedly. 'Most of you I have talked to quite a bit over the years and . . .' He paused, too choked up to continue. 'I . . . I suppose the sun got to me a little bit. I got a little tired, I guess, and a little emotional coming up eighteen. It's been forty years of fun, work, enjoyment . . .'

'You are the king,' Unger said emotionally. 'You not only affected golf, but all of sport throughout the world. Your impact is everywhere. Can you think of one thing you have done, the thing that you feel that you have had the most fun with . . . ?'

'The whole experience,' Palmer said, tears coursing down his cheeks. 'You know, it's been . . . I haven't won all that much. I won a few tournaments. I won some majors. I suppose the most important thing is it's been as good as it's been to me . . . Hopefully, there will be a few more golf tournaments along the way.'

Palmer covered his face. There was a long silence. 'I think that's about all I have to say,' he mumbled. He rose, took several steps towards the exit and then stopped, unable to continue. Towel over his face, he just stood there, his body racked by sobs. The journalists leapt to their feet in spontaneous applause, an ovation lasting until Palmer stumbled blindly out. It had been forty years since he won the US Amateur Championship, thirty-nine since he won the Canadian Open, his first professional title, and thirty-two years since he and Nicklaus duelled to the finish at Oakmont.

Afterwards, we took a long time to recover. We were still subdued when Nicklaus came in with a 70.

'How are you holding up?' Unger asked. 'Are you tired?'

'No,' snapped Nicklaus, resenting the inference that, at fifty-four, the heat should affect him more than it did players half his age. 'I don't have any reason to be tired. Why would I be tired? Are you tired? I don't get tired. I keep myself in fairly decent shape. I think the reason people get tired is [dehydration]. I had two glasses of water every hole today, and I think that's the key.'

'Jack, Arnold Palmer didn't make the cut today,' Unger said carefully. 'Can you comment briefly on the huge contribution that he has made to this championship and golf in general.'

There was a pause. 'What did he shoot today?' asked Nicklaus.

'81.'

Nicklaus's face reflected the war being waged behind it. His performance that week had awakened feelings long buried; had rekindled the flame of old rivalry.

'Well,' he said at last, 'Arnie and I have played a lot of golf together for a lot of years, and I think we are all, you know, sorry to see anyone finish their career anyplace . . . He's been great for the game, great for golf, but I think he probably feels like I do. I think there is a time when you have to sort of pass it on and let the younger guys have it. I'm about at that point, too.' The next day he proved it with a 77.

Americans are in a constant state of denial. They shut out the weather with air-conditioners and sun-lamps; they scorn the finality of Mother Nature by tampering without conscience with genetics and having face-lifts, tummy tucks, collagen implants, silicone implants and sex changes; they forgive themselves their excesses by labelling them individual freedoms; they make icons out of recovering alcoholics (Liz Taylor), sexual ambivalents (Michael Jackson and Ru Paul), social misfits (Woody Allen), drug fiends (Kurt Cobain) and martyrs of Generation X (River Phoenix); and they turn reality into hyper-reality even as it is happening, purely by applying the language and dramatic licence of Hollywood to tragic and deplorable events, such as the capture of O. J. Simpson.

On Friday night, every player, journalist, caddie and USGA official in Pittsburgh stayed up until the small hours, transfixed by the awful spectacle of O. J. Simpson's sixty-mile flight through the streets of LA and his subsequent capture several hours later. The whole mad drama unfolded live on national television, revealing an unhealthy voyeurism on the part of the media. Meanwhile, half the nation wailed and gnashed their teeth at the fall of a great American hero, while the rest shouted, 'Go, O. J., go!' from the sidelines and held Simpson up as a paragon of virtue, despite the wealth of evidence to the contrary.

By comparison, golf seemed as wholesome and clean as newly baked bread the next morning, a sport of graciousness and etiquette, where even those heroes with feet of clay were essentially decent, honourable men and not homicidal maniacs, or drug addicts, or child molesters. At Oakmont, you could stand and watch the finest players in the world tee off in the third round of the US Open and feel nothing but pride to be associated with a game which produces the likes of Els, with his honest, smiling face, and the noble Watson.

Not that golfers are without their flaws. On the golf course a man's soul is laid bare, and every facet of his character, however well disguised, will eventually be outed. Thus, Colin Montgomerie, who in many ways is very likeable and endearing, and who desires nothing more than to be seen as a gifted player and a perfect gentleman, is betrayed at almost every turn on the course by an inflexible nature, which leads to petulance, sulkiness and, all too frequently, bad language. This he freely confesses. 'I admit I am a naturally volatile person and that is what makes me a competitor and a winner. I'm a very quick learner at golf but not so quick at learning the concentration and psychological skills required at the very highest level. Deep down I'm not a bad person.'

Throughout the game's history, there have been infamous tantrum throwers. Tommy Bolt was prone to such violent fits of club-abuse and cursing that the Tour once hired a monitor to follow him round the course and count the number of times he swore. By the end of the day Bolt had accumulated $200 in fines. Knowing his reputation, his friends were amazed to see him sitting at the bar afterwards, grinning from ear to ear. They asked him why he was so cheerful. 'Well,' beamed Bolt, 'I stiffed the bastards $1,500.'

But Bolt was a mere novice compared to Lefty Stackhouse, a Tour player in the 40s. Stackhouse believed that the punishment should fit the crime, and self-mutilation often seemed to him the only course of justice. Anaesthetized by alcohol, he would punch himself so viciously on the jaw after a poor shot, that 'the chewing gum flew from my mouth', smash his head against trees or beat his hand with a club. Once, when he snap-hooked a drive playing in a pre-Second World War event with Ben Hogan, he rushed over to a rose bush beside the tee and began raking his right hand back and forth across it until it was a bleeding pulp. 'That will teach you to roll over on me!' he cried. Hogan watched aghast. Stackhouse stopped and looked at his left hand. 'And don't think you're going to get away

'Why me?' Severiano Ballesteros discusses the finer points of the rule book with John Paramor, the Tour's chief referee, at the Volvo Masters, Valderrama. *Phil Sheldon Golf Picture Library*

'Should I stay or should I go?' Nick Faldo wrestles with the frustrations of perfectionism during a season of turmoil, both on and off the golf course. *Phil Sheldon Golf Picture Library*

David Leadbetter assists Mark O'Meara into the ideal backswing position at his academy at Lake Nona, Florida. *Lauren St John*

Six-million-dollar man: Nick Faldo goes through his paces at the British Olympic Medical Centre. *Allsport/Gary M. Prior*

Bernhard Langer, one of the hardest workers on the European Tour, strives for his personal best under the watchful gazes of former coach, Simon Holmes, and lifelong mentor, Willi Hoffman. *Phil Sheldon Golf Picture Library*

AEROBICIZE: Martial Arts expert, Ted Pollard, takes young hopefuls through their paces at the Apollo School. *Phil Sheldon Golf Picture Library*

WOMEN ON TOP: Kathie Shearer, press officer on the Australian Tour, and IMG's
Ann Farrow, celebrate the completion of another successful tournament
Down Under. *Lauren St John*

Robinson Holloway takes a break from her researches into the hazards of
golf in Florida (drive-by shootings, muggings) during the World Cup at Lake
Nona, Florida. *Lauren St John*

America's Al Wester gets black on white in the purpose-built press centre at Augusta. *Lauren St John*

QUEEN BEE: watched over by the US Tour's famous security guard, 'Tiny', Martha Gay commands operations at the Masters. *Lauren St John*

COMRADES: Ballesteros and Olazabal, the most successful partnership in Ryder Cup history, go on the warpath at the Belfry. *Phil Sheldon Golf Picture Library*

Faldo and Montgomerie, Europe's inspirational leaders at the Belfry, are unable to conceal their despair as Samuel Ryder's trophy slips into the hands of the Americans. *Phil Sheldon Golf Picture Library*

MOMENT OF VICTORY: Nick Price leaps ecstatically into the air as the eagle putt, which would bring him the trophy that had twice been snatched from him, falls into the 17th hole at Turnberry.
Allsport/Jeremy Campion

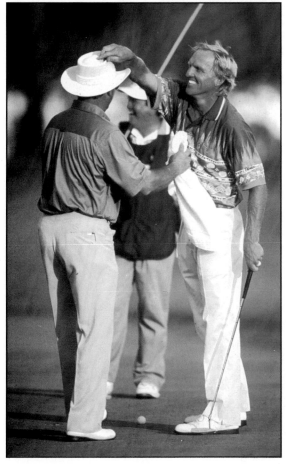

Fuzzy Zoeller waves a white towel in surrender after Norman played some of the greatest golf of his life to beat him in the Players Championship at Sawgrass.
Allsport/Gary Newkirk

VAGABONDS WITH ATTITUDE: European caddies take the train in Switzerland.
Lauren St John

HIGHLIFE: Jose Maria Olazabal, Dave Marr, Ian Baker-Finch and Ian Woosnam enjoy the fruits of their successes.
Phil Sheldon Golf Picture Library

with it, either,' he fumed, and proceeded to do the same to that one. 'Blood was spurting everywhere,' his caddie, Shelley Mayfield, recalled. 'I stood very, very still.'

Neither was Stackhouse against the destruction of property. In Al Barkow's *Getting to the Dance Floor*, Ky Laffoon, who himself had tied his putter to the bumper of his car and dragged it 1,000 miles across the south-western desert to discipline it, recalled Lefty 'sitting cross-legged in front of a fire he had going with every wooden-shafted club in his bag. He turned them all into kindling. The guy who loaned him the sticks was standing over Lefty and chewing him out like you never heard before.'

But as Laffoon pointed out, in his era players 'could afford to be angry and lose our temper. It didn't cost enough to stay cool.' At Oakmont in 1994, a fit of pique leading to a bogey or a three-putt might cost a potential victor prestige and well over £1 million in endorsements and prize money. Of this, Montgomerie was uncomfortably aware. In the third round he was tormented by his driver – 'the straightest club in my bag for the past three years' – which led him astray on a number of holes, most notably the fifth and the seventh, where he escaped from the stranglehold of the rough on one side of the fairway only to descend into hell on the other, and yet he met these trials with as sunny a countenance as he could muster. The attainment of his most precious goal – a US Open victory, which would make him the first European since Tony Jacklin in 1970, and only the fourth foreigner since 1927 (the others being Gary Player, Jacklin and David Graham) to take the title, depended on a clear head.

It was a baking hot day. After five holes Montgomerie was soaked to the skin and his face, beneath the brim of his colonial lion-hunter's stetson, had turned a vivid fuchsia pink. 'Mr Blobby in Incredible Oakmont Melting Drama,' quipped Peter Higgs of the *Mail on Sunday*, who likes to talk in tabloid headlines. When the temperature soared above 95 and our clothes metamorphosed into sponges, we retreated to the media centre, where the American press were watching news flashes concerning O. J. Simpson, and the British were deaf to anything except the US football team's first game in the World Cup. Out on the course, Els had birdied the ninth to turn in 30, which equalled the US Open record. Later, when he scored 66 to move two strokes ahead of the New Zealander Frank Nobilo, on seven under par, he described his round as 'almost flawless. I don't know what happened on the tenth – I think I lost a bit of concentration – but then I regrouped and it was OK from then on.'

Third place was shared by Watson, Irwin, Loren Roberts and Montgomerie, whose 73 had included six bogeys, an eagle and two birdies. 'This is a tough course,' Watson said, admitting that Oakmont trod boldly on the perimeters of unfairness but managed not to overstep them. 'On this course, every green is a rejection green. They don't collect the ball. They make the ball go off the green, from the front to the back, from back to front, over the sides. It's a very penal course. To shoot the scores you have to shoot to win this tournament, you have to be at the top of your game.'

On Sunday, due to an irreversible booking error for which I had no-one to blame but myself, I watched the final round of the US Open on the television at Dulles airport in Washington. When the power-struggle between Montgomerie, Els and Roberts became almost too tense to bear, I clung white-knuckled to the counter in Skooters sportsbar and groaned out loud as Montgomerie, who had the advantage after nine holes, made three consecutive bogeys from the eleventh.

'I don't believe it,' I cried when Roberts took the lead with a birdie at 13, mistakenly imagining that the three foreigners beside me, who had been riveted to the screen for the past hour, would feel as strongly as I did that men who played dull, albeit effective, golf, whose faces never once cracked a smile in four days of US Open play, who described themselves as 'monotonous' and then cemented that impression by listing golf as their only interest in their Tour biography, should not be allowed to win major championships.

One of the trio leaned forward. 'What is this boring game?' he asked the barmaid.

'Golf,' she informed him.

'Gowf?' he queried.

My mouth dropped open. 'Where on earth can you be from that you have never heard of golf?' I asked, when I had recovered sufficiently to speak.

'Ve're from Germany,' he replied. 'Ve don't haf zis game in Germany.'

'Actually,' I said, 'you do. One of the best players in the world is German.'

He reeled back in his chair with an exaggerated air of surprise. 'Who is he?' he demanded.

'Bernhard Langer. He won the Masters last year.'

'Vell,' said Langer's compatriot, 'zey didn't write about it in Germany.'

It's moments like this that bring one down to earth. You travel around the world, glorifying golfers and golf tournaments, and all of a sudden you realize, relatively few people care. Fortunately for those of us who make our living from it, some of them do. Those luckless fools were trailing in the wake of Els, Roberts and Montgomerie, not to mention Watson, Curtis Strange and Nobilo, trying to guess which one of them would win the US Open and disappear.

According to Larry Dorman, Hale Irwin is the only US Open winner in the last ten years who hasn't won 73 per cent more tournaments before his victory than after it. Lee Janzen, the defending champion, made his first top-ten cheque since leaving Baltusrol a fortnight before teeing off at Oakmont, and then won the following week, beating Els into second place at the Buick Classic. 'At some point in the US Open I must have said to God, "If I make this putt, I won't ask to make another putt again," ' Janzen said. 'Because I haven't made a putt since.'

The same could not be said of Roberts, who had spread-eagled the field with a third-round 64. 'If my putter stays hot, anything can happen,' said the Californian ominously. Strange wasn't so sure. He had been paired with Els on Saturday. 'I think I've just played with the next God,' he said afterwards.

Montgomerie and Roberts were sitting in the television studio at five under par when Els arrived at the seventy-second tee. Roberts had missed a four-footer on the last to drop a stroke and tie Montgomerie. Needing only a par to win, Els sent his drive veering away into deep rough. Having hacked the ball out from behind the trees, he watched it bound cheerfully into a sandy divot, 100 yards from the hole. His approach barely made the putting surface and he two-putted from 40 feet.

Montgomerie was relieved, to say the least. 'I've been given a lifeline,' he admitted, 'and I've got to take advantage of it.'

Nobilo finished equal ninth and was desperately disappointed. 'The US Open is really a war of attrition,' he said. 'People talk about the British Open, but that's mainly the weather. At the US Open, the weather is perfect and it's a test of your whole game, which is good. There are four times a year when stroke averages count for nothing and this is one of them. I'd take 300 if it won me the US Open.'

In 1920, during the qualifying rounds at Inverness, Harry Vardon, then fifty, found himself paired with Bobby Jones, an eighteen-year-old amateur from Atlanta, who was studying for a degree in mechanical engineering at the Georgia School of Technology. The oldest and youngest in the field, they were also a pairing whose talent would not be matched until Hogan and Nicklaus played together in the final round of the US Open at Cherry Hills, forty years later. However, neither performed to the utmost of his ability. Vardon had strained his thumb *en route* to America during a pillow fight aboard the liner *Celtic*, and Jones did not have the experience to back up his shot-making skill and youthful enthusiasm. He was so nervous, in fact, that at one point he topped a ball into a bunker.

'Mr Vardon, did you ever see a shot worse than that?' asked Jones, embarrassed.

'No,' Vardon replied drily.

Vardon did not have the advantage of seeing the shots played by Montgomerie, Els and Roberts in the 1994 US Open play-off, any one of which would have put Jones's effort in the shade. Indeed, a couple of them would have shamed the average club golfer into giving up the game. But these were not, as one or two onlookers tried to say, signs of choking, or of men trying to give the trophy away. They were the inevitable consequence of playing one day too many on a course where the extreme brutality of the layout, combined with microwave temperatures, had already fried the brains of many better players than these three.

Nobilo felt that the heat was an important factor. 'In fairness, fitness came into it. I know Monty's been trying to get himself fitter, but still . . . And that was where Ernie was lucky. Ernie had the best start, because he played so badly that he had no choice but to settle down and play. The others then thought it was up to them and they just fell to pieces. But the course was so hard that it was really a question of hanging in there and eventually a victor would emerge.'

Els had begun by pulling his ball into deep rough on the first. He had erred identically on Sunday and been given a free drop because a TV tower was in his line of sight. This time the rule book did not rush to his aid. He put his approach in a bunker and opened with a bogey 5. At the next hole, he and Montgomerie drove into the right rough, while Roberts found the jungle on the left. Els then went into a bush and took a penalty drop, three-putting for an eventual triple-bogey. Monty, meanwhile, had landed on the bank of a bunker, duffed his chip and taken double-bogey. Roberts bogeyed. At the third, Els birdied from 30 feet. Montgomerie put his tee shot in the rough, three-putted and took double-bogey. All three men took bogeys at the eighth, and by the tenth hole Montgomerie was merely marking a card, having taken 42, six over par, to the turn. Els and Roberts had managed comparatively respectable 38s.

As golfing spectacles go, it was not one which might move a generation of youngsters to take up the game. 'It looked like a Saturday morning three ball with a fiver at stake rather than the blue riband of American golf with a total purse of $1.5 million,' observed Tim Glover. But this is where Els's temperament came into play. As a boy, he recalled that while his brother, also a good golfer, would become angry and fall apart when things were going badly, he himself would become ever more patient and determined. He did this now, clinging to his disintegrating golf game with all the fervour of a shipwreck survivor on a storm-tossed raft.

The American, by contrast, internalized everything. Years of hardship and thwarted ambition (after winning just $4,995 in 1985, he became a club pro once more and was finally ready for the Tour in 1990, aged thirty-five) had given him a stoical resolve, and the only evidence of the agony he was undergoing as he and Els tied at three over par – they had been five under after seventy-two holes – was his clenched jaw and suffering eyes. Montgomerie had shot 78, seven over par.

At that point, US television cut away to O. J. Simpson's indictment, and the British media had to phone home to find out what was happening in the sudden-death play-off. Els and Roberts proceeded down the tenth, a par four with a stroke average of 4.62, where Roberts holed a seven-footer for par to keep the match alive. But at the eleventh, his brave thirty-five footer hit the cup and horse-shoed out, and Els became, at twenty-four years and eight months, the youngest player to win a major since Ballesteros took the 1979 Open title at twenty-two years and three months.

In May, shortly before Els finished runner-up to Olazabal at the PGA Championship, he had considered the question of whether or not he was too young to handle the consequences of winning a major. 'Well,' he said, 'when Olazabal had a chance in 1991, some people said that he shouldn't win, that it would put pressure on him. And then three years down the road, they said: "When the hell is he going to win a major?" I would love to win a major any time. I would like to win the US Open next month. You know. Just for my own satisfaction. I know my whole life would change but, hey, that's what we're in this game for. I'll just have to deal with it.'

Els beamed engagingly. 'It'll soon blow over,' he said.

11

NOWHERE ROAD

'I only play one way. Grip it and rip it.'

JOHN DALY, 1992

With John Daly, it's the overall effect that wins you over. First, it's his atrocious rock star haircut, pale gold and sort of spiky on top and long and rat's tailish at the back, which David Feherty said made him look as if he had a divot over each ear. Then it's his Southern drawl and his cries from the heart, and his boyish desire to please and to be loved. Later, you might be captivated by his large, meaty hands, cigarette smoke floating up from their stubby fingers, which are as capable of whaling a drive 300 yards as they are of hitting a delicate chip to the holeside. But it's not until last that you notice his eyes, possibly because they're small, coloured the palest grey-blue and sunk deep into his fleshy face: fish eyes, dead eyes, the eyes of a hunter.

Right now they were staring stonily out at the Scottish Open media. Every other fibre of Daly's being evinced an earnest desire to do only what was best for golf and for his fellow man, but his eyes stayed flat and hard. 'I'm fed up with taking the rap for being golf's bad guy,' he was saying. 'I want people to know that I'm not the only guy to have suffered from an addiction. OK, I don't actually know of anyone taking stuff but I've heard rumours. Everyone has.'

Beside him, Peter Jacobsen nodded agreement. 'Statistics prove there are guys on cocaine in all slices of life,' he said sagely.

The previous day, Daly had sparked a near riot when he

announced to Ben Bacon of the *Sun* that: 'There are certain people on the Tour who do the crazy stuff – drugs, cocaine, some of the other crazy things. I wish we could have drug-testing on the Tour. If we did, I'd probably be one of the cleanest guys out there.'

What irritated him most, it appeared, was the constant peddling of golf's whiter than white image by the US Tour hierarchy. 'I was hurt when I went to rehab and people said John Daly was the only PGA player to do that,' he said at Gleneagles. 'That's so out of whack. There are a lot of guys who have gone to rehab. I'm not scared to talk about problems. In rehab, I learned that if you don't express your feelings, it's going to catch up with you and you'll do something stupid. The people on the Tour who do the crazy stuff are never going to be caught unless they are put in jail. If you're going to test everybody, athletes in the NBA, footballers for steroids and stuff, test the golfers. Let it come out. I think it's unfair that a lot of this stuff has been hidden. I don't think that testing will ever be introduced because golfers are meant to be so right, so on track.'

When Daly spoke next to the press, he was accompanied by Jacobsen, a US Tour player of eighteen years' standing. It was hard to know why. Was Jacobsen there: (a) as a chaperon/child minder, (b) as an authority on substance-abuse, (c) to lend credence to Daly's allegations, or (d) to promote his new book *Buried Lies*?

'I've never even heard rumours but maybe it is time to have drug-testing . . .' was Jacobsen's lame contribution. 'While I was on the board, drug-testing was discussed but we didn't introduce it because it was felt that if somebody had a problem they were probably not doing too well. They are certainly not on the leader-boards.'

Faced with the realization that he may have irresponsibly opened a terrible can of worms, Daly said he didn't in fact know of a single professional golfer on drugs, recreational or otherwise. 'But when you've got 156 people teeing it up, there must be some of them not clean,' he said defensively. 'In basketball there are only ten players in a quarter, and they seem to have huge problems.'

To prove that his heart was in the right place, he then offered his services as counsellor to any golfer with a similar 'problem', concluding: 'I just hope the US Tour take my comments the way they are meant because I don't want any more trouble. I'm not trying to give golf a bad image.'

*　　*　　*

In sport, the compulsion is always to search for precedents. The barest glimpse of new talent is met with a rush of hype and nostalgia, and time and time again humdrum rookies are labelled the next best thing – the most charismatic player since Palmer, the most innovative shot-maker since Ballesteros, the most diligent practiser since Hogan, or the most colourful performer since Hagen – usually with disastrous effects.

There was no precedent for John Daly. Daly came out of nowhere, a bolt from the blue, a rough diamond who embodied his Arkansas roots. His whole demeanour spoke of trailer parks and one-horse towns; of barefoot children with suspicious eyes; of careworn housewives with broken dreams and men with shirts stretched too tight across their bellies; of Southern fried chicken and Dr Pepper cans; of tornadoes and corroded pick-up trucks; and of rebellious youths with no job prospects, who played golf in jeans for escapism. 'My wound is geography,' the protagonist said in Pat Conroy's *The Prince of Tides*. 'It is also my anchorage, my port of call.'

Daly's port of call was Dardanelle, on the Arkansas river, a middle-class town to the north of Little Rock (population 3,621). The son of an itinerant nuclear engineer, he had moved five times by the time he was eighteen, and had spent most of his last few years at high school living alone with his brother while his parents worked in Kansas. 'We were a close family in a kind of faraway way,' John recalled. Though not much of an athlete himself, his father loved sport. When John was seven, Jim Daly gave him a full set of adult Jack Nicklaus MacGregor irons. Away from the silent house, where Jim spent his days sleeping off night shifts, John would while away the hours fishing balls out of ponds and then straining to hit the water-logged balls as far as they would go. Golf was something that could be done alone, something that didn't require fitting in. Like drinking, as a matter of fact. At ten, John had tried his first beer. At twelve, he sampled his parents' homemade wine, but never acquired a taste for it. Jim enjoyed Jack Daniels. Soon John enjoyed it, too. From then on, 'It was always, let's see what Dad has in the cupboard,' he told *Sports Illustrated*.

When he wasn't checking out the contents of the liquor cabinet, John and his father played baseball and football together, and practised for Punt, Pass and Kick competitions, at which he was a natural.

'I don't know where John got this need to win,' Jim Daly told

Michael Bamberger in an interview for *Digest.* 'He's the only one in the family who has it. As far as I know, I only gave him one piece of valuable advice. When we were in these Punt, Pass and Kick competitions, I would always say to him, "Remember, this is your only chance to make this kick. It's now or never." I think that helped him to try his hardest on every shot when he turned to golf. But it also made him lose his temper on bad shots, because he wanted every shot to be perfect. He's still learning that you can hit a bad shot and not have it ruin your entire round. He snapped some clubs as a kid.'

'I can't say that he had a temper,' Lou Daly said. 'He was stubborn, and he still is stubborn. If you would tell John to do something he would rebel. But if you asked him, he would respond. If you use reverse psychology on him, it will work.'

Reverse psychology was, unfortunately, an alien concept to Steve Loy, Daly's new golf coach at the University of Arkansas. Loy looked at Daly and saw a pudgy, immature nonconformist, with bags of raw talent and not an ounce of discipline to go with it. Loy was not from the Robin Williams school of teaching. He didn't believe in the power of individuality. He believed in pounding the creative rough edges out of his boys as if he were sanding down tables, and moulding them into responsible athletes. He set to work on Daly with a vengeance. Daly weighed 230 lbs; Loy wanted to grind him down to 170. It was an impossible demand. But Daly wanted to play golf more than he wanted to eat, so he went on a diet of Jack Daniels, Diet Coke, black coffee and Marlboros. The weight poured off him. He lost 40 lbs in three months. Loy rode him even harder. Daly said nothing, channelling his hatred inward. If he qualified for an away match on merit, Loy would lead him back to the first tee and tell him: 'If you hit this in the rough, you're not going.' Defiant, Daly would deliberately hit it there and cost himself a field trip.

'John is tenacious in everything he does, and as a result he sometimes went to extremes in areas where he shouldn't have,' said Loy; who eventually had to force Daly to start eating again. 'The other thing to remember about John is that he's instinctively gracious. He just wants to please people, and be the life of the party, and that makes it difficult to say no, especially when you're away from home for the first time and everybody wants to be your friend.'

At twenty-one, Daly married Dale Crafton, daughter of one of the best families in Blytheville, Arkansas, at a lavish society wedding. Daly was uncomfortable, he felt out of place. When Dale's grandparents gave the newly-weds a house to live in, Daly said it made him feel 'like a cheap person'. He didn't want anybody giving him anything. 'I did it to please her. I wanted to make her happy,' he said when the marriage ended two years later. As usual, his own happiness was way down his list of priorities.

In spite of the turmoil at home, Daly's golf continued to improve. Two victories on the South African Tour had given him confidence, and in 1990 he won the Utah Classic on the Hogan Tour and finished ninth on the money list with nearly $65,000. That was the year he slipped into a coma, having drunk himself almost to death. His friends were distraught, anxious. Daly's friends were always friends for life; they loved him for his softness and his big heart. Long before he made any money at all, Daly's generosity was a matter of lore on the Hogan Tour. If Daly had $20 in the world, everyone knew he would give away $19. He was forever trying to reach out, to stop others from hurting, forever burdening himself with other people's concerns. And all the while his own problems were being shoved deeper and deeper inside.

The day he received the phone call that changed his life, Daly was a rookie on the US Tour, known to the players who had seen him send balls into orbit off the practice tee but not to anyone else. In a now legendary sequence of events, Daly, ninth alternate for the 1991 US PGA Championship, climbed into the BMW he had bought his fiancée at 5.00 p.m. on the eve of the tournament, and began the long drive down from Memphis to Carmel, Indianapolis. Meanwhile, the wheels of destiny clicked and ground like a giant watch mechanism. Players had already dropped out for a multitude of reasons – mother-in-laws, injuries, Nick Price's wife's baby – and when last he had talked to Ken Anderson of the PGA staff, he was first alternate. In his hotel room in Indianapolis, the message light was blinking. Daly knew that there was a good chance he was only going to be watching his friend Fuzzy Zoeller play golf. He picked up the phone. He was teeing off at 1.58 p.m. the next afternoon with Billy Andrade and Bob Lohr. On Thursday, Daly went out without a practice round on a course Jack Nicklaus had described as the hardest he had ever seen, and returned with a 69. In the second round, he took the lead with a 67. Golf watchers smiled on him indulgently, waiting for him to collapse and let the real winner come through. But Daly refused to go away, shooting a 69 in the third round.

On the final day, a tidal wave of thousands flowed through the gates of Crooked Stick to witness the phenomenon first hand – the earth-shaking drives, the flowing blond mane, the Popeye forearms, capable of playing whisper-soft chips and putts. Daly was in his element. He reacted to their presence like a seasoned showman. There was no nerves, no arrogance, no introspection. He didn't, as his playing partner Kenny Knox observed, conduct himself like any other major champion. And every time his great mitt reached out and clasped the warm hands of the gallery during his hurricane passage along each hole, he bonded himself to their hearts, brought them into his world and made them part of his miracle. The spirit of the game flowed down the fairways. The white ball flattened itself against his clubhead and leapt for the blue. The crowd responded with gut-wrenching roars, and in their excitement Kenny Knox was forgotten, knocked about and tossed to one side, like an unwanted rag doll. It wasn't his day, it wasn't his hour, it wasn't his moment in history. And when it all reached its glorious, and somehow inevitable, conclusion, Daly's fiancée Bettye Fulford completed the picture by bursting from the gallery and flinging her arms around him.

Thus did we witness the unfolding of the American dream. He lived it and he shared it, and he touched us in a way that could not be compared to anyone who had gone before him – not Hagen, not Palmer, not Ballesteros – but was Daly's alone, and was so rare and wonderful that nothing and no-one – not us nor the game – would ever be the same again.

By 1994, the fairytale had turned to dross. Once, Fred Couples had warned Daly that if he wasn't careful he'd wind up becoming a circus sideshow, and that, in effect, is what had happened. Not right away, of course. The magic didn't end at Crooked Stick. Upon receiving his $230,000 victory cheque at Crooked Stick, Daly had announced he would be donating $30,000 of it to set up a scholarship fund to ensure the education of the two daughters of the man killed by lightning that week, and $20,000 to the junior golf fund run by an old Hogan Tour friend of his – thereby earning the adoration of the few remaining people he had not already won over.

For he had become an instant folk hero. In the space of one week

Daly was the kind of household name that Greg Norman only dreams about, his appeal crossing the boundaries of sport, nationality and class. 'I just play for the fans,' was his favourite line, and he meant it. He was down-to-earth, he was sincere and he hadn't forgotten – unlike Faldo et al. – that golf is, first and foremost, entertainment. 'Daly doesn't ignore us,' fans said. 'He makes us feel like we're part of his success.' More importantly, Daly could hit his Killer Whale driver 'further than most of us go on vacation in poor economic times', to quote Nick Seitz. He also hit his three-iron 240 yards, his five-iron 210 yards and his nine-iron 165. These qualities saw that Daly created the biggest commercial storm since Arnold Palmer first hitched up his trousers. Under the guidance of his agents Bud Martin and John Muscatello of Cambridge Sports International he signed a five-year deal with Wilson and a three-year deal with Reebok, which, along with several other endorsements, guaranteed to make him at least $10 million before 1996. That's if he did nothing. If he won more majors, they'd be talking in telephone numbers.

'I'm not going to become a jerk,' Daly said firmly when those around him wondered whether it might all go to his head. 'If I become a jerk, I'll quit golf.'

It was put to him that Elvis had once said that the worst thing that ever happened to him was when all his dreams came true. 'Well, you're right about Elvis,' Daly replied, 'but all my dreams haven't come true yet. In fact, I've only achieved two of them – I got on Tour and I won a major . . . For me, to win the Masters would be amazing but I suppose that for any pro golfer, to win all four majors is the ultimate dream.'

By 1992, persistent rumours about Daly's drinking, gambling and relationship troubles had begun to surface. In between skirting questions about his private life, he whiled away the season demonstrating his Richter-scale-registering drives on *Late Night with David Letterman*, playing golf with Bob Hope, Gerald Ford and Dan Quayle – briefly – before missing the cut in Hope's tournament, and taking 80 at the Players Championship after shooting round the course in two hours with Mark Calcavecchia.

At the centre of it all was his relationship with Bettye Fulford, a hotel executive from Macon, Georgia, whom he had met in the spring of 1990. At Crooked Stick, Daly had introduced her as a twenty-nine-year-old divorcée with no children. They had originally planned to marry in Las Vegas two months after his US PGA victory, but postponed the wedding because of the furore surrounding it. By Christmas, they had broken up. It emerged that Bettye was ten years older than Daly believed, still married and had a child. 'It's hard to believe that anybody could be that crooked or that mean,' he told *USA Today* in January. 'Here I go with this girl for a year and a half, and I don't know how old she is or that she has a kid.' Bettye responded to being jilted with a palimony and paternity suit against her former fiancée. Papers were served to Daly during a practice round at the Masters in April. Daly told reporters that if the child was his he would fight for custody, because 'I don't feel Bettye is capable of caring for it.'

On 8 May, Daly and Bettye were married in Dardanelle. Bettye was eight months pregnant. 'I think it's going to be good for me,' Daly said at the US PGA in August. 'It's going to be good for Bettye, too. Hopefully we can live the rest of our lives together.'

After he had broken a lean spell on the course by winning the BC Open by six shots, Daly, attending a post-victory press conference, called to the back of the room: 'Bettye, you walk all eighteen today?'

'Yes, I did,' Bettye said proudly.

'Amazing,' said the press officer, eyeing the nine months and two days pregnant Bettye with new respect.

'She's a die-hard fan, I guess,' Daly said. 'Not too many pregnant ladies who are about to go into labour would be walking out here. She's a trooper.'

On the surface, Daly worked ever harder to maintain a semblance of normality. It emerged that he had twice demolished hotel rooms and been thrown off a Continental Airlines flight for being drunk and disorderly. 'I'm just fed up with the American press going by what other people say without bothering to find out from me what the real facts are, or at least what my version of the story is,' Daly told *Today's Golfer*. 'That aeroplane incident, for example. The papers [quoted] a Buick official who said that Daly was drunk and had to be thrown off the plane. The truth is I left on my own because the stewardess was so bad. Continental never said anything about me being drunk; I just got off the plane . . . The hotel scene stems from an incident in 1989 before I ever got on the Tour. I trashed a hotel in South Africa and it's the only one I ever trashed.'

He didn't add that that was the day his first divorce came through, that he had fractured his little finger breaking furniture, and that he still managed to shoot twenty-one under par and win the tournament. When the US commentator Brent Musburger raised the issue of Jamaica in 1992, where Daly was said to have wrecked an exclusive Tryall bungalow after being disqualified from the World Championship for signing for a wrong score (he would have recorded an 86), Daly said: 'I stayed in a house with my agent in Jamaica, I wasn't even in a hotel, so how can you accuse me of trashing a hotel when I didn't even stay in one.' As an exercise in semantics, it was exemplary.

'I figure that what I did in college and when I was seventeen, eighteen, nineteen years old is just following me around,' Daly complained. 'I don't deny that I was partying, having fun and enjoying my life, and that's the only reason this reputation for drinking came up. But to listen to some people or read the papers, you would think I was a permanent drunk with a major problem. But I don't think I have a problem with drink or the way I lead my life.'

Away from the limelight, Daly had gone completely off the rails. After one sustained drinking bout, from 5.00 p.m. to 4.00 a.m., his bar bill came to $1,200. He drank an average of sixteen beers a day, laced with one or two whiskies. Tanked up with Jack Daniels, he drove through seventeen straight traffic lights without slowing down. Another time, furious with himself after a poor round, he shot across a busy intersection with his eyes staring blankly ahead and his foot flat on the accelerator. Bettye and their new baby Shynah Hale were in the car. 'If that's not depressed,' Bettye said to Rick Reilly, 'what is?' Daly had only just come out of hospital when he won the BC Open at Kemper, where a nurse told him she had never seen a 27 blood-alcohol count before.

'Seems I used to do everything like I was on a mission,' Daly told Reilly. 'If it was alcohol, I wanted to drink until I couldn't see straight. If it was golf, I wanted to beat everybody's brains out. If it was driving, I can get there faster'n you can. It's not anybody's fault, I guess. I was stubborn as hell, I had no direction.'

No, just a one-way ticket to hell. In an effort to escape the influences and pressures of the city, Bettye and Daly moved to the relative solitude of Castle Pines Golf Club in Castle Rock, Colorado. On 19 December 1992, Daly invited Dan Hampton, the former lineman of the Chicago Bears, his girlfriend Julie, his brother Jamie, and a couple of other friends over to the house. That evening, Bettye accused Julie of trying to 'hit on' Daly. Daly went ballistic. According to police reports, he pushed Bettye against the wall and pulled her hair before smashing a television set, a picture, several trophy cases and punching a hole in the wall. Bettye and Shynah hid in the closet. Someone called the police. By the time they arrived, Daly had driven halfway to Arkansas in an attempt to calm down. He had one final drink at Hooters restaurant in Little Rock on 21 December 1992, then drove back to Colorado where he pleaded innocent to misdemeanour charges of battery and harassment. Deane Beman telephoned him and said that if he didn't check himself into an alcohol rehabilitation centre, he would probably be suspended. Daly signed on for a four-month at a treatment centre in Tucson. He also plea-bargained to a charge of misdemeanour harassment and accepted a two-year probation. Then he and Bettye moved back to Orlando, where the weather would allow him to spend more time in the sunshine, practising his golf.

In 1993, a new, clean-living (relatively-speaking) Daly came out to play. 'John Daly whooshed through a Tucson treatment centre like a roadrunner through a car wash, emerging sober, sobered and afraid,' reported Tom Callahan. ' "I didn't know what was going to happen," he said the evening of his first day back in the mythologically correct town of Phoenix. "I was just going to come out here and play golf, and whatever happened, happened. Thank God it was great. It's been great support." '

If Daly was pleased to be back in the fray, his fans matched his enthusiasm tenfold; an extra 30,000 came through the gate if he was in the field. For a while, he did not disappoint. He continued to drive the golf ball further than anyone else on earth – becoming the first player in US Open history to reach the 630-yard, par five seventeenth at Baltusrol in two. He finished third at the Masters and thirty-third and fourteenth at the US and British Opens. And he signed as many programmes, balls and visors as is possible for a man who still has to sleep, play golf and satisfy nicotine, caffeine and sugar cravings requiring four packs of Marlboros, a pint of chocolate yoghurt, sixteen Diet Cokes and bucket-loads of peanut M&Ms. At one tournament, he ate six bags in a hole and a half. If you are what you eat, what does that make Daly? Sweet as sugar or rotten to the core?

It was these extremeties as much as anything that showed that inside Daly was in turmoil. His marriage – perhaps inevitably – had self-destructed; his golf game was in disarray; and he was struggling to come to terms with the magnitude of his success and popularity. The first outward manifestation of just how close he was to the brink came at an exhibition at Portland, Oregon in August. Daly drove a ball so low over the heads of the spectators ringing the eighteenth green that he almost parted their hair. 'I did it for fun,' he said later, 'and then Deane Beman said, "You could have killed somebody." I said: "I didn't look at it that way. I wasn't trying to hurt anybody." ' Except himself. In October, Daly walked out of the Southern Open during the second round, going straight from the ninth green to the car-park. Then at the Kapalua International in December, he four-putted the tenth, missed a birdie putt at the eleventh and picked up his ball, just hours after Trevino had tried counselling him about his attitude.

'I had a talk to him and tried to explain that all the things he was doing were wrong, but I wasted my breath,' said Trevino, who has known Daly ten years. 'I acknowledge he is a breath of fresh air, but the game can do without him. He has to remember that people will get turned off by his behaviour and then he'll have problems with all his contracts. He is a spontaneous individual who does things on the spur of the moment, but I'm not sure that a suspension will straighten him out.'

'Daly has just pushed it to the limits,' Payne Stewart said. 'He has been very fortunate because of the game of golf, but he has to learn to be proud of being a professional and act like one. What he is continuing to do is to give a bad example to kids. If they see John Daly picking his ball up because he's playing badly, they'll think they can do just the same.'

Beman lost patience. He suspended Daly again, this time for four months. 'I'm just going to basically say there was no 1993,' Daly said.

In March, Wild Thing was back again, full of resolutions. He was going to reduce the number of outings he did from twenty to six or eight, he was going to get involved in a course design project with his good friend Fuzzy Zoeller, and, assisted by the sports psychologist Bob Rotella, he was going to do his best to stay focused on every shot. 'You can't worry about what other people are thinking,' he said. 'You can't please everybody. It's time to start taking care of me. I'm going to do the things that John Daly wants to do. I'm going to live where I want to live, play where I want to play.'

Even the ninety-two-year-old Gene Sarazen was impressed. 'I'm delighted that John Daly is coming back into the fold,' he said. 'It reminds me of when the Yankees played in the 20s and 30s and if Babe Ruth wasn't in the line-up, there was hardly anybody in the crowd. Now comes the Babe Ruth of golf, John Daly. They don't care what he shoots as long as they can watch him play.'

At the Players Championship a fortnight later, Zoeller talked about his relationship with Daly and why he wanted to do anything in his power to help him. He had particularly encouraged Daly's interest in guitar.

'I've heard him play two chords. I think that's all he knows,' Zoeller said with a shout of laughter. 'He's not going to be a rock star any time soon. I played with Eddie Van Halen, President Ford and Bob Hope at the Bob Hope Classic, and that night Eddie came over to the house – I was staying with John, he's got a condo in Palm Springs – and there was a big difference. John picked the guitar up and went bling, bling, bling and then Eddie picked it up and he made it talk. I think Eddie put it in perspective. He said, "John, my guitar playing and your guitar playing are kinda like my golf and your golf. But I'm a better golfer than you are a guitarist." But it's a good pastime for him. He's never had one before.'

He considered the question of whether or not there were similarities between Daly and a young Norman, in terms of public appeal. 'Completely different,' Zoeller said, shaking his head. 'John is a very outgoing young man, and Greg Norman has never been that way. He's always been kind of into himself, and the blond hair and the hats and the clothing he wears kind of made him what he is with his golf game . . . John's very genuine . . . He's one of those you'd want to sit across from at the dinner table because he is such a fine human being. He's a very good kid, doesn't have a bad bone in his body. I mean, he's made a couple of mistakes out here, but hell, who hasn't.'

That had been in March. Now we were at the Scottish Open in the first week of July and Daly had made yet another mistake. He had frankly, if thoughtlessly, suggested that one or two golfers took cocaine. Strange was so disgusted that he told Daly to crawl back under the rock he came from. 'He doesn't realize that it doesn't take much to tear down what it took Arnold Palmer and Jack Nicklaus and others around thirty-five years to build.'

In between, there had been some wonderful moments. He had holed a five-foot birdie putt to finish on 274, fourteen under par, and win the Atlanta Classic by a stroke. 'It's the first tournament I've won on the Tour in a sober manner, so it's a great feeling knowing I can do it sober,' Daly said. 'I don't think two years ago I could have pulled this off.' Having spent the previous day in an Orlando court hearing to decide the visitation rights of Shynah Hale, he dedicated the tournament to his two-year-old daughter. At the Irish Open, he called his mother to say that he had forgotten to buy her a birthday present, but he was two days sober. 'She said that that was the best present she could have,' Daly smiled, adding that she had cried herself to sleep every night while he was in the treatment centre drying out.

But he had been let down by his wild streak, his appetite for destruction – the same one that once made him, when a policeman stopped him and said sternly, 'Sir, you've been drinking a little,' respond with a malevolent grin: 'No, sir, I've been drinking a *lot*!'

Inside, Daly is soft as butter; outside, he may forever teeter on the brink of death and despair.

'Don't hate me,' he says quietly.

12

VARDON'S LEGACY

'I am waiting for the day when everything falls into place, everything makes sense, when every swing is with confidence and every shot is exactly what I want. I know it can be done. I've been close enough to smell it a couple of times, but I'd like to touch it, to feel it. I know it's been touched. Hogan touched it. Byron Nelson touched it. I want to touch it. Then I think I would be satisfied. Then, I think, I could walk away from the game.'

TOM WATSON

History was blowing in off the links, clean and sweet. You could feel it, you could taste it, you could hear its heavy tread. Across the sparkling bay, Ailsa Craig waited, brooding, monolithic, enigmatic. Gannets wheeled about her dark silhouette and tipped towards the red barn standing guard over the sienna loam on the distant hill, or the white yachts straddling the striped depths of the Firth of Clyde, or the remote bulk of the Turnberry Hotel, as pristine as a plaster of Paris model. The smell of cut grass and kelp was carried on sharp-scented gusts of wind. Out by the famous lighthouse, the only sounds were the rustle of brambles, the swish of waves and the cries of the seagulls making spiky footprints in the pale mulberry sand.

In 1977, Jack Nicklaus and Tom Watson locked swords on Turnberry's salt-splashed first fairway and began an electric duel for the Bear's miraculous crown. In what justly became known as the greatest display of shot-making in the history of the game, they matched each other blow for blow – successive rounds of 68,70 and 65 finally tying them on three under par as they putted for birdies on the seventeenth green. When Nicklaus missed from five feet, Watson tapped in to take the lead for the first time. Then, at the last, Watson, freckle-faced and eager, pushed his cap back and played a seven-iron to 18 inches. Unbowed, Nicklaus played a majestic recovery to the edge of the green and holed a 30-foot putt for a birdie, but Watson's 65 gave him victory by a stroke. In the aftermath, Hubert Green, who finished a distant 11 strokes behind Watson, declared that he had won the Open. 'Those two were playing some other game,' he said.

Since the only storm created that year was man-made, Dan Jenkins drew the conclusion that without the hurricane-force 120 mph winds that had reduced the tented village to kindling at the John Player Classic in 1973 (Charles Coody won with a score of nine over par), Turnberry was no great test. 'Under normal conditions, Turnberry is a pushover, not up to championship calibre,' Jenkins wrote, 'which is a truth that was first suggested in 1977 when Watson shot the dirt off the place and broke so many records the sheep even looked up from their grassy hills.'

As if in revenge, Turnberry revealed her true colours in 1986. Witch-like, she whipped up an evil brew of gales and merciless rough. Greg Norman was of the opinion that there should be a law against such conditions. 'I think you should always be able to advance the ball in the rough, but you can't here,' he moaned. 'So what happens if someone breaks a wrist trying to hack the ball out? Would they have a case against the R&A?' Craig Stadler nearly provided a test-case. 'I damn near broke my wrist and I doubt whether I moved the ball an inch,' the Walrus grumbled after pulling a couple of tendons. Even Nicklaus thought the challenge was excessive. 'Did anyone hit the fairway at the ninth?' he asked. '*Is* there a fairway at the ninth?'

On Friday, the wind had dropped to a stiff, swirling breeze, and Norman went round in 63, three-putting the last from 28 feet to miss out on an unprecedented 61. After that, he was like a runaway train, and all the weather in the world could not prevent him from winning the championship by five strokes. Phillip Mackenzie Ross, the Scottish golf architect, would not have been pleased. A man after Henry Fownes's own heart, he liked to tell golfers: 'If you want dull fishing, fish for cod. If you want exciting fishing, go for salmon. My Turnberry is a salmon.'

At Turnberry, Robinson stayed in a trailer park with Graham Spiers. 'White trash hell,' she joked. The *Sunday Times* team were residing in the relative luxury of a farm cottage belonging to an aristocratic artist. A member of Turnberry, he referred to the club as 'an island of privilege' or 'the Savoy moved to Scotland'.

Sam Torrance appreciated his sentiments. He was refused a cup of coffee in the lounge reserved exclusively for past major champions, and Montgomerie was also turned away. 'There is just not enough room for 156 competitors,' Michael Bonallack, secretary of the R&A, explained, adding, 'There is a marquee alongside the clubhouse for players and their wives.' This kept the tabloids busy. 'CUP HEROES BANNED' reported the *Scottish Daily Sport*, making one look around for a third party.

They did a follow-up later in the week when Mark Calcavecchia, who proved that the Shark really is the unluckiest golfer in the world when he won the 1989 Open in a play-off, whined to the *Star* about his £1,000-plus-a-day bill at Turnberry Hotel. 'You have to feel like you're getting ripped off – which you are. They're taking you to the cleaners in there. You go and eat a nice dinner and it costs you £100. When you're charged that kind of dough, the food doesn't taste so good. All the time you're thinking, "One bite of duck has just cost me £7." '

One was left to wonder why the cringe-making Mr Calcavecchia, who has won over £3 million on the US circuit and has two houses – one worth £2 million in Phoenix – and seven cars, wasn't staying in a bed and breakfast. Better still, why wasn't he at home in the United States? 'Basically, unless you're winning this tournament, you're not getting anything out of it,' Calcavecchia concluded. No lightning bolt struck him down.

It is at times like these that one offers up prayers of thanks for players like Tom Watson, who epitomizes all that is truly great about golf: the tradition, the values, the etiquette. On the practice day, he and Nicklaus had taken on Norman and Price over the bright, breezy links. 'Who do you think is winning?' Watson called to gallery, his face alive with happiness. It was eleven years since he won his last Open but he knew he was playing well enough to attempt to equal Harry Vardon's magnificent record of six Open titles.

'You, Tom,' shouted a fan.

'Experience is winning,' Watson grinned.

He and Nicklaus reminisced about their Duel in the Sun. 'We talked about my putt on 15,' Watson recalled. 'He said: "Do you remember when you walked off the green, I said: 'You little son of a bitch!' " I said: "No, you told me that at the US Open." '

The first round of the Open belongs to the underdogs, almost by a special arrangement. It is a day for dreamers, for underachievers, for rookies, journeymen and precocious rising stars. In 1981, the little known Nick Job topped the leaderboard, his opening 70 at Royal St Georges matched only by Vicente Fernandez. Afterwards, thrilled and incredulous, he played down the round as 'a total shock'. But the pressure terrified him. He held on to tie for fourteenth place, but his days on the Tour were numbered. Respected, even revered, as a striker of the ball, he became a nervous wreck on the links. Medication didn't help; neither did *The Power of Positive Thinking*. 'I quite enjoyed it until I discovered the author committed suicide,' Job, now a club pro, said.

Bill Longmuir had more than one bite at the Open cherry. In 1979, he opened with a 65 and struggled to a share of thirty-first place, and in 1984, he shot a first-round 67 to share the lead with Norman and Peter Jacobsen. He ended tied for fifty-fifth place. The next year, Ballesteros, the winner on both occasions, came up to him and offered to give him a lesson before the Open. 'If I see your name on the leaderboard, I know I'm going to win the tournament!' the Spaniard beamed.

'Yeah,' thought Longmuir with a grimace, 'but what about me?'

At Turnberry, the fifteen-minute spotlight shone on New Zealand's Greg Turner, who took a one-stroke lead over Jonathan Lomas with a five under par 65, after eagling the seventh and holing a two-iron from 178 yards for another eagle on 16. Behind them, came Andrew Magee on 67, with his compatriots Watson, Loren Roberts and Daly among those in fourth place. Price and Els were on 69.

Lomas, a twenty-six-year-old chicken farmer's son from Chester-field, had never even qualified for the Open before. He sat on the podium in a state of rapture, with all the world's press at his feet, and cast his mind back to Lytham in 1979 when Ballesteros's fiery brilliance had enslaved him to the game. But it had been a long and brutal haul. He had been to the Qualifying School four times and had slept in his car as he travelled to events on the Challenge circuit. Lomas's face lit up. Those days were gone. In the 1994 season, he had already won $125,000 with four top-ten finishes, and now he had shot 66 on what was rapidly degenerating into a fiend of a day. Asked what had kept him going during the rough times, he said he had been inspired by the example of Ian Woosnam. (By an unhappy coincidence, the Welshman had shot 79 in the first round at Turnberry.) 'I knew Ian had been through what I had, so it was possible,' Lomas said. 'It was just a question of believing in myself and never giving in.'

Out on the wild links, Colin Montgomerie was trying his best not to give up on his new motto: to be sweetness and light on the golf course as well as off it. Recent Montgomerie press conferences had been like confessionals, filled with purgings of his soul. Yes, he would say regretfully, I know I cursed that toddler, glared at that photographer and was a trifle upset after three-putting the sixth, but I'm really sorry, I didn't mean it and I vow I won't do it again. Which, of course, we believed, because he really didn't mean it and he really was trying not to do it again. But now his new leaf was being fire-tested by the golfing gods at Turnberry. All manner of things were sent to try him – clumsy scoreboard operators, whirring cameras and, horror of horrors, a man with a mobile phone – and still Montgomerie managed to maintain a semblance of calm. He looked on longingly as Gordon Brand Jnr, his playing partner, demolished a whin bush when he put his ball in the rough, but he restricted himself to a mild, 'You silly twit,' as his own approach shot came up short. At the sixteenth, where he shanked a six-iron into the Wee Burn – an occasion which might previously have called for the instant decapitation of every toy in the cot – Montgomerie said, like granny dropping a stitch in her knitting: 'Hopeless.' He then hit a beautiful 70-yard wedge shot straight into the hole, sighing as it bounced out to two inches.

Of course, when he walked off the eighteenth, he was simmering like a volcano only seconds away from erupting. His escape route was cut off by a posse of reporters.

'Well, Colin,' said Ken Lawrence of the *Mirror*, 'you've shot 72. Is there a way back?'

Montgomerie tensed. He looked skywards. He made a valiant but fairly brief effort to control himself, and then he became apoplectic.

'IS THERE A WAY BACK?' he screamed. 'WHAT DO YOU MEAN "A WAY BACK"? Only four people have ever broken par on this course. I shot 72 not 82.' And with that, he turned on his heel and stalked off, leaving the *Daily Record* to report gleefully: 'The reformed Monty lasted only 293 minutes.'

As Peter Higgs says, you can say what you like about the Beastie Boys (tabloid reporters), but they are past masters of the art of the guileless question which provokes the exact response they're looking for. Of course Lawrence knew that a 72 in the first round was a perfectly respectable score in the conditions. He was merely testing Montgomerie for reaction. It's like the old guilty by denial ploy. If one asks a palace insider whether it is true that the Queen spends every evening sitting before the television, with her crown on her head, bifocals on her nose and a corgi at each knee, watching *Neighbours*, and he replies, 'That's the most preposterous notion I've ever heard in my life,' one is then free to go away and write: 'A royal spokesman yesterday denied that the Queen spends every evening alone in front of the TV with only her corgis for company, wearing her crown and watching *Neighbours*.' And a large percentage of readers will be convinced that the head of the royal household does exactly that.

No elaborate tactics were needed to elicit a story from Nick Faldo. He managed it all on his own. When mist obscured the island of Arran and icy needles of rain slanted across the fairways, both Faldo and his playing partner, the American Jim McGovern, drove into the rough on the seventeenth. This in itself was not a crisis. Faldo wasn't firing on all cylinders but he was hanging on to a two-over-par score. He marched quickly to the spot where he thought his ball was located. 'I assumed it was my ball because there was no-one on the hill where my ball actually was,' Faldo said later. 'Usually when I hit a shot there are people gathered round.'

The arrogance of this statement struck many listeners as quite extraordinary. It was as though the gallery wouldn't dream of gathering round anyone's ball but Faldo's. 'A guy – I don't know whether he was a spotter – looked at me as if it was mine,' Faldo continued. 'It seemed to make sense.' He admitted that all he could see was white. The rules allow a player to lift a ball to identify it, but Faldo chose not to. He hacked it out just as his own ball came to light 20 yards away.

He was penalized two strokes, pulled his fifth shot into the rough some 135 yards from the green, hit his sixth to 10 feet and missed the putt. A triple-bogey eight left him with a 75 at the end of the day, his worst start in the Open since 1981. 'Not very clever,' Faldo, who had made the identical mistake in practice, said dejectedly. He knew the tabloids would have a field day. But hard as his critics were on him, he was a million times harder on himself – not only because he's the most meticulous man in golf, but because it had been a bad year for him in the events he loves more than life itself: he had finished thirty-second at the Masters, missed the cut in the US Open, and he was in danger of going home before the weekend here.

The caddies laid the blame squarely at the door of Fanny Sunesson, Faldo's Swedish caddie. The majority thought it a sackable offence. 'I'd expect to be sacked for that,' said Martin Rowley, Carl Mason's bag man.

One quality Faldo has never lacked is fortitude. He is not a crybaby. He has courage, he has discipline and he has character, and when golf deals him one of her agonizing blows, he never looks around for people to blame, but simply soldiers on more resolutely than before. In the second round of the Open, he went out onto the windswept links and played sublime golf for a 66. 'It took me seventeen holes to undo what I did on the seventeenth yesterday, but then a nice putt on the last gave me something back,' was all he had to say.

An unpleasant contrast was provided by John Daly, the anti-Faldo. At some point during the morning, we glanced up at the leaderboard and saw with delight that Wild Thing was burning up the course. Immediately, his recent sins were forgiven. There is hardly a soul in golf who doesn't wish Daly well – for the game's sake as well as his own – and when he turned in 32, to be five under par for the tournament, his gallery could hardly contain themselves.

But with Daly, every silver lining hides a tornado. The first sign that all would not be rosy for much longer came at the tenth. He drove onto the beach and never found the ball. The gallery had no luck either, and their hero notched up a triple-bogey seven. Daly took on a slightly unhinged aspect. At the eleventh, he four-putted, missing one putt with an uncaring backhander. 'He was sword-fighting,' said his caddie David McNeilly, after Daly had clocked up a 40 on the inward half and been whisked away by a waiting car. 'I'm going to go home and pull the knife out of my heart,' he said melodramatically. It was hard to feel sympathy for a man who walked round the great links telling spectators: 'I see my ex-wife's face every time I hit the ball.'

The cut fell at 143, taking with it Jack Nicklaus, Open Champion in 1966, 1970 and 1977, Lee Trevino, 1971 and 1972, Gary Player, 1959, 1968 and 1974, and Ian Baker-Finch, the 1991 winner, who failed to qualify by seven strokes. Other big names to get the axe were Payne Stewart, the US Open and PGA Champion, Chip Beck, Corey Pavin, former US Open Champion Scott Simpson, Phil Mickelson, Woosnam and Torrance.

None of this detracted from the magic of Watson's 65. 'Not bad for a forty-four-year-old has-been,' Watson said, wearing an ear to ear grin. His seven-under-par total gave him a one-stroke lead over Brad Faxon and the entertaining Swede Jesper Parnevik, with Nick Price a shot further behind. Turner, Lomas, Nobilo and David Edwards were hanging on to fifth place. Perfect timing had allowed Watson to make light work of the tricky crosswinds, and he had holed out from all over the green. 'It was fun out there,' he said. 'Whatever I tried seemed to work.'

Of all the names to grace the leaderboard, none was more welcome than that of David Feherty, who was on three under par with Fuzzy Zoeller; the European Tour had been a quieter, duller place without him. 'I think I can win,' the Irishman remarked. 'I've got nothing better to do this weekend.'

In a game of two-dimensional nice-guys, Feherty is a true original – quirky, glitteringly intelligent, as articulate as Mae West. It was Feherty who called St Mellion the course that Barbara Nicklaus built, he who described Baltusrol as the Mona Lisa with a beard, and he who said of Augusta: 'It's like a work of art. It's like playing a Salvador Dali painting. I expected a clock to fall out of the trees and hit me in the face.' A former opera singer with an eclectic taste in music and literature, he likes to give the impression that golf holds little charm for him; that given half a chance, he would quit the game tomorrow.

'He's a pro golfer because golf was his passion,' David Jones, Feherty's best friend, said firmly. 'He didn't just fall into it.'

This is one of many Feherty contradictions. His complete reliance on a support network consisting of Jones, his wife, his coach and his sports psychologist, Alan Fine – so at odds with his sophisticated, man-of-the-world demeanour – is another.

'This is a pretty macho game,' Feherty said frankly. 'It's full of crap. Guys quite often invent stuff – it's not their fault. It's *always* my fault. I don't care if it's my fault, that's just the way it is. If I hit a bad shot, it's because I was an idiot or I wasn't talented enough or whatever. There's so much macho behaviour in golf. People have their egos to worry about, particularly the very good players. They kind of build up this wall around themselves, you know, where any admission of weakness is like a flaw in their character. This game's just a mirror, that's all it is. Your weaknesses glare you in the face.'

Feherty recalls the day that golf took over his life. He was sitting in geography class when the smell of the newly-mown lawn drifted through the open window. Feherty stood up. 'Excuse me,' he said to the teacher, 'I'm just going to turn professional.' Down the hall, the headmaster contemplated him across an expanse of mahogany. 'Is your father aware of this?' he asked. 'No,' responded Feherty, 'but he will be in about half an hour.'

His relationship with the game is a turbulent one. 'Have I ever stopped loving golf? Frequently. About twelve times a round. People say I hate the game. I don't. But I don't enjoy the feeling of pressure. I don't enjoy standing over a six-footer, knowing I have to hole it or I'll miss the cut. I don't think that's a nice feeling at all. What I do enjoy is the success and having succeeded. But that's why golf is such a strange game. You have to want to be somewhere where you know you're going to feel uncomfortable. You have to want that responsibility. And that's what separates the guys that win major championships from the guys that don't. It's not the fear of failure that makes you lose a major championship, it's the fear of success.'

Now he was playing the US Tour, far from his beloved Northern Ireland. 'One of the differences in the States is that the guys stay out five or six weeks at a time, even when they miss the cut,' Feherty said. 'It's like: "Haven't you got a home to go to?" You know, I go home every Sunday night. I don't care if it's East coast to West coast, I just can't bear being away. And that's what will make me quit the game.'

He admits to a certain restlessness, a sense of straining against the constraints that the discipline of pro golf puts on a questing mind, a soaring spirit. 'I frequently get bored with it. But it's a love/hate relationship like anything else. I mean, you don't love your wife all the time either. Least my wife certainly doesn't love me all the time. Actually, I *do* love her all the time. It's pretty obvious because I'm still there, I'm in America. But yes, you have a relationship with this game. It's like being married.'

On Saturday, Prince Andrew came to Turnberry to watch play. When the vast gallery had ceased celebrating Ballesteros's arrival on the first tee, the Duke, a ten-handicapper at Swinley Forest and Royal Mid-Surrey, thrust out a hand to the Spaniard and said pleasantly: 'It's very nice to see you again.'

Accompanied by Lord Griffiths, the captain of the R&A, he elected to follow Ballesteros out on the sunlit links rather than hang about waiting for the leaders. But by the fifth hole he was alternating between Ballesteros and Daly in the match behind. 'It's a contrast of styles,' the Duke said. 'Strength versus finesse.'

These assets and many more were to be called upon that afternoon, as near-perfect conditions prompted an all-out charge for the lead. Fittingly, perhaps, it was the forty-two-year-old Zoeller, whistling and wise-cracking in a friendly game with Feherty, who fared best, making seven birdies in a round of 64. 'Hey,' Zoeller said in surprise as he added up his score, 'look what I shot.'

An aggregate of 201, nine under par, gave him a one-stroke advantage with Faxon over Watson, Ronan Rafferty, Parnevik and Price, who had missed a five-foot putt on the last to share the lead. Feherty was on seven under after a 66. 'All I can ask is to have a chance to win,' Zoeller said. 'I wouldn't be playing if I didn't think I had another major in me.'

Trevino, fifty-four, winner of two Open titles, took the low scores as a sign that the set-up of Open courses was making the game too easy. 'A links course is meant to be natural,' he complained. 'You're supposed to walk onto it and there it is, just laid out there with no help from man. Now they are controlling the water on them. What's happened is it's become much easier to drive the ball. If you hook the ball but it finds the fairway, it will stay there. And the lies are perfect. You don't have to improvise shots from the fairway like you used to.'

Bonallack was unmoved. He recalled that Trevino had always liked it when the courses were dry and dusty because he hit the ball so low. Everyone else was happy, he said.

Montgomerie certainly was. One night of uninterruped beauty

sleep – in desperation, he had packed his six-month-old daughter off to his grandparents for the rest of the week – had resulted in a 65, which lifted him to 206. 'I think the tension was very high and I got uptight on the first two days,' he said. 'I only just made the cut. But I'm eight under par for the last twenty-one holes so that's an advantage. I relaxed a bit and I'm enjoying it and playing well. I'm looking forward to tomorrow.' He was thrilled to be informed that his marvellous short game, which helped him to roll in two putts of 40 feet and to chip in from 25 at Turnberry, had made him leader of the putting statistics at Oakmont with 26.5 putts a round. 'If you can putt on those terrifying Oakmont greens, you can putt on anything,' he said.

In his enthusiasm, he had forgotten about the strength of the opposition, the most daunting of whom was Price. The 1992 US PGA Champion had lost the Open to Watson at Troon in 1992, and finished runner-up to Ballesteros in 1988. He was due an Open. Not that the Zimbabwean was counting his chickens. 'If the weather is like this tomorrow, it's going to be a shootout,' he said. 'I'm going to need a 65 or better to win. There's too much experience on that leaderboard.'

At the Nestle Invitational in March, Watson had commented wryly: 'My putting's turned politically correct. I'm on a quota system now. It used to be that I could make everything. Now I have a quota of putts. I can only make a certain number. It's a kinder, gentler Tom Watson now. I don't strike fear into anybody's heart on the greens any more.'

His Huck Finn smile didn't fool anyone, least of all himself. More than a decade separated him from his last major, and six long years had passed since he last saw victory on the US Tour, and yet to see Watson on the golf course was to see a man hit the golf better than he ever had in his life. But for his weakness on the greens, Watson might have won the Masters or even the US Open. In spite of it, he was determined to win at Turnberry. All that was stopping him was his putting. Stubbornly, Watson continued to resist the temptation of broom-handled putters and other new-fangled aids. 'I'll just go at it the traditional way,' he said.

In 1977, when Watson stole a march on the Golden Bear, Nicklaus told him: 'I gave you my best shot and it wasn't good enough. You were better.' That evening, Watson had watched the sun set over the links with tears pouring down his cheeks, tears of joy, 'of love for the game of golf'. Now he had a chance to do it again. 'It's been a delight to come back to Turnberry and relive all the old memories,' he said. 'I've tried to take my time this week. Stopping to look back down the fairways, to look forward to the green, just soaking up the cheers of the crowd. Trying to imagine what it was I knew before . . .'

On the final day of the Open, Watson pitched to two feet at the seventh hole to birdie and share the lead on nine under par. The crowd erupted. Then Watson three-putted from 12 feet for a double-bogey at the next. His agony was palpable, but he forced himself on. At the eighth, he chipped from 20 feet and double-bogeyed again. 'Damn you,' he said to himself, cut to the quick by the realization that he had dropped four strokes in eleven minutes. The gallery turned away. It was painful to see him suffer so much. 'Come on, Tom,' Watson pleaded with himself. But it was over. When Watson took his bruised soul and ruined scorecard to the recorder's hut, he had taken thirty-eight putts in a round of 74. 'That really says it all,' he said. 'It hurts . . . hurts inside.'

The cruellest irony of all is that it was his love of the game, his reverence for its traditions and his rejection of modern crutches that had robbed him of his dream. 'God takes one thing away from you at a time,' Watson said, thinking of his flawless iron play, his flawed putting stroke. 'He doesn't let you have it all very often.'

Strangely, it had been Watson himself who ensured that Price didn't have it all at Troon in 1982, where the twenty-five-year-old Zimbabwean had led by three with six to play. And it had been Ballesteros at the height of his powers who denied him at Lytham in 1988. Since then, Price had won the US PGA Championship and had been named US Player of the Year in 1993. At Turnberry, he was so confident that, standing on the range with David Leadbetter on the morning of the final day, he suddenly announced that he wanted to hit a couple of bad shots. He wanted them out of the way. That done, he teed off and went to the turn in level par 35, playing more cautiously than he would have wanted to. At that point, he settled down to play.

Behind him, the leaders had run into a wall. 'Our game was like sitting in a round room watching paint dry,' Zoeller said of his match with Faxon. 'Nothing ever happened out there – there was no flow, no rhythm and you need that in golf. But it was a wonderful experience. I put myself in contention in the Open Championship which is something not many Americans will experience because they don't have the guts to come over here.'

Was he being facetious? an American reporter enquired.

'Larry, why would I lie to you?' Zoeller asked. 'Hell, I'm not married to you, why should I need to lie to you?'

He scored 70 to finish third on 271, 2 strokes ahead of Feherty, Anders Forsbrand and Mark James. Faldo tied for eighth place after an inspired 64. Daly shot 80 after finishing his round quadruple-bogey, bogey, bogey, bogey. 'John came here to win this championship, and once that chance had gone he didn't care if he was fiftieth or fifth,' his caddie said.

Out in the sunshine, Parnevik, with his Daffy Duck baseball cap and his eager, angelic face set in concentration, was working subtle magic on the links. He had holed a 20-foot putt at the eleventh and an eight-footer at the twelfth to go to ten under, and then slid in an' eight-footer at the next. The scoreboard clicked and altered, but the Swede never glanced at it. He told his caddie, Mike Donaghy, to watch on his behalf, while he devoted his energies to making birdies. Initially, this strategy seemed to work. He holed from 15 feet at 16 and chipped stone dead from the rough for another birdie at 17. Then he arrived at the last. Assuming he needed a birdie to win, he attacked the pin unnecessarily, finding the rough short and left of the green with his wedge shot and failing to get up and down. 'I was trying to get to thirteen under,' he explained. 'That was the figure I had in mind. Maybe I should have had a glimpse at the scoreboard when I was on the eighteenth . . . maybe I should have played a smarter shot.'

Price's patience was finally rewarded at the twelfth, where he holed a 15-footer for birdie. He played a good chip at the next and a great chip at the fourteenth, and suddenly his round came to life. At 16, he made birdie, not by luck but by deliberating for some minutes with his caddie Jeff (Squeeky) Medlen as to the exact spot he should place his approach shot. The momentum shifted. It occurred to him that if he let this chance go by, there may never be another one. 'Sometimes, out there, you have to reach very deep inside yourself, surprise yourself,' Price said. 'Winning a major examines every facet of your character and temperament.'

Then Price came to the penultimate hole, a par five of some 498 yards. He hit a driver and a four-iron to 50 feet. He crouched down and studied the line. Squeeky looked over his shoulder. With his heart in his mouth, Price pushed the ball away. It rushed across the soft green surface, bobbling over the humps, the borrows, the imperfections until, incredibly, it fell into the hole. Price leapt into the air in joyous disbelief, coming down hopping and skipping and embracing Squeeky ecstatically. 'I just about jumped out of my skin,' he laughed afterwards. 'I knew when I walked on the green that I had to hole the putt. But I can't believe I holed it – those sort of things don't happen too often.'

Parnevik, who was convinced he had won, was in the recorder's hut when he was told that Price had gone to twelve under par. 'When that happened, everything just fell apart,' the devastated Swede admitted.

Price played his favourite club, a seven-iron, into the final green, parring the hole for a 66 and an aggregate of 286, which gave him victory by a stroke over Parnevik. 'I had my left hand on this trophy in 1982 and my right hand on it in 1988,' he said, hugging the claret jug. 'Now I've got both hands on it and it's a wonderful feeling.'

As the evening sun shot ribbons of scarlet over the dark brooding hump of Ailsa Craig, Parnevik, pale and sad, dedicated his efforts to his grandparents. His grandmother had died the week before the Open, three months after her husband. 'I didn't have time to say goodbye,' said the twenty-nine-year-old son of a Swedish impressario. 'If you care about someone, make sure they know about it.'

Price stepped forward and lightened the moment, warmly congratulating Parnevik on his achievement. 'You've got age on your side,' he said. 'Use it wisely.'

Afterwards, the nicest guy in golf sat in the interview room and talked us through his round and the disappointments he had endured. 'I can't tell you how much hard work there's been, how much I've wanted this day to happen,' Price said emotionally. 'And then when it comes, you think: "Why did the Good Lord shine on me?" '

13

PASSION PLAY

'I guess it's like being a beauty queen. Suddenly, they wanted me to be an ambassador for golf. Only thing is, I didn't feel like an ambassador. I was just defending myself with a shield. I wanted to know what everybody wanted. I couldn't say yes to everybody.'

US OPEN CHAMPION LEE JANZEN, on the price of fame

'You cannot believe how bananas Tulsa is about the PGA Championship,' Robinson said.

We were at the airport, where I had been arrested by the spectacle of giant golf ball stickers marking the route from the arrival gate to the taxi rank. 'Welcome to Tulsa and the 76th PGA Championship *Colin Montgomerie*' said one. Others saluted Faldo, Norman and Scott Hoch. Tulsa even went so far as to honour nonentities not entered in the tournament. 'Welcome *Paul Goydos*' a golf ball cried.

Not since St Andrews had a place been as golf-obsessed as this, and it didn't just stop at the airport. Nothing in the city, not a Taco Bell, not a Waffle House, not a toolshop, not a supermarket had been allowed to escape without at least a cursory nod in the direction of Southern Hills, venue of the US PGA. Only the futuristic Oral Roberts University seemed immune. Its infamous prayer tower, from where a message was beamed to America to say that unless X-million dollars came the way of the tele-evangelist, God would be taking him up to the sky (there was a shortfall but God relented), looked contemptuously – or should that be piously – down on the traffic heading out to Southern Hills each day, and the landmark hands at its gate, which are supposed to be praying but looked to me like they were closing a business deal, would have no part of any token welcome flag.

For years it was a seasonal sport to disparagingly refer to the US PGA as golf's fourth major. 'The PGA Championship is simply an American tour event with ideas above its station,' chuckled Dobereiner. Even its winners were somehow less great than the Masters, Open and US Open Champions. When Dave Stockton (then the Loren Roberts of the Tour) triumphed at Southern Hills in 1970, it was widely reported that Arnold Palmer had lost to Dave Stockton, as though the latter had been a bit player in the fall of a hero. Stockton was particularly upset by the coverage of Dan Jenkins. At a tournament in New Jersey, he went storming up to Bob Drum in the press centre.

'Is Jenkins here?' he demanded. 'I want to talk to him.'

'I don't think he's coming this week,' Drum said with wide-eyed innocence. 'Whom shall I say is calling?'

Gradually, though, there was a shift of opinion. Unlike the US Open, where nothing functions – not the scoreboard, not the air-conditioning, not the practice ground shuttles – or the Masters, where the press centre is purpose-built, very beautiful and utterly impractical; or the Open, where the catering defies belief, the PGA Championship was a model of efficiency. The same arcane American scoring system was in operation (local volunteers drew pretty but unhelpful drawings of birds and scissors on a scoreboard where microscopic players' names were in alphabetical rather than match order, and birdies, pars and bogeys were all one colour), but at least it was timely and there were television monitors, interview transcripts and plenty of free ice-cream and chocolate sauce. In addition, following the Shoal Creek controversy, the PGA also – speaking entirely relatively – acquired a reputation for progressive thinking.

In 1963, *Golf Illustrated* reported that, 'Those who feel that golf is a game which knows no frontiers will be surprised at the reaction in some quarters in South Africa after Sewsunker Sewgolum's surprise victory in the Natal Open Championship. Reports indicate that the event was not broadcast because a spokesman of the South African Broadcasting Corporation said the corporation's policy was never to broadcast multi-racial meetings. It appears also that the little Indian golfer, who competed in Britain and on the Continent, received his prize in the rain because club officials . . . were advised it would be illegal for him to be in the clubhouse.'

These attitudes were not restricted to Africa; they were alive and well in America in 1990. That was the year that Hall Thomson, founder of Shoal Creek Country Club in Birmingham, Alabama, venue of the US PGA, unwittingly sparked a revolution when he announced: 'We have the right to associate or not to associate with whomever we choose. The country club is our home and we pick and choose who we want. We don't discriminate in any other area except the blacks.'

Golf's hardline élitism had been an open secret for years, but with the PGA Championship only two months away, Thomson's words threw it into the public domain, exposing an ugly skeleton in a snowy-white game. Knowing a damning and potentially explosive situation when they see one, the four golf associations (the PGA of America, the PGA Tour, the USGA and the LPGA) lost no time in embracing policies aimed at eradicating discrimination. Many of these would be in place by the following year, but in the meantime they had to pacify corporate sponsors and try to prevent the collapse or even cancellation of the event. Days before the US PGA was due to take place, the PGA of America was forced to adopt official bylaws requiring host clubs for association championships to have demonstrably open membership policies and practices prohibiting discrimination on the basis of race, creed, colour, national origin or gender. Those golf clubs that refused to comply were dropped from the schedule of sanctioned events.

The long-term effects of this decision were extraordinary; sweeping reforms took place at exclusive clubs all around the country. Shoal Creek threw open its doors just long enough for a single black member to pass through, and the tournament went ahead.

But what really gave the PGA Championship new status in the game was the dawning realization that its finishes were often the most dramatic of any major, and that there had rarely been a bad winner of the tournament. Indeed, in recent years golf's brightest stars had fulfilled their promise on the fairways of the final major of the season: Payne Stewart at Kemper Lakes, Wayne Grady at Shoal Creek, the unforgettable Daly at Crooked Stick, Nick Price at Bellerive and, of course, Paul Azinger.

In 1993, Azinger, touting the label 'the best player in the world not to have won a major', met Greg Norman on the first play-off hole at Inverness. Seven years earlier, the luckless Shark had stood on that same tee box tied with Bob Tway. Norman had been on the green for two, victory a formality, when Tway had holed out from the bunker, exploding from the sand like a jubilant jack-in-the-box while the Australian stood stricken. Now, matched against the nervy Azinger, Norman had a chance to rewrite the past. On the eighteenth green, he stroked a perfect 18-foot putt. It rolled into the cup and hopped out again. Azinger could hardly believe the evidence of his eyes. 'I kind of jumped a little. Two feet from the hole, there was no doubt in my mind it was in. That was one of the nastiest lip-outs I've ever seen.' They went to the tenth green, where Azinger was down in two and Norman three-putted from 18 feet, leaving his first putt five feet short. His putter, arching into the funereal air, symbolized a painful record: not since the 30s had a golfer lost play-offs in all four majors.

Three months later, Azinger was diagnosed with lymphoma. His doctor, who had been nagging him since June about a painful lump in his right shoulder blade, finally persuaded him to have a biopsy. He began chemotherapy. After his first session, he was sick every twenty minutes for eight and a half hours. 'Physically, that was the worst it got for me,' said Azinger, who drew strength from his faith, his family and over 15,000 letters of support. At Southern Hills, he recalled that: 'The reality of my illness hit me when I realized I might die. All my accomplishments meant nothing. All I wanted to do was live. I have won a lot of money, but money can't buy a cure for cancer and it can't bring contentment. I am proud to be called a PGA Tour player and more proud to be a PGA Champion. But there is no greater thing than to be called a child of Christ . . . I am not a preacher but we all have to be prepared to die. God does not intend for this to be a perfect place. He intends it to prepare us for a perfect place.'

Azinger was speaking at a prayer breakfast attended by 850 people on the eve of the PGA Championship. He had already assisted at a fundraiser for a Congressional candidate, and he was planning to go on to visit children with cancer. Later that day, he signed autographs for so long that his practice round had to be rescheduled. He was looking well. His hair was dark and almost as short as John Daly's (Wild Thing had shaved his head as punishment for poor play), but he was eager to get out on the course. The previous week, competing in his first event since being diagnosed with cancer, he had shot 76, 70 to miss the cut at the Buick Classic. No matter. It was enough that he was back.

'Failure still makes me mad,' confessed Azinger with a grin. After missing an eight foot putt at the Buick, he had turned to his caddie and said: 'If you were worried about me losing my desire, I just want you to know I'm so mad right now I could spit nails.'

Out in the shirt-drenching humidity, Daly and Zoeller were practising together. They were accompanied by a six-year-old member of the gallery, whom a marshall had claimed was Fuzzy's biggest fan. Sceptical, Zoeller offered the boy a club and turned to the gallery. 'If he hits this ball, John will give him $100,' he told them. Daly took out a $100-dollar bill and pinned it to the ground with a tee peg. Austin Quentin launched two respectable shots and, before his seventh birthday, pocketed $200 of a former PGA Champion's money.

In the interview room, Montgomerie, Pavin and others came in and assessed their chances of victory at Southern Hills. Their threats and promises dissipated into the thin, artificially cooled air. The name on the PGA Championship trophy was already as inevitable as sunrise.

Greg Norman once remarked that golf's unique challenge is its individualism: 'You're your own judge, jury and executioner,' he said.

No-one understood that better than Nick Price. He had been motivated to turn professional by the responsibility each shot carried and by the money. Picking up a golf magazine, aged sixteen, he thought to himself, ' "Man alive, these guys are unbelievable. Nicklaus made $180,000 last year . . ." And to a kid who needs fifty cents to live on a day, that's millions.' Golf was fun to him, a way of whiling away the hot summer days in Zimbabwe with his friends Mark McNulty, Tony Johnstone, Dennis Watson and Leadbetter; but it became his heart, his life. He thrilled to the flight of a well-struck ball, the sun on his skin, the competition. At seventeen, he won the 1974 World Junior in San Diego. Four years later, after a stint as a radio-communications expert in the Rhodesian Air Force, he set off to Europe to try his luck on the Tour.

Right from the word go, he made money – not much, but enough to carry him through until the next week. But his game was makeshift, unreliable. It brought him victory in the 1980 Swiss Open and then it began to unravel at the seams. 'All I worked on then was timing,' Price told Chris Smith of the *Florida Times-Union*. 'If my timing was good, I could win. If not, I could shoot 80. There was no in-between. There was absolutely no consistency to what I was doing. I would go out there not knowing what I would work on for that day. One day I would turn my grip, the next day do something else. No two things were the same. It was like every day I was making compensations and adjustments to try to play consistently. Finally, I knew if I was going to make a living at this game, I would have to make a change. It was a very simple decision for me to make.'

So Price delivered himself into the hands of Leadbetter, his childhood friend. He hit 1,000 eight-iron shots a day with the sweat stinging his eyes, beginning at the top of the backswing and starting down. He didn't have Faldo's blind confidence, his conviction that Leadbetter was right. Doubt was a constant companion during those long days at Grenlefe, but he kept on. He wasn't sure he knew a better way.

In 1982, leading the Open Championship by three strokes with six holes to play, he double-bogeyed the fifteenth to lose to Watson. Inexperience got the better of him. 'People always say that that was a negative thing in my life,' Price said, 'but for me it was a positive thing because I realized, at twenty-five, that I had the ability to win a major. And that just made me feel so good once I actually got over the disappointment. Probably, the hardest thing for me then was to work out why I had played poorly. I kept saying to myself: "Why did I last for sixty-seven holes and not for seventy-two?" '

Others asked the same question. Price won the World Series the next season, earning a ten-year exemption on the US Tour, and then followed it with a disconcerting number of second places. In 1994 and '95, he finished runner-up nine times in fourteen events on the South African Tour. Mocking hands began to fly to throats whenever Price came down the stretch; but there was a Norman-like element of luck involved in his defeats. Corey Pavin had nineteen putts on the last day of the 1981 South African PGA Championship, and Ballesteros shot a 65 playing the round of his life at Royal Lytham in 1988. Price held on. He knew that if he got into contention enough, he would eventually start winning. He studied the British Open video with his teacher.

'Seve putted unbelievably,' commented Price, with a degree of envy.

'You just didn't make enough putts,' Leadbetter said shortly.

'Instead of giving me the praise I was looking for,' remembered Price, 'and telling me I was putting well, he said, "No, you didn't putt well. Seve putted well. And if you want to become a better player and contest in major championships, you've got to elevate your short game." And that's what happened.'

In May 1991, two-thirds of a decade after his last victory, Price made a 30-foot downhill putt to win the Byron Nelson Classic. 'It was seven years, five months,' he said, 'and it felt like twelve years.' In September, he made up seven strokes on D. A. Weibring with twelve holes to play to capture the Canadian Open title and finish seventh on the money list. The following season, he won the PGA Championship by three strokes with a flawless performance at Bellerive. It was the start of a glory trail that was to take him to the top of the world. When he arrived at Southern Hills, he had won the 1993 US Tour money list, the Million Dollar Challenge at Sun City by 12 shots (the score of the runner-up would have been good enough to win the tournament nine of the thirteen times it was held) and the Open, and he was leading the 1994 money list by a comfortable margin after victories in the Honda Classic, the Colonial and the Western Open.

'Each of my wins has been so significant in its own way . . .' Price said, 'but I hate to categorize them. Each has given me confidence, and an ounce of confidence is worth fifty hours on the practice ground . . .'

In an uncharacteristically expansive mood, Hogan was moved to say of Southern Hills: 'Some golf courses you learn faster than others. This one takes a lot of knowing.'

Jim Lucius, the former club professional, advised participants to study in advance. 'You've got to come out ready to play,' he said. 'If you start out with indifferent shots, you're going to have a hard time scoring. You may wind up with a five, six or even a seven. The man who plays those first three holes better than the rest of the field is likely to be crowned champion on Sunday afternoon.'

Price started with a bogey and two pars. He recovered with birdies at the fifth and sixth, but made five from the rough at the par four ninth to turn in 35, level par. There, he took a breather, gathered his resources and made three birdies coming in for an inward 32. When the sun went down on Tulsa, he was joint leader with Colin Montgomerie on 67, three under par. Phil Mickelson, Woosnam, Couples and Els were a stroke further behind, followed by Watson, Zoeller, Torrance and Floyd, among others.

Montgomerie insisted that losing the US Open to Els at Oakmont would stand him in good stead. 'I'm not disappointed at all. Nobody beat me over seventy-two holes. [The play-off] didn't go the way I would have liked it to go, but it was a good experience. I finished eighth at the British Open and I'm in contention after the first round here. Obviously, I'm learning something. I don't know what it is.'

With six of the fourteen players under par being foreigners, naturally the subject under discussion was whether or not they, for so long the underdogs of the world golf, would make a clean sweep of the major titles of 1994. Couples, as languorous as ever after nearly six months off, refused to get worked up about it. 'I really don't care who wins . . . If they're American or European or from anywhere else, it doesn't bother me much, you know. I don't think Nick Faldo is going to jump up and down if Colin Montgomerie wins, and I'm not going to jump up and down if Loren Roberts wins. If a foreigner wins, at least we won't have to worry about a foreigner never having won all four again.'

After a five over par 75, Paul Azinger had other things on his mind. 'I envisioned shooting 64,' he admitted. 'I dreamed of walking up the eighteenth fairway and winning. But it's been a little harder than I thought.'

One of the delights of travel is the cameos. At New Orleans airport, the man preparing the Nacho Supreme had remarked, apropos of nothing, that everyone has seven angels.

'Why limit yourself to seven?' said a woman customer.

'I have one big one,' he said. 'Gabriel. The worrying angel.'

On the flight from New Orleans to Dallas, a passenger who built flight simulators for F18 jets said that he loved to follow golf. 'As a matter of fact,' he said, 'I used to mow Steve Elkington's mother's lawn.'

On the flight from Dallas to Tulsa, the lawyer in the next seat issued a disclaimer: 'Whatever you've heard about Tulsa, it's nothing like that at all.'

Apparently not. According to a *Tulsa World* editorial, 'Tulsans increasingly realize that dragging the rest of Oklahoma into the 20th century, let alone the 21st, is a nearly impossible job, maybe beyond the capabilities even of the Tulsans. So they say, "Tulsa should just secede from Oklahoma and become its own state." ' The article went on to claim that, 'During the worst of the depression, two hundred men met at the home of one of them and were invited to participate in forming a new and ultra-swank country club at $1,000 each, initial expense. [Never mind that the land on which it was to be built was given to the Indians in 1810 by the US government "for as long as the grass grows and the water runs."] Before the evening was over, 140 of the two hundred had signed on the dotted line.'

The club in question was Southern Hills.

On Friday, Price shot 65 to take a five-stroke lead over Pavin, Jay Haas and Crenshaw on 132, eight under par. In an immaculate demonstration of major winning golf, he had seven birdies and no bogeys in a round in which he sank a 20-foot putt on the third, a 15-footer on 10, a 12-footer on 13, and a ten-foot putt on the sixteenth. Olazabal scored 66 to share fifth place with John Cook, while Montgomerie fell to pieces with a 76.

'The way Nick's played, we're going to have to lasso him,' Crenshaw said with admiration. 'He's striking the ball as well as anyone since Ben Hogan or Byron Nelson. He's a man in full flight.'

'It's not over,' David Edwards said optimistically. 'Nick Price might get sick. He might wake up with a crick in his neck. That would help everybody a whole bunch. If he stays healthy, which I assume he will, he might run off with it . . .'

It was put to Price that he appeared to be in what Norman likes to call 'a zone'.

'I don't really like to be referred to as being in a zone because it sounds like I've been out there for two years walking, eating, drinking, sleeping and thinking golf,' Price said. 'That's not true. There are so many other things in my life that I enjoy doing and I just have a really good knack at the moment of being able to play and give 100 per cent to the next shot. That's why I've done so well over the last two years.'

Among the eight past PGA Champions to miss the 145 cut were Palmer, Tway, Daly, Azinger and Nicklaus, who had shot 79, 71. In describing Thursday's round, one of the worst he had ever recorded in a major, the greatest player in history said that the lingering controversy over a perceived racist comment he made, 'had my stomach tied up in knots.' Barbara Nicklaus said that after a career virtually free of contention and strife, 'This has just torn him up.'

The row broke out after Nicklaus allegedly told a reporter in Canada that blacks gravitated to basketball rather than golf because they had 'different muscles' to whites. He apparently rejected the idea that he could have broken barriers for aspiring black golf professionals by boycotting tournaments held at clubs which discriminated against people of colour.

Chi Chi Rodriguez, with whom Nicklaus had helped to raise $2 million for underprivileged kids, was shocked. 'I know there's not a racist hair on his body,' he said. Certainly, there didn't appear to be. Nicklaus had stopped playing golf in South Africa at the request of the late Arthur Ashe. He insisted that Muirfield Village, his club, be open to minority members, and was ultimately responsible for forcing other clubs in which he had equity to adopt the same policy. He was generous in the extreme to Willie Peterson, the black caddie with whom he won each of his six Masters titles, and was instrumental in helping Peterson to secure the job of caddie-master at Loxahatchee, the course he designed in Jupiter, Florida.

'This hurts my wife,' Nicklaus said. 'It hurts me. I've been upset ever since it came out. All my life I have tried to do right by everyone. I opposed racially-segregated clubs . . . The only point I intended to make was that kids, black and white, gravitate to different sports because of their environment.'

Hale Irwin summed it up best. 'Jack considers himself an authority on everything,' he said, 'and he doesn't know when to stop arguing his point and back off.'

It is a curious thing, but in every four rounds of tournament golf one will always be significantly worse than the others. Comparatively speaking. Of course, if you are Nick Price and your bad round is a 67 in amongst the 66, 66 and 65 you have shot to win the Million Dollar Challenge, then you are not going to lose much sleep over it, but even Price recognized the phenomenom existed.

'You look at a golf championship and figure that you're going to have one really good round – maybe two or three good rounds – and maybe one that is not so good,' he said. 'I haven't had my not so good round yet, but if I have it Saturday or Sunday and I can go out and turn it into a 69 or 70, then I think I'm going to have a good chance. But we've all been in this game long enough to know it's not over until the last putt is holed.'

Saturday was Price's not so good day: he shot an untidy 70 for an eight under par 202, and still managed to leave behind everyone but the forty-year-old American Jay Haas who was on 205. Leading the rest of the field were Pavin and Mickelson on 206, with Norman, Crenshaw and Cook a shot further back.

Price was well aware that he had got away with murder, largely due to the farcical antics of Haas, Pavin and Blaine McAllister, who were chipping into bunkers, falling in water hazards and triple-bogeying all over the place. 'Everything is cut and dried out there,' Price said of his prospects on Sunday. 'I've got to go out and play well. I'll go out there and focus and be a little more determined. I know they're all going to come at me. I just hope I won't be forced into doing something foolish.'

The biggest potential threat was the twenty-four-year-old Phil Mickelson, pretender to the throne occupied by America's finest golfers. A left-hander who won the Northern Telecom Open as an amateur and became the only player apart from Nicklaus to win NCAA and Amateur titles in the same year, he is a golfer of exceptional gifts. Since breaking both legs in a skiing accident in March, he had earned $117,745, taking his earnings in the season to over $400,000. After his third round at Southern Hills, which included an outward 31, he fielded questions about his status as the next American great.

Mickelson's dimples deepened. 'It's a compliment,' he said, 'but I have expectations of myself that are probably higher. As far as being America's been-lately or next young hope and what have you, you know, that's stuff that we as players don't really think about . . . We try and play and improve our game. The top players know that if they improve their games, they're going to have results like Nick Price. I remember three years ago, nobody really knew who Nick Price was. For four or five years, he had a tough spell, and he stuck through it. He worked hard because he knew that if he kept at it, he would have the results that he's having now . . . So I just think about what I'm trying to do with my game and the things that I can accomplish if I get better.'

The only slightly distressing aspect of Mickelson is his manner. It is so coy, so ingratiating, so cloyingly polite and respectful, that it is almost impossible to believe that it is sincere – which it very well might be. As David Feherty once said: 'I don't know him at all but I've seen him smile and that's quite enough to put me off wanting to know anything about him.'

But tradition was on Price's side. Stockton, Green, Floyd and Tommy Bolt had all been wire to wire winners at the PGA Championship. Bolt's victory was notable in that there were no thrown clubs or tantrums all week. The only time the fur threatened to fly was when a local newspaper mistakenly added ten years to his age. When the reporter explained that it was a typographical error, Bolt retorted: 'Typographical error, hell! That was a perfect "4" and a perfect "9".'

Easy game, golf. Easy for Nick Price at any rate. On Sunday – when temperatures rocketed into the 90s and it was so hot that one *Tulsa World* reader claimed 'the catfish were jumping out of the creek already cooked' and another said that a dog had passed the house chasing a cat 'and they were both walking' – Price went out and coolly collected three birdies in an outward half of 32, hitting a driver and wedge to two feet at the third, a two-iron and wedge to six feet at the fourth, and holing a 22-foot putt for another at the eighth.

History tells us that a major only starts on the back nine on the final day, but by then it was already over at Southern Hills. Actually, it was over on the first day. Perhaps awed by his seven-shot lead, Price had one or two rocky moments on the inward half but they balanced out beautifully for a level par 35. His score of 67 for an eleven under par aggregate of 269 gave him victory by six strokes over Pavin, earned him $310,000, took him to the top of the World Rankings (where he should have been for two seasons), made him the first man since Tom Watson in 1982 to win back to back majors, beat the US PGA scoring record of 271 set by Bobby Nichols in 1964, and made him only the sixth man in all championship history to win by leading or jointly leading from the start.

'This is the first time this whole week that I've actually come down and relaxed,' Price said, strolling into the interview room in his usual cheerful, down-to-earth way as if he had just won the monthly medal. 'I was so tense all week . . . I think I won the championship yesterday, to be honest with you, because I just didn't play with any real confidence and I didn't have any direction out there. I was just waiting for something to happen instead of going out and making things happen. It made me so determined last night that I went and hit balls and worked on a couple of things. I did what I had neglected to do and had a chat with Dave Leadbetter and pinpointed the problem.'

As a consequence, Price effectively won the tournament over the front nine, being challenged only briefly by Norman who drew within three strokes of him. 'Everything fell into place,' he said. 'I knew what needed to be done and I went out and did it. That front nine was, considering the situation, the best nine holes I have ever played in my life.'

What was staggering about Price's victory was not so much the statistics, impressive though they may be – since winning the 1992 US PGA, he had won two more majors, thirteen other tournaments, had thirty-seven top-ten finishes in fifty-nine starts and won $5.56 million – but the fact that through it all he had retained the same immensely likeable, considerate and caring personality that he seems to have had since childhood. Jack Newton, the former Australian champion, observed that since the day Simon Hobday told him that Price was going to be the next great Southern African player, Price had not changed one iota.

'Not like fuckin' Faldo and Norman,' Newton said.

Tony Johnstone, who remembers Price as 'the biggest ten-year-old I ever saw – as strong as an ox and very confident,' says that as a boy he was always the one pouring oil on troubled waters. At a junior tournament once, when Johnstone and a couple of other delinquents stole the bus belonging to the visiting Orange Freestate team and went on a joy-ride through the town, all hell broke loose. Price, who had had absolutely nothing to do with the incident, came in and smoothed things over and calmed everyone down.

It was as though he always had a different perspective to other boys – which he probably did have. When you lose your father – a retired Indian Army artillery major – aged ten, when you watch your friends die in the Rhodesian Bush War at nineteen, when you come face to face with your own mortality every day in the shape of a blood pressure tablet, you soon realize that there are more important things in life than hitting golf balls.

'Losing a parent is never easy,' Price told Chris Smith, 'but I learned early on that things are not for ever. That death is an integral part of life and something we have to accept, no matter how hard it is . . .

'The most important thing to me is health and the well-being of my family. If you don't have that, you have nothing. I can handle anything outside of that. If something had to happen to my family, I don't know what I would do. It's funny. Since our son and daughter have been born, my golf has just taken off. Our family is very close; I feel very fortunate. Now, when I practise, I don't just practise for myself, I'm doing things to pay for our family's future.'

Throughout his climb to the top Price has stayed close to his roots, turning down the riches on offer at the World Championship in December and the Tournament of Champions in January to spend what he describes as 'my golden time' in Zimbabwe with his wife Sue and his children Gregory and Robyn. It says much for Norman that Price is such a loyal friend to him, because they are very different characters.

'I would describe Nick as conservative,' Frank Williams said. 'I would describe Greg as aggressive, charismatic, flamboyant, astute, streetsmart, courageous and kind. Nick would never rock the boat. Greg would if he thought he had to. Nick is slightly bewildered that it's all happening to him. Greg would never ever think: "I wonder when it's going to stop." Greg is the most positive person I've ever met in my life.'

At Southern Hills, all Norman was positive about was that Price was the world's most dominant player. In his unassuming way, even Price acknowledged it was true. He said he had nothing else to prove to himself or anyone else, but what he badly wanted to do was win the Masters and the US Open. 'I want to become a Grand Slam golfer,' he beamed.

Outside the interview room, the legions of champions he had beaten out of sight – Norman, Faldo, Olazabal, Watson, Kite and Mickelson – put their hands over their ears.

14

THE GREEN CARAVAN

'There are only two kinds of men in the world – those who stay at home and those who do not.'

RUDYARD KIPLING

In the bar of the Hotel L'Etrier in Crans-sur-Sierre, Switzerland, David Grice, the world-weary Fairway Travel representative, was describing a typical week in the life of a touring professional.

'It's a circus,' he said, by way of introduction. 'What makes my job difficult is that, when a player comes to a golf tournament, everything is free. They get fetched and carried in courtesy cars, and when they walk into the locker-room it's: "Have some free balls, a free shirt, some free clubs." Travel is the only thing they have to pay for, so they expect everything to work perfectly and they get very upset when it doesn't.

'Then you get this false friendliness. But when they phone up to make a booking each week it's very, very rare that they're concerned about what their so-called friends are doing. You get one or two little cliques – the biggest clique being the Scottish – but, apart from that, they'll do exactly what suits them.

'When they get down to the airport on Monday or Tuesday, there's a lot of camaraderie when they come together again. Obviously, not everybody likes each other, but they will always say, "Well done last week," or whatever.

'Then you see them on the plane. I sit in the last row, in smoking, and I look down the aisle and it's like someone's thrown a pack of cards up and just let it fall. You'd expect the ones who are friends to sit beside one another, but they don't. You've got one sitting beside a fat old woman, another sitting beside some kids. The moment we land, at the baggage belt, the whole mentality changes. They become a big family where they'll stick together and stick up for each other. It's like: "We're all in it together, fish out of water."

'Tuesday is when they let themselves relax. They practise, have a few beers, talk about football, have a laugh. On Wednesday, it goes quiet. They're thinking about the tournament, they're on a mission. Even best friends – if one's off early and the other's off late, the early one will stay in the hotel and have a bit of room service. Wednesday night, nobody's around the hotel after nine o'clock. On Thursday, it changes again. The ones that have shot 65 will be happy and intense and want to go to bed early. The ones that have shot 75 will be depressed, and they'll either go out on the piss or they'll sit in their room and phone their wife six times and want to slit their wrists.

'Friday's their big day. The players who have made the cut are overjoyed, they're thinking about the next two rounds. The guys who have missed it are miserable, demanding, cross. They're in a hurry to get home. The players who have qualified on the line are moping around. They're thinking: "What am I doing here?" I've seen players miss the cut and be happier than those who have just scraped through.

'On Saturday night, the professionalism comes in. They're thinking about the money. The guys in the top ten are looking to win, the ones lying twentieth or thirtieth are aiming for the top ten, and everyone else wants to finish in the top twenty or at least better than reserve money.

'On Sunday night, the atmosphere at the airport is the way it would be between four or five o'clock on Friday in a normal job. They're happy because their weekend's coming. They're all jovial and relaxed and they're having a few drinks. They've done the week's work and, whether they've won £2,000 or £20,000, they've accepted it. You get one or two that have a bad last round that just sit in the corner. They're obviously going to carry it all the way home with them. But the majority are happy with their lot. They just want to get home. It's: "Get me out of this fucking circus." '

*   *   *

If it's Tuesday, it's not necessarily Rome. It might just as easily be Phuket or Puerto Rico, or Munich or Montego Bay, or even Berlin or the Czech Republic. Today, as it happens, it is Geneva. The sky is awash with a delicate blue, the ground is damp and aromatic, and the courtesy car is willing and able to take us on the two-and-a-half-hour drive to the skiing village of Crans-sur-Sierre, high in the Swiss Alps. Thank goodness for Swiss efficiency.

A curious mentality attaches to lifelong golf circuit travel. Weeks are not divided into weekdays and weekends, but into laundry days, travel days, practice days, pro-am days and tournament days; and years are not years in the conventional sense, with Easter and Father's Day and Christmas – only seasons. Springtime begins with the Masters; summer exits at the Open; autumn is called to an abrupt halt by the arctic conditions synonymous with the Dunhill Cup; and winter signals the coming of the off-season and the departure of the top players, like snow geese, for exotic locations like Bali and Sun City, and the lesser players, for Argentina and Nigeria.

Now it was September and we were on our way to Crans for the European Masters, the first qualifying tournament for the 1995 Ryder Cup, and thus the first of several million occasions over the next fourteen months when we would be forced to write on that meritorious match. Also in the car was David Probyn, a blond-haired, blue-eyed, squeaky-clean tournament director, immaculately attired in the pin-striped shirt, navy blazer and red, green and blue tie that is the Boss-endorsed apparel of the European Tour. Probyn had been on the circuit five years. Previously, he had done contractual work for Sovereign Golf Holidays, but when an administrative position became vacant at Wentworth headquarters, he'd been taken on by the Tour.

Even Probyn conceded that, with one or two exceptions, Tour officials are peculiarly clone-like: short-back-and-sides; Boss uniform; bland, inoffensive and mildly arrogant character. No doubt he is right when he says that the interviewers are looking for a particular type of person: one who will be able to deal with the lifestyle (which combines the existences of a millionaire, a bank clerk and a travelling salesman) as well as working with the same people week in and week out. 'It's almost a twenty-four-hour-a-day commitment because you have to keep sponsors happy in the evening, which, if you've been out since five-thirty on the golf course, is not always what you want to do.'

Probyn's first real test of character came when he was despatched to Darkest Africa to deal with the circuit there. The Safari Tour takes in Kenya, Zambia, Zimbabwe, Nigeria and the Ivory Coast (subject to local currency fluctuations, military coups, etc.), and has a long and scandalous past, which in its early days was oddly reminiscent of a Hollywood B-movie, in which the lions are moth-eaten, the dames are dizzy, and a group of camp white men dress up as gorillas, Tarzan look-alikes and caricaturish tribesmen with spears and leopard-skin loin cloths. Probyn's experiences were fairly typical. In his capacity as tournament director, he was stationed in the middle of a Nigerian golf course beside one of only two available loos. In between rulings, he would watch people racing from all directions clutching toilet rolls. When a storm blew in, Probyn's job was to hop onto the back of a dilapidated motorbike and buzz along the fairways, tooting the horn to stop play. All went smoothly until he discovered that the self-appointed chief referee, a local government official, had taken it upon himself to tell players that anyone within two club lengths of the hole on the water-logged greens could declare their putt a gimme.

There were the usual collection of travel nightmares. No Safari Tour event would be complete without them. In one instance, Probyn and his flock of fledgling pros set off on a flight from Lagos to Yamoussoukro, which was alleged to take an hour and a half but clocked in at forty-two. He and the players spent the night at the airport hotel where, upon finding excrement and insects on the sheets, they decided that their health would benefit immeasurably from a sleepless night spent playing cards in the lounge. The next morning, they embarked on a three-hour bus ride through the jungle on uncharted roads. Returning, Probyn came within a whisker of being faced with telling sixty players that, due to over-booking, they would not be home for Christmas after all. It would have been more than his life was worth. Tour players might be adept at dealing with plugged lies or lateral water hazards, but let there be a hitch in their travel arrangements and they quickly become unhinged.

The mid-70s and early 80s, the peak years of the Safari circuit, were a time of great unrest in Africa. Trigger-happy militia men, and government officials eager to stamp their authority on the crumbling monuments of colonialism, flexed their new muscle with glee. Private clubs were an obvious target. Not long after Zambia gained independence, a barbecue and disco was held at Luansha

Golf Club for the Zambian Open players. The party was in full swing when the district governor took offence at something or other and left the club in a rage. Soon afterwards, a well-dressed official ordered the crowd to disperse. Neither the players nor the locals took any notice. Half an hour went by and the order was repeated, with the promise that force would be used if necessary. The party continued. All of a sudden, the doors flew open and forty soldiers in battle fatigues rushed into the room. They cocked their machine-guns. Within seconds, the party was over, the players and expatriates slipping and sliding in their frantic haste to reach the exit.

Anyone who knows Africa knows that such an incident is as likely to end peacefully, with smiles all round, as it is in a massacre. However, when tragedy did strike on the Safari Tour, it came from an unexpected quarter. In 1974, the Zambian Open went to Mufulira, a small town on the Copperbelt. David Moore, a talented eighteen-year-old from Essex, and Gary Smith, also in his late teens, were put up by an elderly couple who lived near the course. Mr X was a miner by profession. A year or two earlier there had been a mining disaster, in which a shaft had collapsed and trapped hundreds of workers underground. Mr X had played a key part in the rescue operation, crawling under the earth to survey the carnage and heroically hauling maimed and dying men to the surface. As a consequence of the sights he had seen, he had taken to drink.

One evening, Moore and Smith returned from the course to find Mr X under the influence. He began to shout at them, accusing them of flirting with his wife. He disappeared into his bedroom and returned with a shotgun. Everyone scattered. Moore was slower than Smith and Mrs X, and Mr X shot him in the head. Smith dived into the bathroom, whereupon Mr X banged furiously at the door and threatened to kill him, too. Eventually, his wife managed to calm him down, and the three of them took the unconscious Moore to the local hospital. A senior British surgeon tried to save Moore, but it was hopeless. When Mr X heard the news of the young player's death, he went out into the hospital car-park and shot himself.

It was the unanimous decision of the players that Moore would have wanted the tournament to go on, and therefore it did and was won by Christy O'Connor, Jnr. A memorial service was held for Moore, the unfortunate victim of a terrible tragedy.

Back in the sanitized, eerily normal environs of Lake Geneva, Probyn was considering the small problems he faced in his role on the European Tour. 'The toughest thing about administering a golf tournament is making the right call in adverse weather conditions,' he said. Already his thoughts were turning to the Czech Open in the third week of October. Tour agronomists and greenstaff would be on site five weeks before the tournament to try to cure, or prevent the onset of, the grass diseases common at that time of the year, but they could not control the weather. Shorter days would mean that first tee-off would be around 7.00 a.m., and frost, not to mention rain, sleet and fog, would almost certainly be a factor. Groundsheets would be laid over the greens each night.

'It's very difficult because you've got such a wide range of guys,' Probyn said, not knowing then that the Czech Open would set a new bench-mark in weather-related chaos. 'Some who are very easygoing and some [who] are not so easy. The toughest thing is, your relationship with them can change in an instant if you give a ruling that they dislike intensely. But by the same token, we're there to run golf tournaments by regulations set by the committee through elections. So you have to govern them at the same time as being employed by them, which can be a strange balance. But you also get quite a buzz from being associated with them. Some guys are good to have a beer with, but you can't get too close to them, because if you're out drinking with the same guy every night, somewhere down the line, someone's going to ask questions about how impartial you're going to be.'

We turned off the highway and began the steep climb up to Crans-sur-Sierre. Wooden chalets and snow-capped peaks crowded the chocolate-box scenery. 'The Swiss are a neat and industrious people, none of whom is under seventy-five years of age,' Dorothy Parker reflected in *Constant Reader*. 'They make cheeses, milk chocolate, and watches, all of which, when you come right down to it, are pretty fairly unnecessary. It is all true about yodelling and cowbells. It is, however, not true about St Bernard dogs rescuing those lost in the snow. Once there was something in the story; but . . . the present dogs are of such inclinations that it is no longer reasonable to send them out to work, since they took to eating the travellers . . . Skiing is extremely difficult, and none of my affair. The most frequent accident, among ski-jumpers, is the tearing off of an ear. The edelweiss is a peculiarly unpleasant-looking flower.'

Probyn stared unseeingly out at the vineyards and the mossy, vertigo-inducing mountainside. He was thinking about the way in which the Tour tends to rob its followers of whole years; of how the speed of it steals away youth and the size of it swallows lives. 'Look at me,' Probyn said, his voice tinged with the resentment common even to golf's most ardent devotees, when they consider how much the game has cost them. 'I joined the Tour at twenty-four and now all of a sudden I'm approaching thirty. OK, in terms of my career, I've moved on, but outside of golf my life hasn't benefited. You don't do anything at home. You just exist. You spend two days recovering and then you're gone again. You almost feel like an intruder. *Is* there life outside the Tour? I wonder about that sometimes.'

At Crans-sur-Sierre, I stayed at a small, family-run hotel called L'Etrier. There are three travel operators on Tour, Fairway, Traveleads and Randy Fox, and which of them one chooses to travel with generally has a lot more to do with the reps one is friendly with than the price. The average cost of a week on Tour is £450, including flights, accommodation and transfers. Players, who have the additional burden of their caddie's wages and, of course, meals, don't leave home for less than £1,000, which can easily become £1,500 or £2,000 if the tournament is in Dubai or Manila, or even, for that matter, in Madrid.

Small wonder that players become disconsolate when the European Masters rolls round and they are suspended between one-hundred-and-fifteenth and one-hundred-and-thirtieth on the Order of Merit, with only two or three official events left in which to save themselves. On the European Tour, only the top 120 players keep their cards each season. Unless they are exempt through past victories, the rest of them have to return to the Qualifying School at Montpelier in the South of France in November, where they compete with 168 other would-be Faldos, over six rounds (in invariably filthy weather), for forty Tour cards. It is a grievously sad week and hard to stomach. Nowhere can one turn without seeing broken dreams and broken spirits and lives ruined for the love of an uncaring game. One mother sold her home so that she could pay for her son to realize a lifetime ambition at the School. He failed.

This was the subject under discussion when I joined Gary Evans, Richard Boxall, Derrick Cooper and the travel rep David Grice at the bar of the Hotel L'Etrier. They were talking about the nail-biting insecurity of their profession. Cooper, winner of the 1988 Madrid

Open, was dangerously close to losing his card, and on edge. He listed the names of players who had come near enough to glory to smell it and then watched it ebb away: Denis Durnian, Nick Job, Phillip Parkin, Ove Sellberg, and so on *ad infinitum*. In Europe, at that very moment, a host of fine players were poised to return to the Qualifying School. There was Roger Chapman, who had won the Zimbabwean Open and notched up a string of second places in top-class European events, there was the promising Irishman Eoghan O'Connell, and there was De Wet Basson, the South African of whom great things were expected – to name just a few. Even if your card was secure, there were other humiliations. In America the previous week, Ian Baker-Finch, the 1991 Open Champion, had finished fourteen over par at the World Series after shooting 82 in the second round. Too embarrassed to face the other players, he changed his shoes in the car-park each day. The general feeling seemed to be: there but for the grace of God go us all.

We moved into the dining room, where ensued a lively discussion on the value of everyone's watches. Mine cost £20, so I wasn't eligible. Elsewhere, Ebels and Rolex were placed on the tables for inspection, with prices ranging from £2,000 to £7,000. On the men's Tour, these are the things that symbolize status: your wife, your car, your watch and your position on the money list – and not always in that order. They also represent the extremes. They show how chillingly easy it is to be a success story with a gold watch and cherry-red Porsche one year, and a wet, despairing face bound for Montpelier the next.

'This may sound harsh,' Gary Evans said, 'but if you can't make it through six rounds at the Qualifying School, you don't deserve to be out here.'

He spoke as one of the brightest prospects on the European Tour. Beside him, Cooper looked pale beneath his tan.

On Friday, play was suspended for several hours as milky banks of cloud settled over the fairways. The topic of conversation in the press centre was not the weather but John Daly, who had withdrawn from the European Masters following an alleged assault upon a spectator at the World Series in Akron, Ohio.

According to Robinson, who witnessed this latest outrage, all week long Daly had been driving into other players. 'Are you in such a hurry to shoot 80?' Greg Norman's caddie Tony Navarro queried sarcastically, after Daly's ball had bounded through the Shark's group for the umpteenth time. Daly just ignored him. In the final round, he hit several shots into the match of Jeff Roth, head professional at the Flint Golf Club, Michigan, on his way to a score of 83. Afterwards, Daly passed Roth's parents in the car-park. 'Where did you learn your etiquette?' Roth's sixty-two-year-old father Bob asked contemptuously. Daly rounded on him. Words, as they say, were exchanged. At one point, Daly is alleged to have called Bob's wife, Dolores Roth, an effing whore. Her husband seized Daly from behind and both men fell to the ground. They were separated by onlookers, and Daly strode away furiously. 'I hate this fucking Tour,' was his parting shot.

Now it seemed that an old back injury had been aggravated by the scuffle, and Daly was voluntarily taking the rest of the season off to sort out his personal problems. Unsurprisingly, Reebok and Wilson, with whom Daly had signed a ten-year agreement worth an estimated $2 million a year in the summer, had taken the news badly. Jan Thomson, vice-president of Wilson Golf in the States, commented: 'We regret suspending John's contract and, while Wilson empathizes with his personal and professional challenges, we believe that it is just as important to assure our customers and employees that the company expects the highest level of sports-manship, decorum and professionalism from its professional advisory staff . . . Wilson and John will resume their relationship under a newly-structured agreement when Wilson is satisfied that John has met specific behavioural and performance objectives.'

Zoeller thought the suspensions were unfair. 'I think John has taken a very bad rap for this latest episode,' he said. 'I'm not sure suspending him is the right way to go about it. He had a couple of hecklers, people in the gallery who got carried away. If they had security around John like they were supposed to have, it wouldn't have happened. What we didn't read was that John was the second guy to hit. That means the marshals in front had already waved those guys down. That's what bugs me. Nobody wrote that. He's playing with Neal Lancaster and Neal hits first. Then John hits.

'It's life in the fast lane. When you're on top, they're shooting at you. And they're shooting bullets. This one here was a direct hit.'

John Daly was not the only discontented player in the world. Like Wild Thing, Severiano Ballesteros's relations with the establishment were, to say the least, strained, and he had been unhappy with the general order of things for some time. Never one to let an opportunity go begging, he broached the subject in a roundabout way, informing us on pro-am day that he was considering playing more golf in America.

An air of bewilderment greeted this announcement. Ballesteros is not just an integral part of the European Tour; he is its lifeblood, its heart and soul.

'But why do you want to leave Europe?' queried one slightly anguished voice. 'What are you fed up with? The media?'

'No, no,' Ballesteros said. He smiled wanly. 'I wouldn't get fed up with you. Don't put everybody in one basket. I'm fed up with some things. In general, I'm not too happy.'

Gordon Richardson raised the matter of the BMW International Open. 'In Munich, when you were going to be fined for slow play, you said that you felt you were being driven out of the Tour. Was that said in the heat of the moment?'

There was a pause. 'There are a lot of things I would like made better,' Ballesteros admitted. 'The players are a bit unhappy. I don't want to go too deep into the problem.' He studied his fingernails.

'What exactly do you mean?' Dai Davies asked.

'Well, when you say things to the committee, like, five, six or seven times, about why the players are unhappy, and nothing happens . . .'

'What are *you* unhappy about?'

'You want to know too much,' Ballesteros said firmly and politely. It was clear the discussion was at an end. 'So,' he said with an attempt at brightness, 'the weather's very nice this week . . .'

Outside, mist and intermittent drizzle continued to disrupt the event. There were cold players, cross players and players throwing in the towel. Colin Montgomerie, who had been bidding for his third successive victory, missed the cut comfortably and afterwards exhibited his usual sense of diplomacy and decorum by referring to Crans-sur-Sierre as 'a dump'. One of the caddies – who, admittedly, has a tendency to embellish things – claimed that when a member of Montgomerie's match tried to cheer him up by urging him to think of all his millions, the Scot retorted: 'I haven't even spent last year's money yet.'

Meanwhile, the travel agents ran about like headless chickens. Due to the disruption in play, their bookings were now invalid, and they were desperately trying to accommodate the wishes of dozens of disheartened, I-want-to-go-home-and-I-want-to-go-this-very-minute pros.

'What do you do in a situation like this?' I asked Mark Watson, the Traveleads rep.

'Panic,' came the reply.

Later in the day, John McHenry came into the press tent to stare anxiously at the scoreboard. A former Walker Cup player once tipped as a future star of Irish golf, he was now contemplating the unappealing prospect of a fifth visit to the Qualifying School. 'It's demoralizing more than hard,' McHenry said, without much conviction. He was thirty years old and had a new wife to support. 'I think if you go there with the right attitude, you'll get through. But it's hard to come off this Tour and go back to the School. The people who are there for the first time are up for it, because they view it as the opportunity of a lifetime. But if you've had a long, hard season on the European Tour, and you're a bit browned off with it all, it's very, very difficult to make it through.'

The Tour is relentless, forward-looking, shallow. It takes no account of friendships, relationships, marriages, children, pets or responsibilites. Whether you're fighting to make the cut, survive a deadline or earn a percentage, when you're ensconced in the warm bosom of your friends by the fireside of some cosy restaurant on a frosty night in Switzerland, home can seem as remote as the moon, and blood-ties as tenuous and ephemeral as silk thread. All that matters is the here and now – which is why some people are able to go conscienceless to red-light districts one week and bounce their babies on their knees and be perfect family men the next. It is an unnatural life and a highly artificial one. The Tour and Home occupy parallel universes, and the former almost always has to take precedent. You know at least a year in advance that, barring an earthquake, you will be covering the Spanish Open on 5 May and the Open Championship on 16 July. But it is by no means guaranteed that you will ever find time to learn to play the piano, write to your grandmother, volunteer for a charity, walk the dog or celebrate your wedding anniversary. Not only are entire weeks wasted because you're always waiting for flights, waiting for play to resume, waiting for shuttle buses, trains and automobiles, but entire wars pass you by simply because technical idiocy doesn't allow you to find CNN on your hotel television. As the season grinds on, procrastination becomes a way of life. Everything not pertaining to the tournament currently taking place is put on hold. On returning to base, travellers without spouses are greeted with in-trays overflowing with un-answered mail, final demands and curt reprimands from forgotten aunts, while answering machines bleep with a dozen messages from concerned parents, hurt friends, angry bank managers and disillusioned publishers. Husbands and boyfriends are met at the door by growling dogs and blank-faced children. Daddy who?

'The problem is, to be a good golfer you've got to be single-minded, and then when you go home, if you've got a family, you've got to not be single-minded,' D. J. Russell said. 'I think it's very hard to bridge the gap between a very individual sporting career and family life. You either have to have a very understanding wife, or your priorities have to change. The little white ball becomes less important.'

'It's big business now,' said Randy Fox. 'Players used to enjoy going to exotic restaurants. Now they can't afford to get sick, there's too much money. Look at Peter Smith [a talented Scottish player whose career never really recovered after he was rushed to hospital with a stomach haemorrhage caused by a chicken sandwich in Spain]. And five players had food poisoning in Germany. No, it's steak and chips or McDonalds, one drink, and then it's back to the room to watch satellite television. That's the No.1 priority on Tour now when you're looking for hotels.

'It's changed a lot,' Fox said sadly, considering the unhealthy interest of the average Tour player in television, money and Nintendo games. 'It's how many millions now. They practise putting in their rooms every night. There's very little messing around – a lot of talk, but not much action. There's too much to lose. On Tuesday nights, there used to be forty players in the discos. Now, there'll be three or four. It's really not the most exciting way of life. It's just an eight-to-ten-hour job. They're a homogeneous group of very serious businessmen. They could be next door to the Prado [Madrid's famous museum of art] and they'd never even know it was there. They hardly ever bring their families any more.'

But that is not to say there are no high jinks any more, just less. The top players like to tuck themselves up in bed at sundown and, with the exception of Ian Woosnam, let their hair down only occasionally with a spell of trout fishing or snooker. Of the rank and file, Malcolm McKenzie plays chess with sports psychologist John

(Psycho John) Allsop, Gordon J. Brand paints, Ronan Rafferty adds to his wine collection, Ross McFarlane brushes up on his table tennis skills (he was once ranked twentieth in England), and Mark Roe, a former diving champion, plays practical jokes. These are not always popular. Some people like Roe's idea of fun and think it makes him one of the Tour's few remaining characters. Others think he is childish, and wonder when he's going to grow up. His pranks have included: a record number of food-throwing fights in restaurants and on aeroplanes; cutting the toes out of Barry Lane's socks; removing the fuses from every single electrical appliance in Lane's room; sitting for forty minutes in a hotel corridor until Lane opened his door, and then drenching him with a fire hose. The Ryder Cup player emptied Roe's mini-bar in retaliation.

Still, there are occasions when the Tour does need livening up. It used to be a standing joke that if twelve players walked into a restaurant on the US Tour, they would sit down at twelve tables, whereas in Europe they'd sit at one or two. Nowadays, even the Europeans take up six or even eight. They are also joined at the hip to their own countrymen. The Italian players eat together, as do the Irish, the Swedes, the Scots, the South Africans and the Australians.

'There's not a resentment,' Fox explained. 'There's just a nationalism.'

In the early days of European golf, few players had the luxury of the five-star service even caddies can enjoy today – i.e. courtesy cars, shuttle services to the golf course, gymnasiums, saunas and forty-two channel televisions, and all the other essentials of stress-free travel. Indeed, most players used to take their cars to Continental events. Des Smyth drove the entire circuit one season with Warren Humphries. 'In hindsight, it was the worst thing I ever did,' Smyth said. 'It cost me money, in my opinion, because we were always sick and we were always tired, so we never won any money.'

'We played for nothing, so we won nothing,' D. J. Russell agreed.

Russell travelled with Ian Woosnam. The Welshman had a campervan and Russell had a car and caravan, so they tended to go in the latter. Later, they progressed to a car and B&Bs. In more stringent times still, Woosnam had travelled with Joe Higgins. Usually, the penniless pair existed on a monotonous diet of chips and baked beans, but at one tournament they found themselves without even the means to afford these meagre rations. In the dead of night, they unloaded their practice ball bags, crept down to a nearby orchard and filled them with French apples. They gorged themselves without bothering to wash the fruit first, and spent the next few days being violently and copiously sick.

On another journey, this time from Scotland to Italy, their caravanette began to labour and wheeze. They prayed that the noise would stop. It grew louder and more persistent. At 12.30 p.m., they pulled over on a main street in Milan. They peered under the bonnet and fretted over the cost of a new engine and the very real chance they now had of being disqualified from the pre-qualifying event for late arrival. At 5.30 a.m. Woosnam rose and begged a ride to the nearest garage on the handlebars of a local's bicycle. A mechanic was persuaded to come and inspect the engine, and it was fixed in a flash for the princely sum of £2. Higgins missed the cut at Monticello but Woosnam finished eighth.

'Did you think then that Woosnam would become as good as he did?' I asked Russell on the flight from Geneva to London.

'I suppose you both think that you're going to be that good,' Russell said. 'But he was always convinced that he was going to be what he has been. Woosie's got a big front to him that makes him look as if he doesn't care. He tends to make light of things. But he works as hard at his game as anybody. He likes to make it appear that he doesn't really work that hard, but to win a major and become the world No.1, you've got to be very determined. He's the most determined person I've ever met.'

Determined Woosnam may be, but at this point in time he had had a very thin season. His – or rather, IMG's – insatiable appetite for appearance money had left him cooling his heels in Jersey for most of the year. When he did appear at tournaments, he came in his private plane and stayed only long enough to enhance his Boozie Woosie image, cemented in the tabloid imagination by a fine, earlier in the year, for drunk driving. The public perception was that he had left his hometown in Wales for the Channel Isles tax-haven purely for mercenary reasons, but Russell said that in Oswestry his life had no longer been his own. Not that Woosnam seemed happy in Jersey. He complained of loneliness and said he had no friends to play squash or tennis or keep fit with. His golf suffered through a listless and negative attitude.

'I think the difference between Ian and Faldo is that if Faldo's playing badly, he says: "Oh, I'm concentrating on the majors," or,

"Leadbetter and I are working on something in my swing," ' Russell said. 'Ian just says: "I'm playing crap." Faldo seems to make a positive thing out of playing badly, whereas Ian just tells the truth. It's also very difficult for someone like Ian, to have gone from obscurity to world stardom. You can never be prepared for what that presents. He's a very private person and sometimes he'd just like to go somewhere and not be Ian Woosnam any more. It's nice being rich and famous, but at the same time he likes being one of the lads. Unfortunately, that privilege has been taken away from him. There's been a sort of getting used to it period for him. He's had to adapt to something that he finds very difficult.'

Russell thinks back to the uncomplicated days of their youth with a sigh. 'We often wish that we could go back to that time,' he said nostalgically. 'We often talk about it and wish that we could jump into a caravan and have £20 in our pockets for the month. I think the thing you miss from it is just the sheer ambition and looking forward to every day.'

For his own part, he was looking forward to the day when his insurance policy came into effect. The US Tour have an excellent pension scheme which is based on the number of cuts made, but in Europe there's no security for journeymen. 'The hard thing when you're reaching my age is that the youngsters have got nothing else but golf in their life and they give it 110 per cent. All they dream about is golf – they live it and breathe it. Whereas, golf sort of gets in the way of everything else when you get to forty.'

He was biding his time until his own private pension plan came into effect when he reached the magic age of forty, or better still, until he reached fifty and could qualify for the most lucrative pension scheme ever invented for professional golfers not yet tired of delayed flights, lost luggage and airline food: the Seniors Tour.

15

VAGABONDS WITH ATTITUDE

'My own experience as a caddie imparted lasting knowledge in only two areas – sex and poker.'

LARRY SHEEHAN

A filmy curtain of smoke hung across the railway carriage. Ghostly spirals twisted up to meet it from the cupped palms of a red-eyed group of caddies, whose faded Levis and Paul Smith T-shirts gave them a dishevelled kind of trendiness, like that of university students after a night of revelry. They eyed me with scepticism when I sat down. Ever since I'd analysed Jesper Parnevik's defeat in the Open for the *Sunday Times*, quoting Chris Moody as saying that Mick Donaghy's failure to advise the Swede of his position at the seventy-second hole was 'the worst example of professional caddying in the history of the game' – an admittedly extreme statement – my relations with the caddie ranks had been distinctly frosty. Like minority groups, caddies are allowed to criticize each other, but let anyone else find fault with them and they all band together in outrage.

I decided to brazen it out. 'I suppose none of you is speaking to me,' I said, sitting down uninvited in the midst of them all and throwing my bag on the seat.

Alastair was leaning tiredly against the window. He said bluntly, and only half-jokingly: 'Mick will kill anyone he sees speaking to you.'

'Well,' I said, 'you can't have it both ways. You can't, on the one hand, say that a caddie is an integral part of any player's success, and on the other, refuse to accept any responsibility when things go wrong.'

Instantly the mood changed. This was an argument they could all relate to. Professional pride ran high among the caddies present, and there wasn't one who did not want to be viewed as a valuable and necessary part of his golfer's career and not just a bag-carrier and a second-class citizen on the Tour. They relaxed and began to chat. Only Alastair, more usually known as Squirrel, continued to lounge in his seat, sullen and yawning.

'What's up with you?' I asked.

'Argument with D. C.,' he muttered. D. C. is Darren Clarke, a strong, ambitious Irishman with enormous potential. Clarke had insisted that Squirrel, who had no idea how he was going to get back to Geneva but guessed it would be a combination of taxis, trains and buses, should take his golf bag on to the next tournament. 'I pay you fockin' good money,' he told the obstinate Squirrel. Needless to say, the golf bag had accompanied Alastair to the train.

'You two have got the most enduring love/hate relationship since Liz Taylor and Richard Burton,' Martin Rowley teased him.

Alastair laughed and brightened up. He bought himself a drink, despatched a slab of Swiss chocolate and joined in the conversation as we slipped away from Syon.

Rowley, Chairman of the Caddies' Association, was saying that he received some five hundred calls a year from people wanting to know how to break into caddying.

'And what do you tell them?' I asked.

Rowley chuckled. 'I say: "Go to Dubai, and stand around the car-park." '

Alastair sat up. 'Phil was one of the five hundred who called you,' he said slyly, indicating a clean-cut young man with an open, likeable face. 'He was one of the ones who made the big-time.'

'And what did I say to you?' demanded Rowley.

'You said: "Can't talk now, my peas are boiling over," ' grinned Phil.

Rowley was Carl Mason's caddie, a big-boned man in a yellow Pringle sweater, with overlong blond hair and a public school accent. Eight years ago, he was holidaying in Paris when he saw a poster advertising a golf tournament in Madrid. Having only recently been discharged from hospital following a stress-related illness, he was at a professional and emotional crossroads. So he caught a train to Spain, shared a few laughs with D. J. Russell and the other pros, and tried his hand at caddying.

'I thought: "I'm enjoying this, the world is off my shoulders," ' recalled Rowley, 'and I just carried on.'

'Rowley's about forty and he's lived five lives,' Squirrel said.

It emerged that Rowley had once been the youngest councillor in the history of Derbyshire; had beaten six thousand candidates to a Royal Naval College scholarship (regrettably, he was hit by a car and seriously injured before he could take it up); had been a publican; and had been an export account manager at Gordon's Gin.

I guess I shouldn't have been surprised. One thing you notice about the Tour is that people tend to know each another on extremely superficial levels. For instance, Derrick Cooper and Richard Boxall have a friendship of many years standing, and yet after they'd had a squabble in Switzerland – largely due to the fact that Cooper was fretting about keeping his card (which he did) – Boxy remarked to me: 'I've known him for years, we've even stayed at each other's houses, but I don't really *know* him.' On Tour, players, caddies and riff-raff come and go at the rate of high-speed trains. They lose their cards, they lose their jobs, they get divorced, they get deported, and on the day that they reappear, whether it's a month or ten years later, everyone will greet them as if they've only been gone for the weekend. Indeed, it's unlikely that a soul outside their immediate families realizes they haven't. The pace of life and level of self-absorption in Europe is such that you can follow the circuit for six years, give it up without telling anybody and no-one will notice you're missing until one night when they're telling stories around a dinner table in Stuttgart and your name comes up in conversation.

This is even more true of caddies than it is of everyone else. Ian (Two Bags) Wright had a two-season reign of glory as Ballesteros's caddie when the Spaniard exploded out of the doldrums to win the 1988 Open, the World Match Play and the Order of Merit. During this period, he was interviewed by dozens of influential newspapermen, radio stations and even a documentary crew on his experiences, all of which he subsequently described in a book entitled *Summers with Seve*, and yet he vanished altogether after he and Ballesteros parted company. He is alleged to have popped up a few years later on the US Tour, but I've never seen him. As for poor Two Shots, whom I interviewed in *Shooting at Clouds* as one of the up-and-coming caddies on Tour, he is now driving taxis in Melbourne.

Rowley was talking about players he had known, including a saturnine and eccentric American. He, the American and Robert Lee, the English player of whom so much was expected, had been in a Monaco casino (during the much mourned days when the Monte Carlo Open was held at Mont Agel, and our nights were spent gambling, dining at the Sporting Club and going to the palace for cocktail parties with the royal family) when Rowley hit the jackpot at the roulette table. The caddie was jubilant. After giving most of the money to Lee's girlfriend for safe keeping, he bought drinks all round.

'What can I get you, J?' he asked the American.

'I'd like some coke,' J told him.

'Would you like ice and lemon?' Rowley said, knowing what he meant but ignoring it just the same.

'It wouldn't fit up my nose,' drawled J.

J, it seems, deserves his own chapter in the annals of caddie lore. 'He used to hit it further than any guy in Europe.' 'He had a big following in Asia.' 'He had a very rich girlfriend.' He also, so Squirrel maintained, had weak bowels. At some stage during almost every round, he would dart into the trees to answer a call of nature. One morning, he disappeared with the bag-towel.

'Where's that towel, J?' queried Alastair when they reached the green, picking up J's ball and looking round for the cloth he needed to clean it with.

J raised one eyebrow. 'I didn't take it in there to wipe the sweat off my brow,' he told the startled Squirrel.

Another favourite is Simon Hobday, winner of the US Seniors Open and a legend in his own lifetime. Hobday is a Zimbabwean and, by definition, a man's man. Not only does he object to doing chores of a domestic nature, he really doesn't know how. In the wilder days of his misspent youth, when he roomed with players like Jack Newton, Tertius Classens and John O'Leary (who was full of fun before he became a fully-paid-up member of the Tour's morality police), who were of a similarly romantic and hard-drinking bent, it was his habit to put his dirty laundry in a neat pile on the floor at the end of each day and then start again at the beginning when he had run out of clothes to wear. Sometimes, he was forced to actually wash things. Newton remembers him putting everything he owned, colours, whites, cottons and woollens, into the hotel bath and stirring them round with some soap. Then he draped the shrunken jumpers and multi-coloured whites over the room-divider. Articles would fall to the floor during the drying process, attracting floor polish and dust, and Hobday would just hang them right up again, pulling them on proudly when they were ready, unironed and dramatically stained.

Hobday was prevented from going as far as his exquisite ball-striking might have let him by the yips. These he had tried every way in the world to cure, even resorting to hypnosis. The hypnotist managed to convince him that he was the game's greatest putter but failed to provide him with the necessary tools. Hobday went out the next day and took forty-two putts and still walked off the course thinking he was the game's greatest putter. But he didn't give up hope. At a South African event, he tried a more inventive ploy. He teed off wearing a Mexican sombrero. On the first hole, he sank a 25-foot putt for birdie. On the second, a 20-footer saved par. On holes three through six, birdie putts of 15 feet, 10 feet, and 12 feet dived into the cup as if they had no option. But on the next hole, he went to tap in a two-footer and saw it lip infuriatingly out for bogey. Hobday fell to his knees on the green. He ripped off his sombrero, looked heavenward and shook his fist. 'It took you seven holes, but you recognized me!' he cried in anguish.

It is a caddie's role to be supportive at such times. He should not, as Fishfinger is reputed to have done, clutch his head after a bad shot and say: 'I'm surrounded by spastics.'

'Well, there's one less now,' Bill Longmuir assured him as he sacked him.

Fishfinger, who rose to become a chauffeur for the footballer Dean Saunders was oddly suited to his nickname. He was tall, sunburnt and rather floppy, like a Captain Birdseye special splashed with a dollop of ketchup. 'Where's my lump of cod?' Mark James would say affectionately when in search of him.

Other nicknames are equally apt. Kelloggs is so named because he looks like a serial killer; Saddam is a dead-ringer for President Hussein; the Judge is an excellent judge of racing form; Overkill, Tom Lehman's caddie, gives shot details in unbearable detail; Wobbly, Ian Woosnam's caddie, is named after a cartoon character who walks the way he does; Spock bears a passing resemblance to the Star Trek actor; and Opium, who works for Ian Pyman, is a slow-moving dope. It is possible that by now Bullet, Fulton Allem's caddie, has been renamed. He visited a portaloo during an American event and was approaching the green on the next hole when he realized with horror that he had lost his yardage book. He summoned a lady marshal and appealed to her to retrace his footsteps. Off she went. Frantic minutes ticked by before she returned – clutching her nose and the dripping yardage book. Still, there was nothing else for it, the yardage book had to return to service. Bullet wiped it off as best as he could, and peered at the numbers beneath the dark patches. Allem selected a club and aimed a shot at the green. At impact, his hands slipped and the ball careered off into the rough. He looked at the club with distaste. He picked it up and sniffed it.

'Bullet,' said Allem in a tone of deep displeasure, 'there's shit on these grips.'

Yardage books are a symbol of the modernization of caddying as a profession. Gone are the days when caddies hauled themselves drunken and bedraggled from beneath hedgerows, squinted at the lines of putts and said, 'It's slightly straight, sir.' Actually, some of these men were geniuses at reading greens and eye-balling distances, but Sam Snead was so untrusting of their methods he used to tell his caddie: 'When I ask you what club to use, look the other way and don't answer.' Modern players don't have that problem. Graeme Hinch, a New Zealander, puts their minds at rest by going ahead of the Tour, measuring every contour of every course, making intricate diagrams, and printing them up in yardage books which retail at £5 each.

'It's not about being a good caddie now,' said Paul Stephens, who is known as the Singing Caddie because he has cut several records, including an Elvis tribute album and a single called 'Magic Book' which made it to No.16 in the UK charts. 'It's about compatibility with your golfer, watching your ps and qs, watching what you say. We're bending more the other way – not speaking your mind as opposed to speaking your mind, holding your tongue for the sake of keeping your job. The best caddies have not got the best jobs now, whereas in the old days it used to be that way. It's easy now. We used to have to eye-ball and then it was down to your own judgement, and you had to get your own pin positions and yardages. A twelve-year-old kid could go out and caddie now and do just as good a job because everything's done for you.'

Only the royal 'We' remains unchanged: i.e. 'We made birdie at seven, and then *he* hit the ball in the trees.' A caddie on the train told the assembled company: 'I'm not being big-headed, right, but the only time he fucks up is when he doesn't listen to me.'

'Caddying has changed because the players have become more professional,' Rowley explained. 'Five years ago, all the boys would have been partying all night. Now there's too much money around. Most caddies fly and stay in hotels. On an average week, you've got to pay £150 for flight, £220 for your accommodation, £40 for incidentals, and then you've got to eat. You're looking at around £500 a week. So the whole job has become more professional. The players pay more but they expect more.'

The average wage is £350 per week, plus 7 per cent for a win or 5 per cent for a place. The rising cost of keeping afloat on the Tour means that it is extremely difficult for the bottom-rung caddies to survive, but it also means that the top caddies earn more than a lot of players. They are also more image-conscious. Lambswool sweaters and ugly trousers are still the norm among players, whereas many of the caddies sport Chinos, Keanu Reeves haircuts and smart polo-shirts with white T-shirts underneath. Fitness and weight-training has become a craze among the younger generation. One older caddie confessed, 'There's still large amounts of alcohol being consumed,' but the gym is slowly taking over from the pub and the strip joint.

'There comes a point when you've been in so many bars, drinking, you just get bored,' said Damien, one of the Wentworth caddies, who has lost nearly two stone by running and working out. 'Plus, the women like it when you're fitter. There's always a motive!'

Damien has travelled the European circuit since the days when Silly Billy drove a busload of caddies from venue to venue. 'Everyone drank on the bus,' he recalled. 'You look back now and you think: "How could we do that every week?" But you did.' Even so, most caddies still prefer to stay at different hotels to the pros. 'It's no good for your relationship with your golfer if you mix with the players,' explained Damien.

I was a caddie once. I volunteered for the job at the 1990 Monte Carlo Open after a South African rookie told me that he was going to have to give up the Tour mid-season and return home because he could no longer afford to play. My heart went out to him. My own position as a freelance on the Tour was growing more precarious by the day, and the fact that I was still out there at all was entirely due to the combined charity of my mother, my landlady and my bank manager.

'I'll make a deal with you,' I told him. 'I'll caddie for you for nothing unless you make the cut. If you qualify, then you have to pay me £100 for the week if we finish outside the top twenty, £250 if we finish outside the top ten, and 7 per cent of your winnings if we finish tenth or better.' Agreed, said the South African, and off we went. Five days later, we were walking up the seventy-second fairway towards a share of seventh place and £9,158.22. I was overjoyed. While he was sinking the crucial putt, I was busy calculating how my 7 per cent would save me from eviction, save me from bankruptcy, and still leave me change to spare. The South African shook my hand and gave me a £100 note. 'Thanks very much for your help,' he said. And that was it. Not another penny was forthcoming.

The other caddies were up in arms when they heard. Indeed, a number of them offered to 'sort him out' on my behalf. But there was nothing to be gained from brute force. Our agreement had been verbal; there were no witnesses. I learnt the hard way about caddying's biggest drawback: exploitation. Unless you are Fanny Sunesson, with a six-figure salary and multiple endorsements, or Squeeky, Nick Price's caddie, who's 'won' four majors, all contracts are verbal and come without a pension plan, a medical scheme or security of any kind. There is no such thing as a month's notice. It is a matter of honour whether the player who fires you sends you home with or without pay.

Dave Renwick and Jose Maria Olazabal had been together for nearly eight years when they split up in May, just weeks after the Spaniard had won the Masters. 'It's over,' the forty-year-old Scot said. 'The divorce is final. I have my principles and pride.'

Olazabal had stood by Renwick when he was jailed over his involvement in a car accident in 1989, when two caddies died. But Renwick had also stood by Olazabal. The Spaniard had appealed to him to stay on after Dave had walked off the course in tears during the 1992 Volvo Masters, so he did. But Renwick said that his tantrums were as bad as ever at the 1994 B&H International in May. 'I've said for years that Jose's fiery temper has held him back,' he told reporters at the Spanish Open. 'His behaviour at times has been disgusting and I am not taking any more.' Renwick's biggest complaint, however, was Olazabal's attitude towards money. He received only 7 per cent of Olazabal's $360,000 Masters cheque, while most caddies agree that a major is worth 10.

Percentage payouts are always a sensitive issue. Seve Ballesteros used to justify a paltry wage and just 5 per cent for a win, by saying that he earned twice as much as most other players: 'Five per cent of nothing *is* nothing.' It doesn't take long for a player to get a bad reputation, because he is mean with money or bad-tempered. 'Greg [Norman] intimidates caddies . . .' Pete Bender told *Golf* magazine. 'You're afraid to say stuff to him, even if you're right because you don't want to be fired for it.' Bender was sacked by the Shark little more than a year after winning the Open with him at Turnberry. 'The day before Thanksgiving, 1987, he called me from his car phone in Australia,' Bender recalled. 'He just said: "It's time to change." I said: "Give me one good reason why you're firing me, what's your excuse?" He said: "I don't have an excuse." '

But according to Frank Williams, Bender's biggest problem was that he was indiscreet, not to mention arrogant. 'He forgot who was boss.'

This was borne out by Bender's savage criticism of Chip Beck, after the American had chosen the safe option at the fifteenth hole and lost the Masters to Langer. Bender had been there at Beck's side while he decided whether or not to go for the green: 'I gave him the yardage and he kind of looked at me like, "What should he do?" I was ready to pull the head cover off the three-wood when he said, "Not so fast, let's talk about this."

'So I said, "You've got a perfect lie, 235 yards to the front." I said, "You know, Chip, in certain situations you're going to have to go for it, and this is one of them. You have a chance to win the Masters."

'Then he started stalling. He walked up about ten yards past his ball and kept trying to wait for the breeze to pick up. Then he walked back and said, "Well, there's a little breeze blowing in our face, you know." And I said, "Yeah, but it's not a strong breeze. Downhill makes up for it." I told him I could give him more reasons he should go for it than he could to lay up. I asked him why he didn't want to go for it. He looked me straight in the face and said, "I don't want to mess my round up." '

Beck laid up and made par, and failed to catch Langer. Bender and he parted company three months later, by which time poor Beck had been inundated with hate mail. Fortunately, Mike Donald says that the American journalism graduate is so maniacally sunny that nothing would throw him. If he came home and found his cat had been run over and was lying in the driveway, he'd say, 'Ah, doesn't she look peaceful.'

Malcolm Mason, Torrance's caddie, is more used to mercurial players, having spent four seasons with the Zimbabwean Tony Johnstone, and two with Howard Clark. 'Tony is a very bad tempered person, and his temper comes out in his game,' Mason said. 'But he only ever gets angry with himself; whereas Howard, who is arguably the most ferocious person to work for, directs his anger at his caddie and anyone else in the vicinity. He's such a perfectionist that he doesn't like to think that he might be at fault. It's because of his intensity. I mean, when you come off the course, he can't apologize enough for his behaviour.'

Malcolm, a salesman before a spell of unemployment drove him onto the Tour, has spent the past six years with Torrance, a comparatively easygoing player. 'He's what would be commonly classed as a man's man. He loves all the things that most men like. He's interested in all sport. I think that's probably why we get on so well. But he does get cross. I think that to be a winner, you have to get cross; you have to have aggression to win tournaments.'

John (Scotchy) Graham, who caddies for Mark James, found himself on the receiving end of Lanny Wadkins's temper at the 1989 Ryder Cup when he inadvertently stepped on the Texan's line. 'Get off my line,' growled Wadkins, directing such a venomous stare at Graham that he promptly did it again. 'Well, at least you can say that you've danced all over Texas,' Tony Navarro, then caddying for Wadkins, said drily as they walked down the next hole.

Max Cunningham, Sandy Lyle's caddie, feared for his job for a different reason. Having been invited, along with his wife, to stay with Sandy and Jolande in their fifty-six-room mansion in Scotland, he repaid the hospitality by shooting Lyle's dog. Not intentionally, of course, but by accident whilst hunting rabbits. He was mortified. Luckily, the adored pet – a crossbred Labrador – survived the disaster, albeit with a broken leg which cost £500 in vet's bills to put right.

Back in the Swiss railway carriage, the caddies were discussing the harsh realities of career caddying. 'You know what I hate about this Tour?' Wayne said suddenly. 'There's too many pricks.'

Alastair nodded. 'There used to be a good bunch of guys out here.'

'There still are,' I protested.

'No, they're idiots,' Alastair said shortly.

'The problem with this Tour,' said Phil, 'is that if you're a good chiseller, you'll get to the top, regardless of how good you are on the course. You have to be a slime-ball. I was working for Jonathan Lomas this week, and every time I turned around somebody was trying to talk to him about a job.'

A gloom fell over the group. They began to think about the drawbacks of caddying – the back-biting, the financial insecurity, the gypsy lifestyle, the skivvying, the blame they took for mistakes that weren't their fault. On the US Tour particularly, caddies keep a close eye on each other, watching for caddies who aren't getting along with their players, who are thinking of quitting or are about to get the sack.

'You have to watch those flying knives don't get you,' one caddie remarked cynically.

'It can't be all that bad if you're still doing it,' I said.

'You're doing it because you're hanging on for those big cheques,' Phil responded.

'You're doing it because there's nothing better at home,' agreed Woody, who works for Ian Palmer. 'You don't earn anything but you don't lose anything either.'

Pete Coleman, Langer's caddie, who writes his own cheques, told me that the youngsters who aren't yet making a living look at the superstar caddies and aspire to their wealth and fame. 'I bought a Porsche in 1985, Wobbly has a car contract with a company, and a couple of the guys drive BMWs, and I suppose they look at that and they think: "That's a nice way of life." It's in the open air and every day is different. Every tournament is different. It beats a nine to five job.'

'I wouldn't know what to do if I quit,' confessed Mason, forty-five, whose wife is expecting a child. 'When you're caddying for a good player you know you've got a chance of winning every time you tee it up. The average caddie, there's not another job he could do and earn the money that he does caddying. The winning caddie at the Volvo Masters will make more than the average man does in a year.'

He doesn't feel that the constant travel is a disadvantage. 'Somebody said to me the other day: "Don't you get fed up with being away from home all the time?" But I'm home more often than the average man. I only work thirty-four weeks of the year. I get eighteen weeks off, plus two days a week.'

Apart from that, Mason, like every other caddie, is a gambler, a vagabond and an incurable optimist. He lives for the thrill of the final day and the high induced by victory; for the comforting squeak of leather and the birdsong that fills the cold, clean air on early tournament mornings at Wentworth or St Andrews; for the strange chemistry and interdependency that defines a relationship between a caddie and his player; and for the camaraderie that warms the endless nights, from Madrid to New Orleans and back again.

'Cosmopolitan, that's what the Tour is now for caddies,' Damien said.

16

DANGEROUS LIAISONS

'It is most undesirable that an organization should be able to represent a governing body, sponsors, a significant number of top players, negotiate television, cable and satellite contracts, and sell merchandising rights. The situation is pregnant with conflicts of interest and cannot carry public confidence.'

1983 Report of the Committee of Inquiry into Sports
Sponsorship, chaired by Denis Howell, MP

CONVERSATION IN A COURTESY CAR

Player A: 'What are people saying about the course?'

Player B: 'That it's a field with flags.'

Player A: 'They shouldn't even have flags on it, they should have windmills. The greens are like concrete circles. We should play crazy golf, that would make it more interesting.'

Player B: 'Why have we come here?'

Player A: 'Well, they looked at about six or seven golf courses in the area, and this one had the best facilities.'

Player B: 'You mean, it was the only one with an inside toilet.'

Player A: 'No, this one had the best car-parking facilities.'

Player B: 'Are you sure we aren't playing on the car-park and the cars are parked on the golf course? I think it's a very sad day if the European Tour has reached the stage where we're going to courses because the car-parks are good, and we come away from tournaments saying:

"That was the best car-park we've ever been to." But then the rumour is that this course is owned by the sponsor.'

Caddie (glancing at me): 'Careful. This is developing into a story.'

Player B: 'That's all right. I'll just deny it.'

All season long, there had been murmurings of discontent. Off the record, players, managers and committee members had hinted at a looming crisis and had talked of the dangerous liaison between Mark McCormack's International Management Group and the PGA European Tour, but Seve Ballesteros was the first to publicly express that disenchantment, commenting darkly at Crans-sur-Sierre that 'the players are not happy.' Ballesteros is, of course, given to making veiled threats and innuendos, and if nothing else had occurred to provoke him, the matter might well have ended there. It didn't. The very next week, IMG made an announcement so astounding it took one's breath away: Ballesteros, the winner of five major championships and over seventy titles world-wide, would not be invited to the World Match Play, an event he had won five times.

'How long do you go on past performances?' McCormack said unapologetically. 'Do you wait twenty-eight years before not inviting someone? Or more?'

Well, hell hath no fury like Ballesteros when he has been scorned, and seldom had he been shunned so publicly or so brazenly. 'It looks like it's going to be the McCormack Tour very soon instead of our Tour, the players' Tour,' Ballesteros told journalists at the European Open, his voice icy with sarcasm. 'It looks like he owns it. A lot of political things happen. You give me a little piece of the cake here and I'll give you a little piece there. That sort of thing.'

These observations were not simply a product of Ballesteros's fevered imagination. He was articulating the very real fears of the non-IMG players, many of whom became concerned when the European Tour tossed virtue out the window and climbed into bed with IMG. Their main worry was a monopoly situation. It is pointless to deny that European golf would not be where it is today without IMG, but by the start of 1994 it had become a kind of golfing empire where it managed a significant number of the world's top players, controlled ten or eleven tournaments in Europe alone, negotiated television, cable and satellite contracts (through TWI, their television arm), sold merchandising rights, and had become inextricably bound to the Tour through a series of joint ventures.

Nowhere could the potential for conflict of interest be seen more clearly than in the allocation of tournament invites. At IMG events, IMG players were given priority treatment. Within strict limits, a sponsor can pander to whomever he chooses, but employing a system that doesn't reward form or past achievement is not only guaranteed to cause resentment among the players who are discriminated against, it is also not good for the game. For instance, while the gifted Scottish rookie Andrew Coltart was not invited to the IMG-run British Masters, there were invites distributed among South African unknowns, some of whom didn't even bother to show up.

'I can honestly say that all [my clients] are affected by not getting invitations to IMG tournaments they deserve to be in,' said Coltart's manager Chubby Chandler. 'I can handle the fact that they will try to nick my clients all the time and approach them at the wrong times, but when it starts to affect their careers . . .'

IMG's self-serving invitation policy also makes a nonsense of events like the 'World' Match Play when their fields are full of half-baked Americans and token Japanese. 'They should call it the International Management Group Invitation[al], not the World Match Play Championship,' Olazabal said after IMG failed to invite him when he was the world No.2. One IMG spokesman told me that the reason that Brad Faxon (IMG's highest ranking American client at No.25 in the world), Woosnam (IMG), Parnevik (IMG) and Singh (IMG) had been invited ahead of Ballesteros this year was because the Spaniard had broken down in tears after his 7&6 defeat by David Frost in 1993. 'Quite honestly, we wouldn't want it to happen again,' he said.

This mercenary attitude extends into other areas, some career influencing, but most of them petty. One player-manager claimed that until 1994, 'IMG didn't let anybody know that they could put logos on their Dunhill Cup team sweaters. You'd get to the tournament, and all the IMG clients would have Pringle, etc. on the sweaters, but no non-IMG clients. They almost seem to drop you in the shit on purpose.'

Interviewed in 1992, McCormack appeared to take a strange pride in these tactics. 'If you took a hundred of these stories about our being ruthless or sharklike, ninety of them would centre on attitudes we have taken on behalf of our clients,' he said. 'I think being ruthless, in the context in which it is applied to me, is really a sort of compliment.'

Who could have known then that two years on it would have all gone spectacularly wrong? That what they didn't teach even McCormack at Harvard Business School was what to do when you think you're holding all the cards and you suddenly find that you've lost the aces.

In the first six months of the 1994 season, Norman dropped a small atom bomb on McCormack's perfect world when he announced that he was leaving IMG and taking Frank Williams with him. Hardly had IMG taken the lid off the smelling salts when Price had defected to Masters International, Lyle had signed with Advantage and Irwin had opted for better things, which effectively left Leadbetter and Palmer as IMG's biggest golf clients in America. Rumours abounded about who might be next. 'If I was IMG I would make sure John Simpson was so well looked after that he would never contemplate leaving,' Williams said of Faldo's manager, 'because John has a very good relationship with his clients. They're not just clients, they're friends.'

Amid scenes of rejoicing from the anti-IMG contingent, it was speculated that the cause of many players' dissatisfaction was the percentages IMG demand – 10 per cent of all prize money and 20 per cent of off-course earnings. According to *Golf Australia*, Norman ceased to be a financial client of IMG's in 1992 – that is, they stopped dealing with his accounts and tax affairs – but remained a merchandising client, meaning that IMG continued to negotiate deals for him for its standard 20 per cent fee (including 20 per cent of the appearance fee it charged its own golf tournaments to have Norman play in them). 'Norman has never publicly discussed why he finally severed practically all association with IMG and hired Williams, IMG's former Melbourne boss, as his personal manager,' said the magazine. 'It has been suggested that Norman looked at the books and saw how much IMG was making on him alone each year. IMG sources say it was around the $3 million mark, but those outside reckon it may have been closer to $6 million.'

To Peter Higgs of the *Mail on Sunday*, Williams commented: 'IMG don't have the clout they used to have, nowhere near. They can't guarantee the top players at tournaments because they don't have them. The players are in control of their own destiny. The dog is wagging the tail again.' To me, he said: 'I would say a lot of it has to do with control. The top players want to control their own destiny.' And to Jerry Tarde of *Golf Digest*, he added: '[Greg] wanted peace of mind with no hidden agendas.' Hidden agendas? 'Leveraging,' explained Williams. 'IMG telling tournament sponsors, "We'll give you Greg if you give us TV rights." '

McCormack was coldly contemptuous of these observations, describing Williams as 'a pleasant bloke but not a rocket scientist . . . The job we did for Greg Norman was absolutely phenomenal,' he told Higgs. 'Economically, we rewrote the book. We earned him enough money to do what he wanted to do. What he chose to do was to have someone working for him alone. I'm a loyal person but everyone in the world doesn't treat loyalty the same way, and I was deeply disappointed when Greg left. It hurt me because I knew what a good job we'd done for him. When a guy is forty and has won two major championships, to accomplish what we did for him was extraordinary.'

The split with Norman has not been total. Until October, the Shark and IMG were still in partnership in three ventures: the Holden Classic (which is no longer a qualifying tournament for the World Championship), the Shark Shootout, and Norman's course design company. This company is now wholly owned by Great White Shark Enterprises.

'Player management in golf is about six or seven per cent of our business,' McCormack told Higgs. 'And you take out of that what we would have made from Norman or Price. Although it's considerable monies, in terms of affecting IMG's business it's not a big deal. But emotionally it's a huge deal because golf is so close to me.'

Back at East Sussex National, Ken Schofield was being interviewed on his meeting with Ballesteros. Schofield is a born politician. His knack of turning straw into silk thread, verbally if not always in actuality, has played a key part in the Tour's success, and if one heard that, like Gary Player, he listens to Winston Churchill's speeches in bed, one would not be in the slightest bit surprised. He is more adept than any cabinet minister at pirouetting away from unwanted questions, which can be exasperating when one is trying to pin him down on a serious issue.

But Schofield refused to be rattled. On Ballesteros's claims that the Tour was too long and too weak in parts, he said: 'I asked him to name the tournaments we should kill off. He would not do that.

We have 434 players who are entitled to play in our Tour School, who pay six-hundred-and-fifty pounds each for the privilege. Some are club professionals but the great majority would like to be like Seve or Jack Nicklaus.'

On the subject of Faldo's failure to support the European Open, one of the best events on the Tour, not to mention his insanely small schedule, which had seen him compete in only seven of the thirty-one events held in Europe by mid-September, Schofield said: 'The Tour remains strong with assets like that in hibernation.'

Finally, he came to the dramatic rejection of Ballesteros by IMG. 'All I would say is that we have a lot of business with IMG, as we have with a lot of other companies . . . The Tour continues to expand and continues to advance in times that have been difficult. We have no sponsor this week, for example. To continue to be strong, we need strong partners and strong promoters, and there are not many stronger than IMG. They are very reliable. Seve did get picked eighteen times for the World Match Play. Then he did not say too much. It seems to me that eighteen times is a long run.'

And away he went to America, confident that order had been restored. He could not have been more wrong. The very next week at the British Masters at Woburn, Faldo announced that he was abandoning Europe for the US Tour. 'It's unfortunate that we have not made as much progress as America has made over the last ten years. The interest in golf has been phenomenal since the 1985 Ryder Cup, but we've never had a major injection of cash from the big companies. Our business approach needs addressing. When you have a great event like the European Open and you haven't got a sponsor, that's a bit of a worry.'

Faldo is a bit like Prince Charles in that, however laudable his intentions are, he almost always succeeds in annoying people. This time, Mark James was the offended party. Faldo had tried to be constructive by saying that something had to be done about the courses and conditions in Europe. 'We're struggling,' he said. 'Mount Juliet is a good example where, given an injection of money, you get a great tournament venue. That's the only one I can think of apart from Dubai, Valderrama and French National.' He conveniently forgot that he had passed up the chance to play the latter because he wasn't getting appearance money, but had gone without a qualm to Crans-sur-Sierre, one of the worst courses in Europe. 'If we make the courses so we can't resist them, we'll be out there playing them,' he continued. 'It's money – money grows grass. That's the bottom line.'

James was disgusted. 'I can't believe the things Nick said,' he told journalists after presenting himself in the media centre, unasked, for interview. 'I think a lot of the top players are dominated by money to a ridiculous degree. Some of them won't contemplate playing where they are not guaranteed money for doing something . . . It's strange that none of these players is ever at the smaller events. We can ban appearance money, but if they get paid for doing something else at a tournament – if they think they need the money that badly – then there is nothing that can be done. It would be better if the sponsors got together and made the fees more reasonable.'

Mark Roe agreed. 'Unless they're giving Nick his fee for doing his Wednesday clinic, which is maybe $100,000 a week, Nick is not going to go to the relevant course.'

'The wishes of the top players are different from the bulk of the membership,' explained James, a member of the Tour's tournament committee. 'For the players from the Qualifying School or at the lower end of the Order of Merit, more tournaments mean they are playing for more money. Those at the bottom end don't make a fortune. It's not handed to them on a plate.'

And this is where European golf stood when Ian Woosnam swept to victory at Woburn in September 1994.

On a raw January day in 1973 (at a time when the European Tour Order of Merit winner was lucky to clear £20,000), Colin Snape walked into the offices of the Professional Golfers' Association. Halfway in, he paused in disbelief. Having been interviewed by men of seeming distinction in the plush splendour of the Mount Royal hotel in London, he was expecting something rather more grand – a museum case of gutta perchas, perhaps, or a few oil paintings of Vardon or Tom Morris. But the scene before him was grim and uninviting. Snape sat down and tried to come to terms with his surroundings. He was young and ambitious. After nine years as a golf club secretary, a position he had taken on at the age of twenty-three, he was looking forward to getting his teeth into his new role as the PGA's deputy tournament administrator. Previously, much of the work had been done on a voluntary or part-time basis, but the PGA had been forced to change its approach after an embarrassing crisis at the Esso tournament at Moor Park in the autumn of '72. Eric Brown, the Ryder Cup captain, had been disqualified for cheating. He had handed in his card unsigned, realized his mistake and persuaded the tournament administrator to give it back. Such had been the furore that the PGA decided that it had no choice but to employ full-time staff who could administer the rules and enforce them where necessary.

'It was a very cosy, old boy network,' recalled Snape, 'because the PGA was run on a shoe-string. When I joined it had £17,000 in the bank, it had an eight-year, short-term lease on a small dingy office under the main stand at the cricket ground at the Oval, and it had a staff of four. So it was long in pedigree, name and reputation, but very short on assets . . . I joined in a climate where the tournament players wanted more power – they were the public perception of professional golf – and the committee that I inherited was a great unwieldy body. If one ever does the script for *Carry on Golfing*, you could do about five episodes on the people round the table at the Oval. There were twenty-four club pros and four tournament pros. The club pros, the expenses they earned going to and from London for committee meetings were probably their main source of income.'

Almost immediately, Snape earned a reputation for being fair but very tough. At his first tournament, he telephoned Henry Cotton, a figure of near-divine status in golf at that time, and informed him that he was going to disqualify a player from the Portuguese Open. 'Who?' demanded Cotton. 'Don't you mean, what for?' Snape said coolly, before informing the great man that he was going to eliminate the defending champion Antonio Garrido for not handing his card in within the time allowed.

But even Snape was not prepared for what happened next. On 17 April, three months to the day after he stepped across the threshold of the PGA, John Bywaters, head of the association, dropped dead in the office. Six weeks later, Snape had been appointed secretary in his place. At that stage, the PGA was the most powerful body in professional golf, controlling the Tour, the Ryder Cup and the club professionals, and there was utter dismay in several quarters that the club pros had been unwise enough to recruit him. 'It caused immediate alienation with Jacobs,' Snape remembered, 'and I can understand it looking back on it because he was John Jacobs, tournament director general, and I was nobody, literally. Nobody had ever heard of me.'

This set the pattern for their relationship. Jacobs was a highly respected golf teacher and an enthusiastic, popular man, largely responsible for the launch of the European Tour as we know it today, but he was also an old-school traditionalist, and he found it well-nigh impossible to deal with the visionary and anti-establishment Snape. Uncaring, Snape gravitated towards other free-thinkers like Cotton and Henry Longhurst. 'Longhurst was seen as part of the establishment, but he wasn't really. I mean, he loathed Jacobs – the rows that went on. Because it was just at that time that Jacobs had become golf adviser to ITV, and the BBC had always had a monopoly. It's funny, you listen to BBC and Sky now – in 1973, ITV were the upstarts coming through and Jacobs, who was tournament director general of the PGA and could position this, that and the other, gets himself appointed golf adviser and immediately puts tournaments into ITV. The row that caused with Longhurst! That was the atmosphere I came into in '73. And Jacobs sailed serenely on. The Ryder Cup in '73 was the first ITV tournament. It was a complete and utter shambles in television terms, in that ITV never understood golf. I mean, they soldiered on for another ten years until they sort of bowed out in '79. In 1973 at Muirfield, for example, when the Ryder Cup was building up to a climax, we went away to watch the three-fifteen at the races.'

Early on in his term as secretary, Snape put forward a plan for a national golf centre. He wanted to persuade a golf club or a company to build new PGA headquarters, rent-free on a ninety-nine year lease, and in return the PGA would guarantee to bring two Ryder Cup matches to the course and endeavour to stage major events. 'I couldn't see myself living in the Oval, anyhow,' admitted Snape. 'It might be considered selfish in that respect but I was single, I didn't give a damn about anything and I was ambitious. I wanted to change the old order.' In 1974, he began to look at four possible venues in the North of England, one of which was the Belfry, a grotty hotel so rat-infested that it was in danger of being closed down. Eager to get his staff and the pros away from their London connections, Snape opted for the Belfry in the heart of the rapidly developing Midlands. The owners had agreed to provide land and buildings if the capital could be found elsewhere, and a shipping company had agreed to put in two golf courses.

'Politically, the PGA was breaking apart. Jacobs was daggers with me. It was all bang, bang, bang. He was propagating the idea that I was a threat to the Tour, which I wasn't. It was hard. And there was a series of meetings, throughout '74 and '75, where revolution was on . . . It was decided in 1975 that the PGA would go to the Belfry, the Tour would stay at the Oval and a new PGA European Tour was to be formed . . . There was a great belief, even then, that the Belfry would never happen. It was the wish of many people in the business to see me fall flat on my face – being frank about it.'

In 1976, the situation with Jacobs came to a head. At a tournament in York, Jacobs called a players' meeting and said: 'Look, I'll go if he goes,' according to Snape. Snape ploughed on, fearless and determined. When he went to the golf trade, cap in hand, and begged for their assistance in furnishing the new headquarters, they laughed in his face. So Snape found help elsewhere. The shaft company Apollo agreed to provide furniture to the tune of £100,000 if their name was put over the door. Financially, things were beginning to look up. Snape had made it a priority of his to expand the PGA's involvement in the regions, and within five years he had a staff of forty-four and an income of over £1 million. Schofield was making equal progress with the Tour.

'In everything that I did in pro golf, I just applied normal business acumen,' explained Snape. 'Golf is a product to me. So many people, the ego! I used to have to go to the Masters and the Open Championship, and it used to bore me silly. The same old crashing bores were there talking about the same old things. And it's the ethos of the game. I used to see them flying into the Masters – Brikash Bandari, who hadn't got tuppence to rub together at the Indian Golf Union, but Brikash, *first class*. It's a joke. All of that was anathema to me. I've got no other interests and I just immersed myself completely in the job. I used to go to all the tournaments. I was always there to stroke the sponsor and attend the meetings . . . I was secretary of the world PGA as well, which covered thirty-five countries. After the Ryder Cup in '85, they said, "You'll be having a couple of weeks holiday now." Christ, by the following Tuesday I was bored.'

In the mid 80s, Snape began to pay a heavy price for his radical views and rejection of the old guard. Everywhere he turned, he encountered vitriol and opposition. But in business terms his methods could not be faulted. He had transformed the fortunes of the PGA so that by 1985 its annual profit was well over £500,000, and he had rescued the women's tour when it went bankrupt in 1981, and created a £2 million twenty-event circuit, which had reached a peak never attained since when Snape departed in 1986.

'That was always a disappointment for me when I left, that the women's tour went backwards for about seven years,' Snape said. 'They've got an opportunity now but they have to be careful. You must never let anything be committee-led. Pros should be out there on the golf course. When they get in a political situation, they're a disaster because they've got to protect their own selfish interests. And there's a danger of that happening again. As an executive director, you've got to have a lot of courage and confidence and whether you're giving rulings or whatever, once you've [said what you've got to say, get out of there]. Don't hang around, because if they're going to hit it fat or career off a tree, you can be guaranteed that you're going to be the first to hear about it. You can never please people. You've got to do what you think is right and get out of there.'

Snape gazed out of the window at the smooth green lines of the Warwickshire Golf Club – where he hopes one day the Ryder Cup will be staged – which ultimately came to replace the PGA as the project closest to his heart. He was thinking about the years he had invested into pro golf and the happiness and searing pain that had come with them. 'You know, you're only as good as your last game,' he observed. 'Ken Schofield's done tremendously well. *Twenty-four million pounds*. And they're all as selfish as hell, and he'll get knifed. He will. I go down to Wentworth and see him. I say, "Make sure your pension's paid up because you can't win." Anyone working in pro golf – same with Beman. It happened to me. Anybody that is a representative – I had 3,500 members when I was boss of the PGA, well, how the hell can you keep them all happy? And Ken's gone on and on and yet Seve's saying this, and Faldo: "The practice facilities aren't good." And then there's these [Chris] Moodys and all the rest of them who never win tuppence. There's always 90 per cent losing. In any Tour, the good players usually don't have time to go on committees. It's this quaint British tradition. Whether it's in local government, parliament or whatever, the only people who want to get on the front row are people who are failures. If they were any good, they'd be earning a better living somewhere else.'

I studied him as he sat in the empty conference room at the

Warwickshire, surprised by his passion and his bullheadedness, his military bearing and oddly humble manner, the scope of his vision and his articulate, well-reasoned arguments. On the way down from Coventry station, his assistant had told me that she had taken on the job with trepidation, having heard tales of his rapid progress through secretaries, but had since been completely won over by him. She admired his honesty; his commitment to seeing his goals through.

'Why do you think you were such a controversial head of the PGA?' I asked Snape.

'Umm . . .' He grinned. 'It's my North-country upbringing. I can be an awkward sod, I would hold my hand up to that, and if I believe in something then I'm a real terrier in that I'll see it through. I trust people – often wrongly – implicitly . . . I can't stand deceit, and I've seen more of it in this business than anything else I've been in . . . But I do get . . . yeah (softly), I get up people's noses. I don't deliberately intend to. But I've mellowed . . . Even I blanch at some of the things that you do when you're younger. I can take a much better, balanced view now.' Regret crossed his face. 'It's been said to me that I haven't been able to play a part since I left,' he said quietly.

'Why did you leave?'

'I was fired.'

'What were the circumstances?'

'I don't really know to this day,' Snape said, and his eyes were dark with an emotion that could have been bitterness but seemed far more like pain and incomprehension. 'You'd say one would have expected it. But the chairman walked in with the captain at twelve o'clock – Derek Nash and Charles Hughes, who I'd put there – they came in and said that there was dissatisfaction expressed, and would I leave. I was out at two minutes past twelve and I was never even allowed in to clear my desk. I've never been in the place since.'

'Have you any idea what might have precipitated it?' I asked gently.

'No. I conjectured, I asked, but it's been a well-kept secret . . . It was Peter Alliss who, I would guess, played a part, and we had been friends. I'd done a lot for him. I'd put him in as the next captain elect but I think there was just a general dissatisfaction that I was too powerful. I *think*. But I can look back on it subjectively. No doubt I did alienate one or two by not watching my ps and qs, but I was the type of person, whether it was Laura being fined £50 or whatever, it was all done straight from the heart. But anyhow. And in many ways it's been good for me. It's a tremendous shock for your family. I'd married going to the Belfry and reared three children there, and to go home and say . . . And we were ostracized. We had to sit in that house for eight months. The PGA cut us off completely and we had to go through all sorts of lawyers just to get a pittance of compensation. You know, you do all that and . . . I say to Ken unashamedly: "Make sure your pension's paid up." Because they'll knife him. It's a cruel, cruel world is pro golf.'

Increasingly in professional golf – and not only when one sees what happened to Snape – one gets the distinct impression that almost everyone at the top of the game has lost complete touch with reality. Take an arbitrary scenario like Ian Woosnam's press conference at the Scottish Open at Gleneagles. There we had a man – who in another life might have been a cowhand, or at best a club pro giving lessons to high handicappers, but in this one happens to be a Tour player with career earnings of £4 million in Europe alone and endorsements worth almost as much – informing us that one of the reasons he had been playing badly was that the fabric his last clothing sponsor had provided didn't breathe properly and there were only four or five colours to choose from. With Hippo, he said, he would have all the colours of the rainbow and thus would feel happier starting the day. His golf would undoubtedly benefit. Since then, we have seen him in nothing but black and white which, as we all know, are not colours.

The atmosphere of unreality that leads to this kind of nonsense stems from the belief, largely induced by the circus-like structure of golf tournaments and the unnatural lifestyle that results from it, that the Tour is an island.

'The bottom line is, the power within the Tour has been held in the hands of so few people for so long that they have begun to believe that they don't need a consensus,' said one source high up in the European Tour. 'And what tends to happen is that they believe in their own infallibility, so that any critic of the system, anybody who refuses to accept the diktat of the ruling cabal, is immediately branded a rebel. There's a siege mentality. It's like, if you're not for us, you're against us, and within the hierarchy of the

Tour that makes for a poor working atmosphere. The field staff are afraid to give a full overview of what happens because they fear for their jobs, and the people at ground level, the players and the caddies, have this feeling of helplessness because if they line up against the closed ranks of the Tour they're going to get nothing out of it except a reputation as a trouble-causer. Which is OK if you're Seve Ballesteros and you can't be beaten into submission without a good deal of attendant publicity, but is not so good if you're a bit player and you don't have the contacts or the reputation to take on the combined might of the Tour.

'So that manifests itself in a number of ways. At board level, you have the permanent board basically instigating Tour policy, with regards to joint ventures with IMG, etc. And at the other end, you have this widely held perception among the players that it's one rule for us and another rule for them. Why hasn't Ballesteros been taken to task for some of the more outrageous criticisms he's made this year – his complaints about slow play or his allegations of bribery and corruption over the Ryder Cup course once his own company failed to get it? He's been critical of the Tour for getting into bed with IMG, whereas he'd probably be quite happy if IMG were in bed with Amen Corner [the event arm of his own company] to the same extent.'

Of course, millions of companies are conducted in precisely this manner to the detriment of nobody. But the Tour is not a self-contained unit with the sole purpose of making money for a single owner or group of share-holders. It is employed by the players, for the players, and that places a very different reponsibility on it. It means, for instance, that a certain amount of honesty and a straightforward approach to issues concerning the players in general, is desirable. But openness is not the Tour's strong point.

According to one source, at the 1993 PGA Championship, the level of dissatisfaction among Tour members – which stemmed from the perception that the board was out of touch with the players – was such that for the first time ever there was a contested election at the AGM for seats on the tournament board. James resigned and Tommy Horton and Peter Townsend were replaced by three Tour players, namely Chris Moody, Keith Waters and Glen Ralph. Schofield apparently felt this was tantamount to a vote of no confidence, and thus the remaining members of the board pushed through a change to the articles of association, taking away members' rights to re-elect board members directly, and removing their right to vote by proxy. From that point on, players were only able to elect members to the tournament committee which acts under the remit of the main board. Simultaneously, in the interests of 'continuity', the original board members (Coles, Gallardo, Gallacher and O'Leary) were given semi-permanent positions not subject to the normal rules of election by rotation. Schofield justified this by saying that the events of the AGM were normally only associated with bad times, and since the European circuit was riding the crest of a wave any future disruption to the activities of the board would be unthinkable.

Another example of the Tour's reluctance to respond frankly and positively to negative issues is appearance money. In 1971, when Jacobs was trying to promote the European Tour Players Division and needed Jacklin's support, he came up with the idea of persuading sponsors to pay the player inducements of £2,000 per event. It was a stroke of genius. Jacklin was the US and British Open Champion and a huge draw, and European golf took off. Then came Ballesteros with his fire, his artistry and his movie-star looks. His manager demanded £10,000 per tournament. The sponsors went crying to Schofield. Ballesteros resigned from the European Tour and was left out of the 1981 Ryder Cup team, and the appearance money war began. Since then, the Tour have alternated between denying its existence and publicly stamping it out.

'We can't get rid of it,' James admitted. 'We can say, "appearance money is no more", and we have said that, but if a sponsor wants to pay a top player $100,000 for appearing in the tournament programme, or coming to a cocktail party, or giving a clinic to five people on a Tuesday, there's really nothing we can do about that. It's beyond our control.'

'Who does the Tour think it's kidding about appearance money?' one player queried. 'There's a rule that says that only 25 per cent of the prize money can be used to induce players. Who is abiding by that rule? Is it the Irish Open? There you have a £500,000 event with only £125,000 left over, and they manage to entice John Daly, Nick Faldo, Jose Maria Olazabal, Ernie Els, Seve Ballesteros, Bernhard Langer and Colin Montgomerie. Well, what great value that is, ho, ho, ho. All those players for the knock-down price of £125,000? Or is it possible that the rule isn't being administered correctly?'

There were other problems, some of which may have been caused by too much looking across the Atlantic. In June 1992, the US Tour committed themselves to eighteen course developments, eight of which then faced financial difficulties, ranging from 'builder default and savings and loans insolvencies to general recessionary problems', according to a report by *Golf Digest*. The magazine also said that the Tournament Players Clubs, as they were called, were the PGA Tour operation most questioned by the players. Is it wise, the players wondered, to get into real estate development? Is it a good idea to get into political battles with local councils and planners? Is there a danger that conflict of interest would occur if the Tour ended up competing with its own members in the field of course design? And what, if anything, did the players stand to gain?

Nine years previously, Deane Beman had almost lost his job over the Tour's contentious expansion into golf course development. Palmer and Nicklaus had sent a letter to the tournament policy board telling Beman that his plans were 'unauthorized' and 'ill-conceived', and accusing him of wanting to be the 'Czar of Golf . . . The Tour should not own, manage, operate or endorse golf courses . . .' they wrote. 'The Tour's responsibility should be limited to support and advice for others to develop such projects. The Tour should not be an equity participant.' But despite the fact that the letter was signed by fourteen of golf's greatest players, the policy board would not be dissuaded. Between 1983 and 1986, some eleven new TPC courses were opened, and in 1992, Beman reported that he had turned a $1 million investment into a $200 million empire, with benefits to players, charities and fans.

It is possible that, seeing this, Schofield decided to embark on a design project or two of his own. One of these was Caldas, a blighted development outside Barcelona, which was originally intended as a possible host for the 1997 Ryder Cup. Needless to say, this did not come to pass. Caldas and a number of other sites became a steady drain on the Tour's resources until IMG breezed in like knights in shining armour and established European Tour Courses. ETC is one of the joint ventures that the Tour has been criticized for, but these marriages definitely have their advantages. There is no doubt that IMG run many of the best events on the European circuit for the simple reason that they have experience, marketing skills and the best brains in the business behind them. They also have television and the means to attract the top players. The same applies to their joint ventures with the Tour. They have money, they have muscle and they have the expertise that the Tour is often lacking. But there is a very fine line between a mutually beneficial relationship and an incestuous one open to possible abuse between an organization with vested interests and a governing body which should, at all costs, remain impartial.

These concerns aside, the inescapable fact is that Schofield has turned what was effectively a clearing house for entries and a supplier of rules officials into a £130 million business. He is a brilliant executive director. If one counts the European Tour, the Seniors Tour and the Challenge Tour, there are currently more than a hundred tournaments and prize money in excess of £26 million annually, as compared with only £1 million in 1977. Faldo said at Woburn that the Tour's business approach needed addressing, but as James responded: 'I'd be surprised if Faldo knew an awful lot about the business approach of the Tour.'

Faldo also said that the Tour needed to look to its laurels where courses and conditions were concerned, and other critics, myself included, questioned the loss of several sponsors, including those endorsing the Scottish Open, the European Open, the Madrid Open and the Rome Masters.

James refused to believe that the 'crisis' in the Tour was any more than a storm in a teacup. 'We've got a greater turnover of sponsors now than we had in the 70s because we've got more tournaments,' he said. 'When we had seventeen tournaments, ten of them were long-term British sponsors and six of them were national opens, many of which are still with us. We have a lot of very long-term sponsors. The ones that are more transient are the smaller events on the Continent, and they've been turning over at the same rate since they started appearing. It may be that since the recession they've become slightly harder to find, but it's minimal, and I believe that the Tour uses its own money [to finance them] occasionally, but we've done that for years. Now suddenly, I think because of the recession, players are starting to look at the Tour and pick holes in it. They're expecting it to weaken and it's not happening.'

Back in his office, Schofield was fighting his way through a barrage of unflattering articles and wondering, like Snape had done, where it had all gone wrong. 'I've always felt, in a practical sense, that our Tour had to win over our very best players,' he told me in the halcyon days of 1992, 'by putting on bigger tournaments, in better conditions – in terms of the golf courses – and actually running something which, in general terms, can compete. A person in my job must always remember that these guys are self-employed. We don't employ them. They are their own men. It could be fatal to become possessive of them.'

17

THE LONELINESS OF THE LONG DISTANCE RUNNER

'Why does Nick Faldo have to be like this?'

RICK REILLY, *Sports Illustrated*

This is how it started. All that morning the sweeping green sea of St Nom la Bretêche, venue of the Lancome Trophy, had been as lively and picturesque as market day in Bridgetown, Barbados. Stylish Frenchmen and women in impractical shoes had surged excitedly around the first tee; birds had skipped and danced and sung their hearts out in the courtyard of the old chateau; aeroplanes had droned lazily overhead; and golfers in primary colours had moved up fairways bathed in autumn sunshine like mechanical men in pin-ball machines. But within the cold rectangle of the press centre it had stayed stubbornly dull. We read old newspapers, took a long lunch, drank sixteen cups of black coffee and looked vainly to the scoreboard for inspiration, but no matter how we tried our screens remained stubbornly blank. Singh and Ballesteros were yesterday's news; Miguel Angel Jimenez was no news at all; and the most interesting thing that had happened all day was when Alastair Johnson, McCormack's No.2, had wandered into the tent and, putting one large, and not particularly clean, foot on the table beside BBC radio's Tony Adamson, had commenced tutting over *Golf Weekly*'s 'Crisis? What Crisis?' piece on the state of the Tour, which singled out IMG as a problem the Tour needed to address. It was, without question, the slowest Saturday in memory.

'Faldo's going well,' Tim Glover said suddenly, closing the lid of his computer and giving up his attempt to make a silk purse out of a sow's ear of a story. 'We'll have to have him in.'

Tony Greer, the press officer to whom this remark was directed, paled. 'What for?' he demanded. His loyalty to IMG is surpassed only by his devotion to IMG clients and he guards their interests with a missionary zeal. 'He's five under par.'

'He's on for a 66,' I said, 'and we've all got early deadlines. We have to have a story for the first edition.'

'What makes you think he's going to be a story?' Greer said weakly.

The answer was, nothing at all. At Woburn the week before, Faldo had vented his frustration at the media's treatment of him by saying: 'This is the problem. You try to say something constructive and you get a verbal bashing.' He felt that his observations about the European Tour hardly progressing in ten years, and there being only four good courses on the circuit, had been misinterpreted and falsified. 'I've been misrepresented for nineteen years,' he cried bitterly. 'I'm going to go back to just talking about birdies and bogeys. That'll be it.'

So, you see, we weren't expecting much out of a post-round interview with Nick at an IMG tournament in Versailles at all. Indeed, it was a measure of our desperation for material that we were prepared to call in a player five or six strokes off the pace, merely to glean a few round details. And to begin with, that was all we got. Faldo was in an obliging enough frame of mind and he reeled off his recent history, telling us how he had misjudged the wind and found the water at the ninth, and explaining that he was still putting with his left hand below the right – 'cackie-doodle-doo.'

We were gathering our notebooks when Glover said in passing: 'Was it a difficult decision for you to make to commit yourself to the US Tour next season?'

He might as well have tossed a match into a can of petroleum. '*Difficult?*' snapped Faldo, blue eyes flashing with anger. 'Easiest one in the world after all the *shit* that was thrown at me last week.' He raised an accusing finger. 'You lot,' he said disgustedly. 'I came in with the intention of saying something and you took the wrong end of the stick. You got another player involved. To coin a famous French phrase, an *oeuf* is an *oeuf.* The Alliss incident at the PGA

Championship was the last straw. From now on, it's just birdies and bogeys.'

He was referring to an article which had appeared in *Fore!* magazine in May, in which the television commentator Peter Alliss described Faldo as a would-be comedian and 'the classic only child . . . The thing about Faldo is that you don't want to give him a cuddle, unlike, say, Sandy Lyle. Faldo struggles to get people to like him, and he doesn't create excitement. He's a hero, the finest golfer there's been for many, many years, but he doesn't fully understand that he is a hero.'

Alliss's antipathy towards Faldo had as its source an incident at the 1993 British Masters, where Faldo, irritated by a comment Alliss had made about his game, questioned his qualifications as an armchair critic. 'I think Faldo would like to be loved,' Alliss said. 'He's admired, rather like Lester Piggott, but he's not loved. It disappoints me for his sake that Faldo has not made friends with the media. He's had umpteen run-ins with the press and he still hasn't learned to use them. When the press tell him that Peter Alliss says his swing looks off, he replies: "What does he know? He climbs fourteen steps to the commentary-box and suddenly he's an expert." Now that's an insult. I was never as good as Faldo, but we could have played a dozen rounds and I'd win five of them. You don't go to America and beat the likes of Arnold Palmer and company in their heyday if you can't play a bit.'

At St Nom la Bretêche, Faldo had not paused for breath. He had gone on to say that although there were those among the media whom he respected and even considered friends, there was 'a small minority' who spoiled it for everyone else. 'You have to get your house in order,' he told us. '*I'm* certainly not going to change. That was the last straw. I try to be constructive and try to help and you make me sound stupid with a capital F.'

By now, of course, it was terrifyingly close to our deadlines. There was a tense, horrible silence. None of us had the faintest idea what to say, what to do or where to look. I felt sick, Greer was paralysed, and Faldo just glared at us through narrow, hostile eyes. We shuffled our papers and looked anxiously towards the door. Mike Britten was the first to get to his feet. Faldo exploded. 'You see,' he shouted, gesturing wildly towards Britten, 'he's in a strop, he's in a strop. This is what I find so fabulous. I criticize you in a twenty-foot by twenty-foot room and you can't take it. You're walking out the door.

I can be criticized in front of twenty million people. Twenty million people think I don't know what the hell I'm talking about.'

Nick Faldo was fourteen years old when he discovered golf. Sprawled on the sofa before the television – a rare moment of stillness in amidst the mad whirl of swimming, cycling, fishing and cricket that filled his days – he caught, by chance, the closing rounds of the 1971 Masters. Already he was drawn to the individual sports. Tall for his age, supple and athletic, with a smile tugging at the corners of his mouth and the intense, introverted, slightly fanatical look of a boy with big dreams, he was a county swimming champion, relishing the lonely discipline and the exhilaration that came with accomplishment. Now he looked at Nicklaus and he liked what he saw. The velvety fairways of Augusta National were appealing to him, but he was particularly struck by the sound of a well-hit shot and the magnificent solitude that seemed to be an integral part of great golf. He watched the Golden Bear triumph and others fail, and it captured his imagination. Fortuitously, the Easter holidays were just beginning. Here, thought Faldo, is a sport I have to try.

In those days, Faldo lived in a two-bedroomed Welwyn Garden City council house in Knella Road, the street where his mother Joyce had spent her childhood. George, his father, had grown up in the East End of London, in a dank flat with no running water and a bathroom shared with the neighbours. After they married, Joyce became a cutter and pattern drafter for Cresta Silks, and George, a laconic former military policeman, worked in the financial planning department of ICI Plastics.

Nick was born on 18 July 1957, altering their lives out of all recognition. Through him, they saw a chance to realize their most cherished ambitions. Joyce had never forgotten how, as a young girl, she had been invited to play at an exclusive tennis club and had been left feeling shamed and humiliated. 'I haven't had the proper grounding,' she had told herself, vowing then that any child of hers would have every opportunity she could provide. Her plans for Nick soared high above the suburbia she inhabited.

'First we wanted him to be an actor,' Joyce recalled in John Hopkins's biography, *Faldo in Perspective*. 'We thought he'd be another Sir Laurence Olivier. We took him to dancing and elocution lessons. We tried to interest him in piano lessons. We knew he would win the Tchaikovsky piano prize. He had smashing legs and I wanted him to be a model so I used to take him to Harrods fashion shows. Finally, we realized he was only interested in sport.'

As a teenager, Faldo had a quick temper, easily provoked by defeat. His parents found these tantrums amusing, indulgently nicknaming them Nick's Maria Callas's. 'We'd hear the gate go boing, boing, boing and then the bike would be thrown aside and we'd laugh to ourselves,' George said. 'We were with him if he lost. We were sympathetic. There's no point in playing games if you're not going to win.' But it was a silent ride home on the days when Faldo's best was not quite good enough. 'We just left him alone for an hour,' Joyce told the *Mail on Sunday*, 'which is what his wife Gill does now. One time I tried to cheer him up and went to see him in the bathroom and put my two fingers in his back and said: "Do you want me to end it all now?" He laughed.'

When Faldo expressed an interest in golf, Joyce offered to pay for lessons. He spent three months hitting balls into a long-jump pit before being taken out onto the course at Welwyn Garden City. 'Where do I hit it?' he enquired of his instructor. 'There,' came the reply. 'Right,' Faldo said, and went round in 78 (not counting three lost balls). When he was sixteen, he told his parents that he wanted to quit school and concentrate on golf. 'By all means,' chorused Joyce and George. So Faldo found himself free to do nothing but pursue his obsession. Encouraged by his mother, he embarked upon a strenuous regime of daily practice, while Joyce ferried him to and from tournaments or stood frozen in the back garden and told him where the club was at the top of his backswing.

'I might have been a firm disciplinarian, and he told me I was bossy when he was ten,' Joyce said, 'but I gave him lots of care and support, and now he's his own man and no-one would ever tread on him.' Some outsiders saw it differently. One described Joyce as domineering, overbearing and arrogant. 'Talk about the Oedipus Complex. She idolized Nick, and she told him to his face.'

In 1976, with a glittering amateur career behind him, Faldo went to the US with Sandy Lyle and Martin Poxon to sit entrance exams at Houston University. Lyle failed, but the others won scholarships in the region of £450. Faldo was unhappy from the word go. It had come as a shock that he was actually expected to study, and the idea of attending three-hour lectures on Physical Education and Public Speaking was anathema to him. He began cutting class to practice golf. He telephoned Ian Connelly, the Welwyn Garden City teacher with whom he had worked since 1973, and told him he was thinking about dropping out and turning professional.

'I told him to stay there,' Connelly recalled. 'In retrospect, he'd probably say that he did the right thing by giving it up, but I never ever agreed with it. I'm a great fan of the American collegiate system. I thought it was very much in his interests to stick it out because you're living in a different environment, you're mixing with different people, you're independent, and the Americans are the best people in the world at public relations and that would never have done Nick any harm. He's very successful but I still think he would have been even more successful, from a PR point of view, if he had stayed.'

But Nick had no intention of sticking it out. Ten weeks after setting foot on US soil, he boarded a plane for Britain. There, he prepared to turn pro and settled back into the cocoon-like routine of his parents' house. The threesome had been restored. Faldo and his father even went together to give his professional application to the PGA. One former official can remember Faldo being ordered by George: 'Now you sit down there, Nick, and let me handle this.'

And so began a pattern that has continued to this day, where Faldo, pilloried for making a decision that seemed ludicrous to his critics, proved he had done what was best for his career. In 1976, he won the thirty-six-hole Double Diamond event, in 1977, the Skol Lager, and in 1978, he swept to victory in the first of three consecutive PGA Championships. 'The true feelings of winning can last for ages and ages,' Faldo enthused. 'It starts at the prize-giving where you can sense that people are looking at you. They're not looking at the guys who have come fourth tied, they looking at the winner . . . After that there's the time when people are saying, "There's Faldo, he won last week . . ." There have been pressures on you to win, and so finding that you have met them is rewarding. You've pushed yourself and you've found that you're not scared of winning.'

It was while he was defending his second PGA title at Ganton that Faldo suffered the first of many disillusionments. Having beaten Neil Coles and Ken Brown by four strokes and Norman by seven, with a glorious display of attacking golf, he was fined £50 for slow play. According to the 1981 Pelham yearbook: 'The whole affair was unfortunate, badly timed and over-officious. It is true that the round had taken four and a half hours but this included considerable time wasted by crowd interference and marshalling that was often inadequate. Faldo maintained that they had to wait thirty-six times for the galleries to be cleared and that in itself must have accounted for some thirty-six minutes' delay that had nothing to do with the players. Quite rightly he observed that instead of getting a slap on the back after retaining the title, all he received was a slap in the face.'

Peter Dobereiner remembers the incident with a shudder. 'It certainly wasn't his fault at all, and he absolutely collapsed. There were tears and dreadful scenes. His moment of triumph was totally ruined.'

Into this turbulent atmosphere stepped Melanie Rockall, a pretty young journalist who had interviewed him for a women's magazine. Melanie was the polar opposite of Nick. Where he was single-minded and absorbed in his golf to the exclusion of all else, she was vivacious and outgoing; where he was a homebody, accustomed to having his every whim catered to, she loved parties, loved people and loved to travel. But on Valentine's Day in 1979, after what Joyce described as 'a fiery courtship', Nick proposed, and they were married in June the same year.

'We were happily married for eight months,' Faldo told *Sports Illustrated.* 'Unfortunately, we were married for four and a half years.'

In 1981, when Faldo went to the States to play, Melanie went with him. Her days soon took on a pattern. She would read by the pool, write in her diary and play 'secretary, press officer, maid and good little housewife' to Nick. Every day. Boredom suffocated her. 'When I realized that I only had one choice and that was to be with Nick as much as possible and to a large extent take care of his affairs, then I did that for the first three or four years and enjoyed it,' Melanie recalled. 'But there was always a little voice inside me that said, "Something's wrong . . ." Being a golf wife is a terribly secondary existence. You're always orbiting around an enormous star. You're never shining on your own. You exist only as a satellite.'

Faldo was helpless, as little able to mend the cracks in his marriage as he was to relate more warmly to tournament galleries. 'On the course, I'm good at blocking things out,' he said. 'I don't think of anyone or anything that isn't to do with golf. People think I'm rude because I don't answer them but actually I often don't hear them.'

But Connelly had warned him from the earliest days of his career that that simply wouldn't wash with the public. 'I always wanted Nick, obviously, to be a great player, but also to be a sportsman and a gentleman. I held Nicklaus and Palmer up as examples. And it's bothered me over the years that he never took that advice. I remember when he first became successful on the Tour, people would applaud him and his hand would rise about two inches. I said: "Come on, Nick, these people are dying to love you. You're the great white hope of British golf. Why can't you raise a smile and say thank you?" '

By the end of 1982, Connelly's relationship with his star pupil had broken down irretrievably. 'Ian was my biggest fan and my biggest critic,' Faldo was to say later.

But Connelly remains a staunch supporter of the man who first came to him as a lanky and ambitious fourteen-year-old, even though their parting was less than amicable. 'The last time I ever spoke to him was at the '83 Open at Birkdale, when I bumped into him by chance,' Connelly remembered. 'We had a twenty-second conversation before he was enveloped in autograph hunters. Eleven years have passed since then and I've never heard from him, never spoken to him, never had any contact with him whatsoever. Don't you think that's a bit strange?'

In 1983, Faldo won £140,000 in prize money and had the lowest stroke average in the world. He entered six tournaments in Europe and won five. But all he was concerned about was that he had fallen apart on the closing holes of the Open Championship. The next April, he did the same at the Masters. Having gone into the final round sharing third place with Crenshaw and David Graham, he made four expensive errors to take 40 to the turn. A total of 76 left him in fifteenth place.

Gill Bennett was walking with him. Formerly secretary to John Simpson, she had arrived at the Hawaiian Open with Faldo in February, hotly pursued by reporters. When news of their affair reached Britain, Melanie began divorce proceedings.

'Gill and Melanie are total opposites,' Faldo told Hopkins. '[Gill] enjoys travel, perhaps because she is the daughter of a pilot. When I say we're going away, she says, "Oh, good, we haven't been on a plane for a week." She gets on better with the other wives. We both like the same sort of music. We make instant decisions, where before we used to have a stewards' enquiry before we did anything. Life is much less complicated now.'

But even Gill found it difficult to deal with the torment Faldo underwent on the course. At Augusta, she recalled wanting to burst into tears or run away and hide, to do anything but watch. 'But I knew in my heart of hearts that I had to stay with Nick. I knew I must support him in bad times as well as good.'

Faldo was disappointed but not devastated. 'Don't get too upset,' he said soothingly to Gill. 'You may have worse times than that, but you will also have better times. What's happened has happened. There's no point in worrying about it.'

The following week, he won the Heritage Classic, his first US Tour title. For many Europeans, that would have been the making of a career. But not for Faldo. Faldo only wanted majors. That winter he had an intense discussion with Leadbetter, whose pupil Nick Price he had long admired, at Sun City. He came to a decision. If perfection was possible in golf, he would attain it, and the way that he would do that was by starting over from scratch. He asked Leadbetter to throw the book at him. The journey to greatness had begun.

When Alfred Perry won the Open at Muirfield in 1935, his oration at the prize-giving was, as Longhurst observed, a model of its kind. 'I'd rather play a round of golf than make a speech,' was all he said. If only Faldo had done the same. If only Faldo had admitted to himself that he is 'nowhere near as capable of looking after himself verbally as he is with his golf clubs,' (to quote Bruce Critchley, author of his autobiography, *In Search of Perfection*), then the world's media would not have been arrested in mid-flow at Muirfield in 1992, where smoke was rising from their typewriter keys as they attempted to rewrite Nick Faldo's image before deadline time. Nor would the sportscaster Steve Ryder, who was the first to interview the Open Champion after he had walked sobbing off the eighteenth green, have had to ask him to remove the white hankerchief which he had knotted at four corners and, for reasons never explained, placed on his head. And millions of viewers would not have had to suffer the worst speech in the history of the Open Championship, during which Faldo, in an attempt to appear magnanimous, suggested a whisky company join him in giving a bottle to every golf club in Britain, thanked the press 'from the heart of my bottom', and urged the galleries to join him in a chorus of *My Way*.

In his defence, John Simpson claimed that after winning his third

Open title at Muirfield, Faldo exhibited every medical symptom of shock. But it was hard to believe that the allusion to the media – at the very least – was not premeditated.

Faldo's declining relationship with the press dated back to 1979, his first big year, when his behaviour had led him to be labelled as sullen, spoiled or surly – the anti-Sandy Lyle. In America, Andy Prodger, one of his caddies, walked up to him at the Heritage Classic and said: 'What's all this about a nickname you've been given by the British papers? El Foldo?' It wasn't true, but Faldo wasn't to know that and it cut him to the quick. 'I think the trouble is, he kind of carries these scars with him and uses them to have a poke . . .' one source said. 'He has his shortcomings, but he's actually very shy. That's why he makes these jokes . . . He takes [newspaper articles] very seriously – he's wounded by them – and he's always looking for opportunities to even the score . . . He has a persecution complex but he doesn't have the intelligence to work out that, maybe if I took a step towards them [the media], it would be better . . . I think a lot of it comes down to . . . arrogance and this feeling that, "I'm famous, why should I change?" And that was fostered by his parents, who wanted him to become famous, it didn't matter whether he was an actor or a golfer or whatever. In a way, he's led a charmed existence. You can't knock him for that.'

'It's very easy to take the downside of the man,' Critchley said, 'which I think is wrong. Here is a man who has an enormous gift and he finds it difficult to express himself. He actually feels pursued by the media, who are looking for the wrong things. They're not interested in his golf; they're looking for quotes. My own opinion is, if you'd said to the press a dozen years ago, "How would you like a British golfer who will win five majors but unfortunately he won't be able to speak?" they'd have said, "Fine." You've then got to be Dr Johnson and Oscar Wilde rolled into one . . . A lot of our sports heroes are "dull" in this other role they're supposed to have as entertainers. He's not a funny man, he's no great wit. He's not in the top ten of that league. But he's a thoroughly decent guy with a real talent to concentrate on what he does best, which is play golf.'

But even when Faldo proved he was the best player, if not the best politician, he could not escape his critics. His reward for hitting 1,500 balls a day until his hands bled, during his swing change, was to watch the gradual desertion of friends, long-term supporters and all but a couple of his sponsors. When he justified his decision to gamble with his career by making eighteen pars in hellish conditions to win the 1987 Open, people said how defensively he had played. When he made eight birdies on the final day of the 1989 Masters, and another one to beat Scott Hoch on the second hole of a play-off, they said that Hoch had choked on his two-footer on the first hole. When he beat Raymond Floyd in a play-off the following year, they focused on Floyd's mistakes, not Faldo's victory.

Tellingly, his closest friends – Simpson, Leadbetter, Sunesson – stood by him through thick and thin. 'We have fun,' Leadbetter says of his brilliant pupil. 'We really haven't had any arguments at all that I can think of. I mean, over the past five years there have been periods of time when he's been frustrated, and I've written him letters and said, "Hey, come on." I gave him that book, *Be Happy*, and that really helped him a lot. He started to look at things in a better perspective. A lot of times in this game, you don't realize what you're doing yourself – how you're acting or reacting.'

Gradually, the tide of public opinion began to turn. It was difficult not to respect a man who could win the 1990 Open by five strokes, demolishing the St Andrews tournament record by six shots. It was impossible not to have the highest esteem for a golfer who could win four majors, become the No.1 player in the world and still want more. For a time, Faldo even worked to build the perfect body, enlisting the help of Paul Ankers, a supposed Olympic medal-winning judo expert. This went well until Renton Laidlaw, the *Evening Standard* correspondent, received a letter from the Judo board saying that they had never heard of such a person. 'Ankers away!' Laidlaw said cheerfully, as the physiotherapist, who had been courting Fanny, disappeared without trace.

Nevertheless, Faldo's image continued to improve. He smiled more, he talked more, he gave ever more time and money to children's charities. 'He does good by stealth,' Dobereiner said, 'which I always think is an admirable trait.'

But then came the 1992 Open at Muirfield, where Faldo, who had been at pains to change his ice-man image, did exactly that by throwing away the Championship, clawing it back and bursting into tears of relief on the final green, then ruined it all with his speech.

'I really would like to express myself more,' Faldo told Reilly. 'I'm a totally different guy to how I'm portrayed. I just can't seem to smile much on the course. I think of funny things to do, but I don't do them. Sometimes my wife will come down the stairs looking ravishing in a red dress, her hair all done up perfectly, and I'll think, My God, she looks so gorgeous. But before I can think to say it, she'll say, "Well, don't you think I look nice tonight?" Then it's too late, isn't it?'

Too little, too late. It was the story of his relationship with the media.

On the final day of the 1994 Open, Faldo scored a six under par 64, which gave him a share of fifth place when the Championship was over. When he came in for interview, his face was lit with the shy pride that always comes over it when he touches, however briefly, the perfection in his mind's eye. He sat down and stared hard at his card. At 6 foot 3", with shoulders almost as wide, he cuts an imposing figure, and yet whether he is walking down the fairway or crossing a room, there is an awkwardness about him, a self-consciousness, as if he is always aware of being watched. He ran his fingers through his hair. There was a wistful note in his voice as he detailed his round for the media. He said: 'When I got to the sixteenth, I thought: "Well, if I hole this, that'll be 62 and that's never been shot before." But it didn't last very long. Soon as I missed the putt, I knew . . .'

On Saturday evening, Faldo had worked for more than three hours in the gathering gloom on his putting. Between them, he and Leadbetter had studied an apparently flawless stroke and found the hidden imperfections: his right hand was too strong, it wasn't natural; the grip on his putter needed changing. Faldo explained this with lip-smacking satisfaction. There is nothing he relishes more than taking things apart, fixing their imperfections, polishing them lovingly and putting them back together again.

But the season had been a frustrating one. 'I haven't produced anything like what I wanted to produce,' Faldo admitted. A tiny frown creased his brow as he considered how all the sweat, all the ceaseless striving for nirvana had come to naught. 'It hurts him *so* much,' Melanie Faldo had said, 'one missed putt, one second place. That's what makes him great.' That and his quest for the grail. At Turnberry, Faldo smiled as a thought occurred to him. 'As Lead said, "We're preparing for something," ' he said. 'And I think that's the way I've got to look at it. I've got to keep grinding away. Once I get the putting going, that makes a massive difference to your morale.'

That afternoon, a dedicated band of followers had held a banner aloft as the former Open Champion passed. FALDO'S LOYAL FANS, it said. 'I threw them a banana skin,' Faldo reported. 'I said: "There's a souvenir!"'

He leaned back in his seat, flushed with pleasure. Once he had recalled: 'By the age of ten I began to experience that wonderful glow that spreads through your body when you know you are the best.' But somehow, somewhere, he had lost the capacity to share that feeling. 'Come on, Nick, these people are dying to love you,' Connelly had told him, but Faldo, shy and easily wounded by criticism, had chosen to withdraw. He never understood that curiosity is one of the most powerful urges in human nature: that the more reclusive you are, the more intrigued people become; the more blanks you present them with, the more inclined they are to fill them in without your assistance.

He was asked how long he intended to keep playing golf.

'As long as I've still got the desire to keep striving to hit a golf ball the way I want to hit it,' Faldo answered, and his face, so often shuttered and expressionless, was alive with the love of the game. 'That's what I really enjoy most. Every shot is a target, a mini-goal, because I'm trying to do something . . . I'm trying to hit the ball there . . .' His hands mapped the flight of a perfect golf shot through the air. 'Obviously, there's more to it than that. There's all the preparation, all the practice. And I *love* the practice. The day I wake up and think, "Oh no, I've got to practise today," that'll be it, I guess. But I've never been bored with this game at all, not one single moment. I've been frustrated, but I've never been bored with it. I feel that my best point is the fact I practise hard and then I get a moment when I think: "I'm going to practise harder."'

We were spellbound – carried along by his extraordinary passion; mesmerized by the picture he painted of a life lit from within by devotion to a game. All of a sudden, it was clear why at times he seemed introverted, taciturn or unsocial: golf filled his world and his family made it complete. He didn't want, or need, anything else. You couldn't imagine the day would ever come when Faldo wouldn't want to drop a ball onto the wet, emerald grass, and hear the satisfying whoosh as it cut cleanly into the blue. And it seemed churlish beyond words to question his tunnel-vision simply because he was a sportsman and not a composer, or a musician, or a great artist. Was Mozart a well-rounded person? Was Hemingway? Was Van Gogh?

Faldo laughed out loud at the thought of quitting, the joy of the round and the high of achievement still bubbling up in him. 'Who knows what will happen in six or seven years time,' he said. 'Arnold Palmer hasn't been able to give it up and Nicklaus says: "If I was smart, I'd have retired at thirty-five." I guess it's just something in your blood with this game . . . There is no such thing as just one last practice ball. There's always going to be another one. You *have* to hit one more, just in case . . . you get it right.'

18

GRAND FINALE

'The less I practise, the luckier I get.'
COLIN MONTGOMERIE, 1993 and 1994 Order of Merit winner

It is not only in the movies that giant birthday cakes are wheeled onto dance floors, to the accompaniment of thunderous rolls of drums, whereupon lissom young women clamber out clad only in fish-net bodystockings. Yes, this was the treat we had in store for us at a Spanish hotel on the eve of the Volvo Masters, the final event of the season. But the icing on the cake (so to speak) was a troupe of Brazilian dancers in feathers – a guaranteed crowd pleaser – and several people took a turn around the floor.

For some reason this brought to mind a story that may or may not be apocryphal that the golf teacher Eddie Birchenough told me about Doug Sanders, whose fate it is to be remembered always as the man who missed a four-foot putt to lose the 1970 Open to Nicklaus at St Andrews. Sanders, it would be fair to say, loves to surround himself with exotic accessories, be they women or shoes. A decade or so ago, when the B&H International was still held at Fulford in York, he was eating lunch when his eye was caught by a table full of women. Unable to resist the opportunity to brighten their day, he sauntered over.

'Would you mind if I joined you, ladies?' he asked charmingly.

One woman gave him a cold stare. 'Yes,' she said, 'we would.'

Sanders was taken aback. Nobody ever turned him down. Embarrassed, he returned to his friends just as dessert was being served.

A plan for revenge formulated in his mind. Addressing the waiter, Sanders said: 'I'll give you £100 if you tip trifle on that lady's lap when you serve her table.'

The waiter pursed his lips. 'That's more than my job's worth,' he said. 'I want to work here tomorrow.'

Faced with a second loss of face, Sanders became more insistent. 'Two-hundred pounds then,' he tried

'No,' the waiter said stubbornly.

At the table was a young IMG manager, who had only just started with the company. 'For £200, I'll do it,' he announced to the surprise of his colleagues.

After the meal he disappeared, returning dressed as a waiter. When the time came for dessert to be served to the women, he contrived to pour trifle down the front of the one who had been reckless enough to reject Doug Sanders. He pleaded clumsiness, but she was virtually in tears. Matters got out of hand when it was discovered that she was a hostess for B&H. The promoter went berserk and the 'waiter' was forced to own up and apologize. He paid to have the dress dry-cleaned from the money won in the wager.

The Volvo Masters is the PGA European Tour's showcase event. It is the only tournament, besides Augusta, where officials in designer uniforms comfortably outnumber players, where the champagne flows more freely than Gatorade, where there is no halfway cut, and where an end-of-term atmosphere of relief, rapture and goodwill usually prevails.

All things considered, it had been a wonderful year. For the first time in history, foreign players, all of whom had played or were playing the European Tour, had made a clean sweep of the four major championships; and through their achievements we had seen the emergence of the next generation of golfing greats: Olazabal, Els, Price, Montgomerie, Mickelson and Tom Lehman – of whom Nicklaus said, 'Mr Lehman plays a game with which I am not familiar,' after the American's landslide victory in the Memorial. We also saw the recovery of Paul Azinger from cancer and the welcome return of Ballesteros, who added the German Masters, won in a play-off from Els and Montgomerie, to his B&H title and only narrowly missed preventing the Scot from winning the Order of Merit for the second time. In the space of just six events, he had worked his old, fiery brand of magic and had played his way into the 1995 Ryder Cup team before the '94 season even ended.

Over the course of the year, we witnessed the coming of age of a crop of new talent, including Jonathan Lomas, Andrew Coltart, Lee Westwood and the Swedes, Gabriel Hjerstedt and Pierre Fulke. Carl Mason, one of the most loved players on the European Tour, surprised himself by winning a tournament for the first time in his twenty-year career at the age of forty-four. He enjoyed it so much he promptly won another one, this time the prestigious Scottish Open. Canada shocked everyone by snatching the Dunhill Cup; Ballesteros made a mockery of IMG's decision not to invite him to the World Match Play by thrashing David Frost 8&7 in the first round and almost winning the event for the sixth time; and Price proved he is the game's most dominant player by winning the PGA Championship and the Open, four US Tour events, and topping the US money list for the second consecutive season.

The contributions of the journalists to the whole circus are, of course, small fry by comparison – as the players are so fond of reminding us, we make the cut every week – but even by Norman Dabell's high standards, it had been a particularly good year for Inspector Clouseau-like disasters. 'They just follow me around,' confessed Norman, whose first misadventure came at the age of four, when he rode over the edge of a quarry on his tricycle.

In the Royal Navy, Norman was nicknamed 'Snags' because he only had to glance at a radio for it to blow up or go out of frequency. After running a six-man cutter aground on a sandbank on the River Stour, and bringing about the capture of his cadre when he kicked a booby-trapped shoe polish tin, he decided that the upper ranks of the Navy were not for him, and turned, quite naturally, to golf journalism. But his troubles had only just begun. Attaching himself to a group of British university students *en route* to a tournament in Malmo, Sweden, in the hopes of saving money, he was detained and strip-searched on arrival at the airport under suspicion of drug-smuggling. 'I was doing nothing of the sort,' insisted Norman, 'but those bloody Swedes don't miss an orifice. It was most undignified.'

In 1994, Norman's catalogue of woes had been unending. Having survived being stranded in Madeira and the subsequent journey to Morocco – a thirty-six-hour trip involving five airports – some four weeks had passed before anything untoward happened. But at the

Extramadura Open in Badajoz, he was climbing out of a courtesy car when the driver, thinking he had gone, reversed at speed, trapping Norman between the door and a lamp-post. He avoided being flattened only by throwing himself onto the lap of another passenger. The door was almost wrenched off its hinges. For the rest of that week, he was banned from using the cars, because he was 'a liability and worse than Mr Bean.'

Undaunted, Norman proceeded to the next tournament in Jerez, where he was 'set upon by two Spanish wretches demanding money.' Norman felled one with a karate chop that he had learnt in the Navy, and the other ran away. At the Italian Open, Norman was given the only telephone in creation without a bell, and had to spend the week guessing when BBC Radio or Radio Kent were waiting to go on air. At the Open, rushing to do a live broadcast, he rounded a corner in his car and was caught up in a cycle race. Norman's face was redder than the two hundred cyclists 'buzzing like bees' around him as he crawled the ten miles towards Turnberry, arriving late and very excited.

At the Honda Open in June, he kept a low profile. The year before, he had returned to his hotel in the small hours, pressed what he thought was the light switch but was in fact the fire alarm, and brought all the guests screaming out of their rooms in their nightgowns. At the Lancome Trophy, the courtesy car driver issued those fatal words, '*Je sais un* back route,' and ended up speeding like a demon along pavements and verges. The atmosphere when they reached Charles de Gaulle, some twenty minutes after the flight was due to take off, was such that the driver sprang from the car and ran away, never to be seen again. Norman made his delayed plane easily. Finally, at the German Masters, a clumsy photographer poured an entire stein of beer over Norman in the midst of a Radio Five live interview.

But the lifetime jinx had not ended there.

'This is where you need to park if you want to avoid getting a parking fine,' Norman informed Charlie Mulqueen, the Irish reporter with whom he was sharing a hire car, on arrival at their hotel in Marbella for the Volvo Masters. The following morning, Mulqueen emerged to find the car had been towed away to the pound. Norman was unrepentant. 'Well, you never got a parking fine,' he told the agitated Mulqueen.

Alan Fraser, the *Mail* feature writer, also stumbled inadvertently into the Dabell twilight zone. He and Norman were sitting at the bar one night when the old sailor recognized a face in the crowd.

'Why don't you go over and say hello,' suggested Fraser.

'I can't,' said Norman.

'Of course you can,' Fraser insisted. 'Don't mind me.'

'I can't,' Norman said sadly, 'I've had my finger stuck in the chair for half an hour.'

And with that he wrenched his finger, scratched and bleeding, from the wickerwork seat of his stool.

After all this, Norman claims he is very lucky. This would seem to be borne out by his winnings for the season, which included a £2,000 watch, a £900 set of golf clubs, a £100 driver, a putter and a holiday for two in Australia – not quite as much as Els had acquired but no small haul, either.

But there were more important things to consider at the Volvo Masters than the confessions of golf writers. There was the first round of the tournament, for example. Out on the pristine emerald contours of Valderrama, a diabolically difficult course, Sam Torrance, Peter Mitchell and Miguel Jimenez were in the process of shooting 65s, taking apart Jaime Patino's 'Augusta of Europe' with consummate ease to share the lead.

There was also the 1995 schedule to think about. These had been unusually difficult times for European golf. Having sailed along in a state of bliss since the launch of the PGA European Tour in 1975, rarely drawing even the mildest censure, the Tour's top brass had been flung without warning into unimaginably hostile waters. Ballesteros was accusing them of accepting bribes from Patino and allowing McCormack to run the circuit. Feherty, Singh, Parnevik and Craig Parry had joined the US Tour; Faldo, Els and McNulty were about to, and Ballesteros, Olazabal and Langer were thinking about it. And Schofield was being criticized for everything from the Sky television deal to the lack of prospective Scottish and European Open sponsors, and from the struggling golf course ventures to appearance money, which he could no longer deny the existence of since James, one of his own committee members, had told us it was alive and well and inflating Faldo's bank balance as he spoke.

Is it any wonder that we were waiting with breathless anticipation to see whether or not the new schedule redeemed the Tour's flagging image? But no, it seemed we had to wait a little longer. The schedule, which is guarded like a state secret, would not be unveiled until noon on Saturday. Under no circumstances could we see it before then.

Thursday morning found us sitting around Sergio Gomez, Olazabal's manager, drinking coffee and discussing the future of Jose Maria, who had decided not to play the US Tour after all. 'So,' Sergio said in his articulate, heavily-accented English, plucking the not-to-be-seen schedule out of his top pocket and spreading it on the table for our inspection. 'When Chema joined the Tour, he used to start after the Masters. Appril [*sic*]. Now he's starting meedle of January. We really think that even if you don't want to go to the States to start your season – and not everyone has a chance to do that – the situation is we should start last week of February or first week of March. So what I am saying is, top executives of the Tour are not listening to the requirements of players, sponsors and the venues.'

Renton Laidlaw pointed out that the golfers didn't have to play before the Masters if they didn't want to.

'But Sergio makes a very valid point,' interjected Dermot Gilleece of the *Irish Times*, 'and that is, if you have five tournaments in Spain . . .'

'Which are shit tournaments,' Sergio said. 'Well, don't quote "shit" please. In fact, I know you are clever enough to mention that fewer tournaments in Spain will result in a better quality of event. Because I'm always very straight.' He chuckled. 'I mean, I suppose Shakspeare [*sic*] used to speak one way and write another way.'

'. . . with £250,000 prize money,' Dermot continued, 'they couldn't fill these tournaments. Why not have two or three with a greater amount of money?'

Somewhat outlandishly, Sergio then suggested that the Johnnie Walker Asian Classic, the second event of the season, be held in Europe in late February or March and broadcast to Asia. 'The porpoise is to sell Johnnie Walker, OK?'

'You can't have the Asian Classic in Europe,' Renton said reasonably.

'We've talking about the European Tour,' Dermot interrupted. 'The whole basis of the thing is that the European Tour has become totally artificial because we're trying to create a year-round tour when it is not climatically possible to do that.'

'We're lucky because some four or five years ago the Canadian

Open wanted to join the European Tour,' Sergio told him. 'That would be great. Canadian Open, Argentinian Open, South Africa, Philippines, Dubai. We'd be missing only Australia.'

This was Schofield's dilemma: to go or not to go. In 1995, the Tour would stage thirty-seven events in seventeen countries, worth upwards of £25 million in prize money. Climatically and financially it was not possible to do this in a recession-hit Europe alone, and therefore the executive director had cast his net globally and produced a schedule which began in Dubai in mid-January, travelled to the Philippines, Madeira, Spain, South Africa, Portugal and Morocco in its first six weeks, and ended with the Volvo Masters in late October. Schofield reasoned that it was better to have a patchy ten-month schedule, where Qualifying School and restricted category players could earn their spurs by competing in events such as the £250,000 South African PGA in Johannesburg, than return to the old April-through-September season.

The top players disagreed. Free to play in an unlimited number of special events during the off-season (i.e. the World Championship in Jamaica in December, where last place is a guaranteed $50,000), they argued for quality over quantity. They complained that too much long-haul travelling was bad for their backs and that the early season tournaments were often held at sub-standard venues for laughable prize funds, despite the fact that since many of these events couldn't pay appearance money, they almost never played in them. Only Ballesteros was honest enough to admit that one's perspective changed depending on where one was on the rankings. 'I believe it's too long, but the guys on the bottom think it's fair, so it's a delicate situation.'

All things considered, Schofield had done a commendable job. No sponsor had yet been found to endorse the Scottish Open, and the European Open had left British shores for the K Club in Dublin, but the overall picture was a positive one. Indeed, when the Eueopean Tour did hold their press conference later in the week, Schofield told an open-mouthed audience that, 'I kind of feel that Nick Faldo's comments, and the comments of Seve Ballesteros and Mark James, all of these things, at the end of the day, I actually think are compliments, because they're at the top of the game, and through our efforts they're going into the United States and they're playing the very, very best championships on the best golf courses in the world. I think the guys are perfectionists, they're champions, and they're trying to urge all of us to go forward as quickly as possible.'

He also said that the Tour's much-criticized course design ventures and the satellite television deal were in fact the key to its success. He maintained that more golf was now seen by the viewing public. He meant by this that more tournaments were covered, not that more people watched golf.

'We're the European Tour, not the BBC's footprints,' he said.

But all that really mattered was that Volvo, the Tour's umbrella sponsor, was happy – which it was. Its initial investment of £10 million spread over five years, followed by a three-year £7.5 million contract, was made at a time when Europe had only twenty-eight events and television coverage was not guaranteed. Since then, European Tour highlights had been shown throughout the US and reached an audience of 54 million in Asia alone. But Mel Pyatt, head of Volvo's event division, stressed that television exposure was crucial to the continued support of his company.

'I don't want to criticize the business direction of the Tour,' he said. 'I can only say that if the Volvo Masters or the Volvo PGA Championship were only seen on BSkyB, that would be seen as a negative return on our investment. Who's playing and what TV distribution do you have – those are the first questions that are asked to justify any type of sponsorship.'

On Friday, Langer shot a nine under par 62 on a golf course where the attainment of par had once seemed a product of luck, not just skill and good judgement. He took only 12 putts on the outward half and 10 coming back, single-putting the last four holes. By comparison, Montgomerie took 29 putts and 36 strokes in his round of 65, and Ballesteros, 28 putts and 39 strokes in his 67.

'Today was Bernhard Langer's day,' Montgomerie said admiringly. 'That is a tremendous golf score. It will be a long time before that is beaten. My 65 today was my best score at this course by two strokes, and I was still three shy of him.'

More remarkable than Langer's score was the news that he owed it to a putting lesson from Anders Forsbrand. In June, Forsbrand had almost become the first player since Mark James at the 1978 Sardinia Open to shoot a three-figure score. James's excuse for the 111 on his card was a sore wrist, which meant he played most of the round one-handed. The Swede's was simply the vagaries of golf. After completing the front nine in a respectable 43 strokes, he took 83 for fifteen holes and, after losing seven balls, five in water and two in the rough, was on 93 when he stood on the final tee. One can only hazard a guess at the number he might have chalked up at the eighteenth, but he was disqualified for failing to complete the hole. Faced with a 115-yard pitch over water, Forsbrand forbore to play his sixth shot and the putt (or two or three putts) that would have pushed his score into three figures.

Still, he had managed a 70 in the second round at Valderrama and had helped Langer to one of the finest rounds in Tour history.

'I expect Mr Patino's hung himself by now,' Pete Coleman, Langer's caddie, joked, not meaning any disrespect to the Bolivian tin magnate, but saluting rather his dedication to preserving Valderrama's image as a place where even angels fear to tread.

But Mr Patino was occupied with a fresh scandal – the revelation that the road which had been a virtual condition of the 1997 Ryder Cup coming to Valderrama, was unlikely to be built. Travel chaos was now a certainty. 'The road is needed, not just for the Ryder Cup, but for humane reasons, because four people died this summer in traffic queues,' Patino told us, adding with a persuasive smile: 'If it is not started next year, there is no way it can be finished in time.' His faith in the power of the British media to influence Spanish town councils was touching.

The journalists had other things on their minds. Michael Williams, the estimable *Telegraph* correspondent, had almost burnt down the press centre when his pipe set his papers on fire. Williams tapped on, oblivious to the blaze. He is not as accident-prone as Norman, but neither is he a stranger to catastrophe. After all, it was Williams who proudly ad-libbed 700 words to a copytaker on deadline from the Curtis Cup, only to find he had filed it to the wrong newspaper.

However, history will remember Williams as the man who silenced Bing Crosby – or as Dobereiner, who likes to call a spade a spade, describes him – 'the man who killed Bing Crosby.'

The scene of the alleged crime was Hilversum, venue of the Dutch Open. Nathaniel Crosby, Bing's son, had been playing in the tournament, and afterwards Bing was to give a small show. A stage had been set up just outside the clubhouse. When the first bars were struck, Williams limped over to the window to get a better view. He was almost there when he tripped, tearing the microphone wire out of its socket and cutting the great man off in the midst of *White Christmas*.

Crosby never resumed singing. He died a week later at La Moraleja in Spain, playing golf with Manuel Pinero and Antonio Garrido. He shook hands with them, thanked them for the game and keeled over.

On the morning of the final round, I wandered down the practice ground to watch the leaders hit balls. Ballesteros had taken the advantage on Saturday, his 68 for a nine under par 204, keeping him two strokes ahead of Langer and Montgomerie. His satisfaction was short-lived, though, for he and Jiminez were both fined £500 for slow play.

In a vitriolic outburst, Langer, who had shot 73, accused Ballesteros of destroying his timing. 'We were waiting on the front nine and then they were put on the clock and they started running. Because of that, we were put on the clock on 15 and I couldn't go through my normal routine. It just upsets your rhythm. Players should not be fined money. That sort of money means nothing to Seve. He's been there before and it just doesn't change. They should introduce the American way: time them, fine them, take shots off, more shots and then disqualify them.'

Which was funny because Langer is one of the slowest players on the Tour.

'Would you mind if I asked you a question?' I asked Montgomerie, who was practising beside Ballesteros. Ordinarily, one would never dream of talking to a player just before he teed off, but at the last tournament of the year, certain liberties are granted.

'No,' Montgomerie said shortly. Then he smiled, revealing a perfect row of tiny white teeth. 'Go on, then.'

'How have you managed the level of consistency you have for so long? On the graph of your career, you've only ever gone up.'

There was a pause. Montgomerie pressed the glistening blade into the grass and smacked the ball away. 'Well,' he said, laughing at his caddie's face, 'the less I practise, the luckier I get.'

There are few more intriguing men in pro golf than Colin Montgomerie. Not one contour in his 6 foot 1″, 15-stone frame speaks of athleticism. One looks from the granite outline of Norman, to the trim rower's torso of Faldo, to the rugby-forward shoulders of Els, and one shakes one's head at Montgomerie's soft pink muscles and cherubic curls. He looks ideally suited to the director's chair in the biscuit factory his father once presided over, or to the members' lounge at Troon, where his father is secretary, but he doesn't seem capable of winning the Order of Merit twice, almost winning the US Open twice, or of striking dread into the heart of every man in contention virtually every week of the year. And all with no practice – or very little of it.

The secret has to do with nature, not nurture. At eighteen, Montgomerie was a six-handicapper, which is fine for the monthly medal at Troon but no use at all if you plan on turning pro. He appealed to his father for assistance. Montgomerie Snr's cheque book paved the way for his son in amateur golf and then bought him a place at a Texas university. 'It was in America I discovered I could actually play the game,' he said.

In 1987, aged twenty-four, he turned professional. An eleven-stroke victory in the 1989 Portuguese Open launched his bid for stardom, and four years later he became the European No.1. By now, his reputation as a firebrand was well-established. Intelligent, articulate and refreshingly pleasant off the course, Montgomerie could be monstrously disagreeable on it. The Americans nicknamed him Mrs Doubtfire.

'He wears his heart on his sleeve,' Alastair McLean, his caddie, said. 'He lives for the moment, for the shot even. If he stands up to hit a shot, he puts 100 per cent effort into it, and if he messes up he's cross with himself because he thinks he's done all the right things and he hasn't got the reward. He tries his heart out.'

Adam Hunter, Montgomerie's fellow Scot, took a different view. 'He keeps saying in the press that he's working on his temperament, but I don't really think he cares. He's out there to do a job and if he upsets some people, too bad.'

But John McHenry, the Irishman who played with Montgomerie in the World Cup, insisted that Montgomerie had not been given due credit for the efforts he had made to change. 'He's been ridiculed for years about his size and his looks – often unfairly and he has just accepted it. He never complains about it and he never gives it back. The only time I've ever seen him turn is when it affects his wife. He's just set out to prove himself, and now people have an awful lot of respect for him. They are no longer saying those things, but just admiring what he does.'

This was not entirely true. There is a humorous element about many Montgomerie stories that make them an integral part of Tour lore. One player recalled Monty saying conspiratorially to him soon after he joined the circuit: 'I'm wearing jeans.'

'So?'

'I'm not allowed to wear jeans at home.'

At the Dunhill Cup in June, the BBC Radio reporter Tony Adamson was desperately trying to pin Montgomerie down for a talk. This is no easy task. Montgomerie is probably more obliging than any other player in Europe when it comes to promising interviews, but more elusive than all of them put together when it comes to finding the time to do them. However, Adamson had finally managed to elicit from him a solemn vow that he would do a live radio piece at Woburn. At the appointed hour, he waylaid Montgomerie.

'Can't do it now, I'm sorry,' Monty told him.

'But Colin, you promised,' Adamson said, losing patience.

'Can't,' Montgomerie repeated. He looked downcast. 'Bereavement in the family,' he said sadly.

Adamson was horrified. 'Bereave . . . in the family? Gosh, I'm so sorry . . . Why didn't you tell me?'

'It's all right,' Montgomerie said in martyred tones. 'You weren't to know.'

Later in the day, Adamson was relaying this story to a Scottish colleague.

'Bereavement in the family? What bereavement?' said the journalist. 'Oh, you mean the death of the Montgomeries' Filipino au pair's mother?'

At the end of the day, the only thing that counted was Montgomerie's scores, and they were the product of long, accurate driving, a rare gift with a putter, and a certain amount of arrogance. Lyle believed it all stemmed from Montgomerie's contentment with his swing. 'He's never messed around with it,' he said. 'He's comfortable with it, and his confidence is the result of playing with the same swing for eleven years.'

It was not Montgomerie's swing that let him down in the last round at Valderrama, it was his luck. He started well, hitting his approach at the first to 2 feet. Ballesteros went one better, hitting his to two inches. Both men birdied as Langer, in the match ahead, holed from 25 feet. Ballesteros conjured up a birdie at the fourth, and the lead swung to and fro between the three of them until they reached the seventh. There, Montgomerie hit an errant second shot, which connected with the head of a spectator and ricocheted out of bounds. His fourth shot found a bunker at the back of the green and his double-bogey six all but removed him from contention.

But this drama was nothing compared to the final showdown at the eighteenth, which Langer watched evolve from the safety of the clubhouse. At the seventeenth, Ballesteros hit a wild hook off the tee. 'He's volatile and hyper-sensitive,' Dobereiner observed, 'which may account for his genius but it doesn't help him with his scores. The real stamp of a pro is always said to be the ability to go round in 72 when you're playing really badly. I don't think he's got a safe game to fall back on.'

This was illustrated at the eighteenth, where Ballesteros, over-compensating for his hook, cut the ball into the trees. It finished flush against a cork tree and nestled snugly in amongst the roots. A referee was summoned. Guy Hunt, a former Ryder Cup player, thought that Ballesteros should play the ball as it lay. So did John Paramor, the Tour's chief referee, when he was called upon to give a second opinion.

But the Spaniard, prowling and scowling beneath the boughs, was having none of it. He insisted he deserved relief under the 'burrowing animal' rule. Paramor squatted down and peered at the base of the tree. He sifted handfuls of dirt between his fingers. Charcoal-faced and fuming, Ballesteros paced back and forth, pointing and gesticulating and citing the rule book. Paramor's jaw tightened. He scrutinized the ground more carefully. His knowledge of the rule book is unrivalled and he, as much as anyone, would have liked to have found a loop-hole. After ten minutes, he stood up. There was nothing else for it: Ballesteros had to play.

Reluctantly, the Spaniard hacked the ball out onto the fairway. From there, he failed to produce the expected miracle shot and found the bunker at the back of the green. His only hope of matching Langer's score now was to hole his trap shot, but that didn't happen either. He bogeyed to finish in second place with Vijay Singh on 277, a stroke behind Langer. Montgomerie and Jiminez were equal fourth, the former topping the final Order of Merit with £762,719. Langer was second in the rankings with £635,483, Ballesteros third with £590,101 and Olazabal fourth with £516,107.

Unsurprisingly, Ballesteros was steaming. 'I think I should have got a drop,' he fumed, which really meant he thought he should have been able to intimidate the referee into giving him a drop. 'With a different referee, I would have got a drop. I was unlucky it was John Paramor who was there.'

'It was a tense situation, and in terms of the tournament, a very serious matter,' Paramor said later. 'There was no evidence of any burrowing animal, although Seve disputed this several times. I inspected as much dirt as I could and there were no droppings of any kind.'

Langer, who had won a tournament for sixteen successive seasons on the European Tour, was half-amused, half-disgusted by Ballesteros's behaviour, which would have aroused wholesale condemnation had it been displayed by anyone else. Langer shrugged. 'I might have been the luckier one at the end, but if you get into contention often enough, you are bound to get the breaks at some stage,' he said.

Afterwards, we rushed excitedly through the airy cream corridors of Valderrama and on down the steps with our golf clubs and suitcases, shouting and giggling like school kids on the last day of term. Across the lawn we struggled and on to the bus, where armfuls of Heineken cans were already being loaded, and the aisle was blocked solid with black fibreglass suitcases and clubs in great Mizuno bags; the golfer who travels light has not yet been born. Anyone with even five minutes to spare had showered and they were spruce and damp in jeans, polo-shirts and glistening combed hair. The driver switched on the music and started the bus. With a shudder, we were off and rolling down the bumpy drive towards Marbella and the distant airport.

Beside me, Eddie Birchenough was talking about the golf swing. 'You can only teach people what they want to learn,' he said. 'If I had a motto, it would be: "I don't know what I was taught, I only know what I learned." When somebody comes to me and says, "I want to be a golfer," I try to explain to them that they're not coming to me to see how good a teacher I am, they're coming to see how good a golfer they can be. So all the time I'm trying to draw from people the qualities that they need to become golfers. There are two things you need to adhere to: At impact, the butt-end of the club has to be closer to the target than the face – that's the only way you can get backspin. The other fundamental is that your weight is on your left leg at impact because you need to be pulling. If you can satisfy those two things at impact, how you swing the club doesn't matter.'

'Mmmm,' I said, only half-listening. All around, the air was filled with music and banter and that intense warmth that precedes the breaking-up of friendships forged in the delights, frustrations and sorrows of the year-long struggle that is professional golf. But it was an illusion. Already, the season just gone was being forgotten and people's minds jumping ahead to family reunions, far-flung tournaments and unseen homes. They were together but separate, just as they always were.

When we reached the main road, I looked back. At the top of the furthest hill, like some remote fairground, was Valderrama, its candy-striped tents wreathed in the pale fire of sunset. Within a minute, it had faded from view.

'Don't forget,' Eddie Birchenough was saying: 'You don't know what you were taught, you only know what you learned.'

I laughed. 'No,' I said. 'I won't.'

And with that, the European season, bittersweet and crowded with memories, drew to a close.

271

INDEX